Mark My Words!

a personal history by

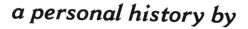

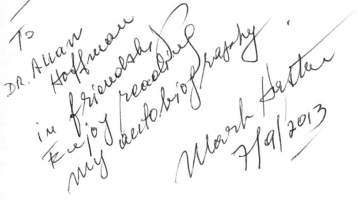

To DR. Allan Hoffman in friendship Enjoy reading my autobiography

Mark Hasten 7/9/2013

Mark Hasten

as told to Peter Weisz

Brotchin Books

MARK MY WORDS!

CONTENTS

To my family

"Then they all accept upon themselves the yoke
of heavenly sovereignty from one another, and
grant permission to one another to sanctify the
One Who formed them, with tranquility, with
clear articulation, and with sweetness."

— *from Shacharis, the Weekday Morning Service*

INTRODUCTION

I have known and admired Mark Hasten for over three decades, but not before becoming involved in this book project did I come to understand the true measure of the man. In many ways, Mark is an uncomplicated person whose effortless style shields a layer of tough complexity. His vivid pictorial memories of his long-lost *shtetl* (little town) in pre-war Poland were lovingly exposed to me as we strove to capture them upon the pages of this book. I truly cherish the opportunities I had to wander briefly through the memories of his boyhood home and that world that was soon to become tragically engulfed in the flames of the Holocaust.

Mark's recollections of his wartime survival in primitive Kazakhstan and his eventual enlistment into the Polish Brigade of the Red Army are poignant and unforgettable. I observed and listened intently as Mark once again traversed the Vistula in war-torn Warsaw and I was overcome as he described the tear-filled post-war reunion with his family. Despite surviving horrors and deprivations that would have sent weaker men into deep depression, Mark never abandoned his optimism nor his deep religious faith.

Listening to Mark describe his exploits as part of the Irgun underground in the DP camps of post-war Europe made my hair stand on end. His voyage aboard the ill-fated *Altalena* provided him—and now me—with a front-row seat to one of history's most controversial, and memorable, moments.

Mark Hasten

Mark's story is not one of constant nobility—not by any means. He never sought to conceal life's low points despite the tendency of the mind's eye to become blinded to the unpleasantness of the past. His willingness to lay it all open—in an uncluttered and forthright manner— impressed me greatly. It was clear as the process moved along, that Mark was truly interested in getting his story recorded just the way it happened. By so doing, he has created not only an engrossing personal testimony, but also a valuable historic legacy.

As Mark's path took him to Canada and the new world, I found his buoyant attitude to be infectious. His wit and humor never abandoned him—neither during his life, nor during the retelling of it. Mark's accomplishments as an engineer and a business leader were well known to me at the outset of this project. What I discovered—and what I hope the reader will discover—are the intrinsic reasons behind the success. Persistence, tenacity, and a highly innovative intellect.

Joining into partnership with his younger brother, Hart, the two men have forged a business partnership that has endured and flourished for thirty-five years. A few years ago, I was pleased to be involved with the production of Hart's biography, "I Shall Not Die!" *(Gefen Publishing, 2002)*. Mark and I specifically avoided recounting incidents described in the earlier book, noting them where appropriate via endnote entries. Hence, this volume serves as a perfect compliment to "I Shall Not Die!" and the two memoirs together compose an amazing and incomparable family saga that serves to document the extent of man's highest capabilities in the face of unimaginable adversity.

During our many hours of discourse about his life, Mark never preached or pontificated. His manner is more subdued— and often quite charming. Nevertheless, I inevitably found great wisdom in his words and a strong undercurrent of faith-based morality in his recollections. It is these lessons from a life lived broadly and abundantly that I consider to be the most enriching aspects of my unique experience. And it is for this reason that I have accepted Mark's invitation to "Mark My Words!" I invite you to do the same.

Peter Weisz
Indianapolis, Indiana
August 1, 2003

ACKNOWLEDGMENTS

I would like to express my deepest thanks to the following individuals without whose assistance this book would not have been possible.

Anna Ruth Hasten, *my wife*
Hart N. Hasten, *my brother*
My four children:
     Mr. Edward Hasten,
     Rabbi Michael Hasten,
     Mrs. Monica Rosenfeld,
     Mrs. Judy Kaye
Yechiel Kaddishai
Rabbi Ronald Gray
Chanan Rappaport
Martha Havely
     and, of course, Peter Weisz

Micaiah declared, "If you ever return safely, the LORD has not spoken through me." Then he added, "Mark my words, all you people!"

— 1 Kings 22:28

PROLOGUE

There is a world that exists only in the memory cells of my brain. It is a world populated by satanic villains and heroes of the highest order. It is the world of the shtetl and the world of the Irgun. It is located at the crossroads of history and personal emotion. At times I am able to pull on my boots and traverse this "memory" world and sometimes I am able to bring along others on my visits. It is the visitors to this world who have encouraged me time and again to record my memories.

This is a world that has vanished, but yet, should not vanish. It was a world that saw enormous evil assembled against the forsaken Jewish people. This needs to be remembered. Stories of the courage and the vision of the many heroes I came to know should also be told and re-told. This world is the place where I go to remember a time I can never forget.

I am writing these words so that the world of my memories will endure even after my brain cells have long been quieted. I view my life experiences, particularly during the 1930s and '40s, as unique in many ways. As those experiences retract further into the past, I am increasingly convinced that I must record the highlights, if not for the sake of history, then at least for the edification of my own family. They should know of my life. Of the idyllic shtetl world of my boyhood. Of the ongoing struggle for survival during the war years. They should know that I was one of the very few Jewish soldiers (other than partisans) to see combat on the Eastern Front during World War II.

They should know that I sailed on the Altalena and that I served in the Etzel as we struggled to reach Palestine and that I fought as an Israeli soldier, awash in tears and blood, to give birth to the new State of Eretz Yisroel (Land of Israel).

More than anything else, I wish for this book to serve as an historic document. Many of the Irgun leaders have written about this fiery and critical period in Jewish history. Their accounts are vital towards gaining an understanding of the dynamic forces at work during this period. I see my words as an adjunct, offering a testimony of those turbulent times as seen through the eyes of a young, idealistic, and passionate Jew thrown in to the fray, and somehow managing to survive it all.

In 2002, my younger brother, Hart Hasten, wrote and published his autobiography (I SHALL NOT DIE!, Gefen Publishing, Inc.). In this excellent volume, Hart covered much of our childhood years prior to our separation in 1943. He also expounded on our business career after we joined forces in 1967. Hence, it is the years between that are the focus of this book—years that included my service in the Polish Army during World War II and my activities with the Irgun Zvai Leumi leading to the birth of the State of Israel.

Permit me to say what this book is not.

This book is not a personal manifesto. I do not intend to expound upon my political point of view. This book is not an exposé in which I tell the "real story" about my adversaries, nor is it an inside glimpse into the private lives of those I have known in the public eye. This book is not prophecy. I do not seek to offer warnings about what might happen in the years ahead. I wish for this book to simply tell what did happen. And I would be pleased, if, as the prophet Micaiah proclaimed, you were to "Mark My Words" as the story of one man who lived through a highly critical era for our people and our world.

Mark My Words!

I invite you to travel with me as I visit this world of memory once again, this time with pen in hand. Why? Quite simply, because I want you to know what happened.

CHAPTER ONE

Brotchin

My father, Bernard Hasten, was a foot soldier in Franz Joseph's Austro-Hungarian army during the darkest days of what became known as World War I. Released from active duty at war's end, he found himself a young man on the streets of Lvov. Like many other such *Ostjuden,* or Jews from the East, *Tatu* (as my brother and I called him) looked to the West for economic opportunity. Tatu's brother, Hermann Geller, was living in Dortmund, Germany operating a small delicatessen. So as soon as Tatu found the train fare, he joined Uncle Hermann, and the two brothers spent the early 1920s slicing pastrami, sorting eggs, and building up their modest business.

Although they were born to the same mother and father, the two brothers had different last names. To understand the reason, one must be aware that in 19th century Poland, as in all areas controlled by the Austro-Hungarian Empire at the time, couples were required to undergo both a civil and a religious wedding ceremony. The civil ceremony carried a hugely onerous tax that only the bourgeoisie and the wealthy were able to afford. Poor couples, such as my grandparents, were forced to marry without benefit of the large tax stamp that was imprinted on an official marriage certificate. Hence, in the eyes of the state, any children from such a marriage were legally considered "out of wedlock." My Uncle Hermann was born during this period and was given the surname of Geller, his mother's maiden name. By the time my father came along, my grandparents had managed to pay the tax and became legally married allowing them to bestow the father's name upon their next son, Bernard Hasten.

After a few hard-working years in Germany, Tatu decided to return to what was now Poland and find a bride. He married my mother, Hannah Halpern, the daughter of a successful lumber mill owner in the Carpathian shtetl known as Bohorodczany, or Brotchin, as it was known to the town's Yiddish-speaking community, which made up roughly half of the little town's population of five thousand.

By the early 1930s Bernard, or "Berish" as he was known in Yiddish, and Hannah had produced two sons. I was known as Munjee and my little brother, Hertz, was known as Hetche. Our last name at the time, however, was Halpern, not Hasten. Like my grandparents, my parents declined to pay the marriage tax and were living in an unwed state according to the government. My brother and I were eventually able to adopt our father's name, Hasten, in the mid-1930s when it appeared that war might break out again. Women, such as my mother, became concerned that if their husbands were called up into military service, they might become widowed. And without a legal marriage certificate, they would be denied a government pension. So, my parents, like many others at the time, scraped up the money and paid the marriage tax which immediately turned all of us into Hastens.

Although my father operated a successful wholesale leather store, he always felt that his opportunities in Poland were limited. He yearned to return to Germany to make his fortune, and he groomed his children by teaching us *Hoch-Deutsch* (formal spoken German) for the day he would bring us all to Dortmund where he could engage in business without the constant pressure of the government tax collectors. How well I recall the days when we got word that the taxman had arrived to our town. The news spread like a virus through the community as we rushed to our homes and stores to hide whatever valuables we might have on display. The tax was based on inventory so the object was to quickly stuff all of my father's leather hides into pre-arranged hiding places before they could be spotted by the tax assessor.

Taxation, and the art of evading it, was a central aspect of shtetl life. Two taxes we were unable to avoid were the tax on sugar *(because the government held a monopoly on sugar production)* and matches that had to carry a tax stamp on every box. These taxes made both commodities very expensive and highly prized. I remember how we would slice each wooden matchstick vertically with a razor into four separate quarters—gaining three extra flames from each match. In order to secure its income stream provided by the matchbox tax, the government outlawed flint stones making cigarette lighters a contraband item. My mother, never above a bit of black marketeering, would deal in illegal flint stones until the day someone *massered* (squealed) on her. Fortunately, she was able to discard the evidence before the authorities questioned her.

I became quite adept at making homemade cigarette lighters out of empty bullet casings. I would attach a little handle, a shaft for the flint and a small wick. Once filled with gasoline, these bullet lighters fetched a few *groshen* (pennies) on the black market and allowed me to contribute to the family coffers.

My father's leather shop was a smorgasbord of smells. He would obtain the hides from the tanners and then cut them to order for his customers, who included the local cobblers and other craftsmen. He also sold leather by weight to individuals who wished to re-sole their shoes or make a belt. In addition to the leather business, Tatu also did some dealing in Persian rugs that he bought by the wagonload and sold by the piece. These business activities were in addition to the livestock he traded in regularly. My fondest memories are of the bustling farmyard, full of horses, cows, calves, goats, chickens, and roosters tended to by the children as well as by the servants. Two workers were kept busy year-round doing nothing but chopping wood and stacking it in the woodshed for use by our extended family. Thursday night was baking night when the *chaulent* (bean casserole) and the *challahs* (traditional Sabbath plaited bread) for the coming Sabbath were prepared in the enormous wood-burning hearth. We kids were kept busy kneading the dough for the five or six families in the neighborhood.

Our extended family all lived and worked in a large complex that occupied an entire city block. What space the family did not require, was rented out to merchants and craftsmen. I recall the sheet metal shop, a hosiery emporium, and a little store that sold only milled flour. Of course, the compound housed my father's leather shop as well as my grandparents' inn and tavern. The tavern was always a place of warmth and joviality and often served as the catering hall for local weddings. Sometimes there was a bit too much warmth and joviality as the 200-proof vodka began flowing too freely. I recall how fistfights would erupt between members of the groom's family and the bride's family. Usually an insult about too little dowry could spark a mini-brawl. Another source of dispute was the value of the wedding gifts that were displayed and publicly announced by the *marshalek*. This marshalek, or interlocutor, would not only announce each wedding present, he would, on the spot, compose a rhyme or a little song about the gift and about the family from whom it came, much in the manner of a rhyming calypso singer.

"The Cohen family will suffer no guilt. They gave the bride this embroidered quilt."

The marshalek would lead the procession to the *chuppah* (bridal canopy) where the ceremony would take place. He would often carry two shiny, crusty challah loaves high above his head, twisting them right and left, and was always followed by a band of colorful *klezmer* musicians. If the marshalek announced a somewhat inexpensive gift from a family that could afford better, this would cause a negative crowd reaction and might easily lead to a fight once the imbibing got underway.

Drunkards were an everyday part of life in those days. When somebody overdid it and could no longer handle the alcohol, I was called upon to assist in transporting the poor fellow around the back to the woodshed. We'd lay the *shikers* (drunkards) there on top of the woodpile and let them sleep it off until they sobered up.

The beverage of choice among our crowd was most often not wine, but a rich, frothy homemade beer. I recall the huge wooden beer barrels that filled the cool basement underneath the inn and how my grandparents would siphon the brew upstairs, through the floor using heavy hand pumps. Customers would bring jugs from home and wait while my grandparents filled them till the foam was overflowing. And although I was too young to sample the beer, I understood that the flavor was something special. Well into her old age in this country, my mother carried with her a memory of that thick Polish beer. She was always trying different types of beer whenever we visited an American restaurant, but she never found anything to compare with the unmistakable flavor of that Brotchin brew.

After my grandmother Toyba (Yonna) died in 1936, my grandfather seemed to lose interest in the inn and closed it down. It was in this space that my Uncle Psachye opened up his bicycle shop. When not working in the yard, I was kept busy at the bicycle shop helping my uncle. He taught me how to build an entire bicycle from scratch. By age ten, I could balance the wheels, assemble the metal frame, put together the spokes and the gears and create a rather passable bicycle that my uncle was then able to sell. After a bit, I was permitted to build a bicycle for me to keep, and this made me the happiest kid in the entire shtetl, that is until I got a look at my uncle's new motorized bicycle. This was the ultimate in technology and I simply could not rest until he let me ride it. After much pestering, Uncle Psachye finally relented, set me on the motorbike's seat, and let me drive it around the courtyard before the unbelieving faces of my friends and family. This was, undoubtedly, the finest hour of my childhood.

Like many other families, we were the proud owners of a family dog. But Wilchur *(Wolfie)* was no family pet or lapdog. Wilchur was a mean and powerful German shepherd and served to protect our property against trespassers and thieves. The beast was kept muzzled and locked up during the day and was released on a cable leash every night to serve as our canine burglar alarm. He had huge clawed paws that he would use to dig the earth around the gate to his pen where he was taken each morning. The dog could only be handled by my father and my *Zayde* (grandfather). No one else was permitted near the animal. I recall the large "Beware of the Dog" sign that graced our backyard. Even years after we had given old Wilchur away to a farmer *(where he reportedly perished when the farmer's barn burned down)*, townspeople would still inquire before coming on our property, "Is that mean old dog around here?"

The religious orientation of our little community was anything but monolithic. There was an official "state-appointed" rabbi, Rabbi Nebenzal, known as the *Rabbiner* who was responsible for conducting marriages, funerals and the like. He was accepted by the Polish government as the religious representative of the Jewish community of Bohorodczany. In addition, our town was also home to the Rav or Chassidic rebbe by the name of Rosenbaum, who was supported by a group of followers and operated without benefit of official sanction. This situation, with its competing alliances, created a large rift among the Jewish citizens of Brotchin. I received a glimpse of exactly how large during a recent trip back to my hometown in the summer of 2002 *(see chapter 20)*. While there, I came across a document—a petition, actually—dated May 1925 urging the Polish government NOT to re-name Rabbi Nebenzal as the official rabbi of Bohorodczany and to appoint Rabbi Rosenbaum in his stead. The document contained a photo of Rabbi Rosenbaum and his two sons Laibel and Tzvi and his beautiful daughter as well. The text read as follows: "We, the undersigned Jews of Bohorodczany . . . do hereby petition the Polish Sejm (senate) to appoint Rabbi Nissin Chaim Rosenbaum to the post of chief rabbi of Bohorodczany for the following reasons . . . " At the bottom of the page, amidst dozens of other signatures, one name stood out. Bernard Hasten, my father, had signed this petition two years before I was born. Despite his wishes, and those of his fellow towns-people, the petition failed to convince the Polish State, and Rabbi Nebenzal was appointed to another term. The petition remains, however, to document the tradition of political and religious activism into which my brother and I were born.

Learning in the shtetl started early. Early in the day and early in life. Public school attendance was required of all children over the age of six, but for the Jewish children, education began much sooner. Jewish parents would employ the services of a *behelfer* or deliveryman. The behelfer would pick up a pre-school-aged child from his home in the morning and, carrying the child on his shoulder or back, deliver him to the rebbe's house. There they would be introduced to the *aleph-bet,* or Hebrew alphabet, so that by the time the child began his studies at the cheder, he was already capable of reading the Hebrew text. There, on the floor of the rebbe's parlor, the age-old light of learning was being kindled in the minds and hearts of these young scholars.

Under Polish law, every child was required to remain in public school through the sixth grade. Classes were held six days per week, including on the Sabbath. Jewish children, of course, did not attend on Shabbat. Boys and girls attended in separate schoolhouses, except during the weekly religion class when the Jewish girls traveled to our boys' school. Our religion teacher was a mustachioed and bald-headed Professor Nadler who, while not an observant Jew, did a good job of teaching us the basics of Judaism. He loved to match up the boys with the girls to make little *shiddachs* (romantic matches). Once he paired up

7

a boy and girl, he insisted they both give him a kiss on top of his shiny bald dome.

All classes in the public school were conducted in the Polish language, and the entire school system was under the domain of the Catholic Church, but all children, regardless of their religion, were required to attend from 8 A.M. to 1 P.M. each day. After lunch, all the Jewish boys went off to an afternoon cheder or religious school that met five days per week. These classes were taught in Yiddish and the prayers, liturgies, and commentaries were studied in the ancient Biblical Hebrew. We became adept at translating the liturgical Hebrew into Yiddish as we searched for meaning in the Chumash, Gemarah, Talmud, and other holy texts. By the mid-thirties, as the tide of Zionism began to rise in our shtetl, many of the young boys began attending modern Hebrew language classes after cheder three or four times per week. These *Ivrit b'ivrit* (Hebrew in Hebrew) classes were taught by an ardent young teacher named Professor Landau. So, during a typical day, I would find myself fluently speaking, and studying, in German, Polish, Ukrainian, Yiddish, Ancient Hebrew, and Modern Hebrew. This polyglot environment did not cause me a moment's dismay and seemed quite normal and natural to me.

The public school classes were free, but our parents were required to pay for both the cheder and the Hebrew language classes. By paying the fee, and by simply studying modern Hebrew grammar and literature, we were making a political statement. We were preparing ourselves for the ingathering when there would once again arise a Jewish homeland in Jerusalem. Like most European Jews, we dreamed of a better world. A world where we would not be constantly taunted as *Zsid* (Jew) by the Jew-hating locals. A world that provided Jews with the same opportunities for success as their gentile neighbors. For example, my uncle Psachye, before getting married and opening the bicycle shop, graduated from law school. Yet, he was barred from practicing law because the very legal system under which he wished to practice included prohibitions that blocked Jews from representing clients, signing legal documents, and serving as legal advocates. To become a lawyer you first had to have the good sense to have been born a Pole or a Ukrainian. Uncle Psachye did find work as a *Metzenas* (paralegal) and that was as high as he could hope to advance in the legal profession.

While the hot breath of anti-Semitism was always felt on our necks, as young teens in the shtetl, we would frequently stand up to our tormentors. Our toughest enemies in school, however, were the local gentile *shtubaks*. A shtubak was a slow student who had been held back one or more grades and was often much older, and much bigger, than his classmates. These giant shtubaks made a habit of taking out their aggressions and their jealousies on the Jewish students. This situation came to head when I was twelve and in the fifth grade. One of these shtubaks, a hulking dunce with short-cropped blond hair, was making it a daily ritual to select a Jewish boy and beat him up without provocation. I convinced my classmates that it was stupid for us to simply sit around waiting for our turn to face this sixteen-year-old bully. I convinced them to join me as we armed ourselves with broomsticks and confronted our overgrown enemy. We gave the fellow the beating of his life and from that day on, he bothered us no longer and actually became our friend and protector.

Our community enjoyed the services of a Jewish physician, Dr. Singer, the son-in-law of Professor Nadler. Dr. Singer was a dapper gentleman who worked from an ornate office right in the center of town. His practice extended well beyond the Jewish community and, despite the ingrained and institutionalized anti-Semitism, he counted many non-Jews among his patients. The irony was that while a gentile mother could call upon a Jewish doctor to assist her in delivering a baby, that same doctor, because he was a Jew, was not permitted to sign the baby's birth certificate. He was one of the first to be killed by the Nazis in their campaign to eliminate the intelligentsia.

While to my wonder-filled eyes this bucolic way of life seemed perfect, my father felt otherwise. Tatu itched to leave the shtetl life behind and travel down the big city boulevards that had opened for Jews since the war. But the shadow of the swastika and the rise of Hitler in 1933 put an end to my father's dream of German emigration and locked our family's fate into the sleepy shtetl of Brotchin. Having lived in Germany, my father had a better understanding of Hitlerism than did many Jews in our town. I recall him preaching to us, "When Hitler says he wants to make Germany *Judenrein* (cleansed of Jews), he really means it. He's really going to do it." I recall how our radio was put on the windowsill as townsfolk gathered around to listen to Hitler's ranting speeches. Most Jews viewed events in Germany as far away and not affecting them. "Even if Hitler tries to come this way," went the common wisdom, "the Polish Army will stop him before he finds us." Looking back, these were years of extreme denial and delusion. My father swam at crosscurrents to this tide of insulated complacency. He was no alarmist, running wildly through the streets, screaming "The Nazis are coming!" Instead, he was a steadfast man who adapted to the rapidly changing circumstances around him in an ongoing effort to stay one step ahead of the danger.

It was from the town of Brotchin that our family was forced to flee the German onslaught in June 1941. My father had secured a horse-drawn wagon into which he trundled us and our belongings, and we joined the steady stream of Jewish refugees heading east towards Russia. In addition to Mamma and his two boys, Tatu had agreed to bring along the four teenaged sons of his friend, Moshe Friedman, the tailor. Eighteen Jews, the number corresponding to the Hebrew numerological value for "Life," trudged out of Brotchin with us that night, on foot and by wagon, leaving behind two thousand five hundred others who were all consumed by the Nazi death machine.

Eighteen months before, Poland had been carved into two by the Molotov-von Ribbentropp non-aggression pact, and our shtetl had fallen under Soviet domination as it became part of the Ukraine. As the Russians assumed control, they shut down all the churches and synagogues and eliminated all forms of private enterprise. The familiar shops and boutiques that populated our main street were either converted to state-run stores or shut down. It was during this period that my father abandoned his business interests and joined the local paramilitary militia. He was issued a uniform and was set to work maintaining law and order, Russian-style, on the streets of Brotchin.

I recall how Tatu was called in to investigate the case of a missing grindstone belt. The town possessed a quaint grinding mill where all the families would bring their wheat to have it milled into flour. After relying upon hydropower for generations, the mill had finally converted to DC electrical power. The huge grindstone was now powered by a massive electric motor to which it was connected by a meter-wide leather belt. The belt was perhaps fifty feet long and had attracted the eye of a master thief from the neighboring village of Sadzeva. My father was called in when the belt was discovered missing and soon his investigation revealed that the Bandit of Sadzeva was seen selling leather shoe soles obviously cut from the purloined belt. The city elders managed to secure another belt, and within a few days the mill/power plant was operating again. Several weeks later, my father received a tip from one of his informers that the Grindstone Bandit was about to strike again and planned to steal the new belt. This time, however, the security officers would be ready. The tip proved to be reliable, and as the Bandit entered the mill in the early hours of the morning, he walked right into the stakeout. The Bandit attempted to flee arrest and was shot and killed by one of the security officers.

It was learned that the Bandit was a "Petlurist," a type of local Ukrainian bandito named after Simon Petlura. Petlura was a gangster and anti-Semite who rose to power after the first world war and was eventually successful in heading the short-lived independent Ukrainian Republic from 1919 to 1920.

During his reign, he slaughtered thousands of Jews in massive state-sponsored pogroms. After the Ukraine fell to the Russians, Petlura took up residence in Paris where he was assassinated in 1926 by a heroic Jewish partisan, Sholom Schwartzbard, in retaliation for the thousands of Jewish lives Petlura had wiped out. By helping to eliminate one of Petlura's followers, my father was emulating the heroic act carried out by Schwartzbard some thirteen years earlier.

The Russians brought something new to our shtetl-hunger. We learned to live under constant food rationing. Thankfully, we were permitted to own a few cows that provided us with a little milk and butter which we now made ourselves since our servants had "thrown of their chains" under the new Soviet regime.

My conventional studies, which had taken me through the fifth grade, came to a halt and I was forced to enroll in a new school created by the Russians. Along with my classmates, I donned a red neckerchief and became a Komsomol or Young Pioneer I could not get over the irony of the communist education. All students were forced to attend a daily class in "Atheism" where the evils of religion, the "opiate of the masses" were constantly drummed into our heads. *Bez borznik* (There is no G-d) was their motto repeated endlessly at every turn. The teachers also continually scorned and berated all religious practice and worship as "decadent" and "counter-revolutionary." Yet, before entering the classroom, each student was required to bow deeply before the statues of Lenin and Stalin and pledge his undying fealty to these founders of the Soviet state.

The school was administered under the stern hand of a giant Russian redhead in a black dress who made it her business to whip her unfortunate students into respectable comrades of the socialist state. She would pick up a student by the throat just like a feather... and often did just that. On top of that, I did not get along well with my classroom teacher, a Mrs. Pincus, who liked to scold me with her face so close to mine that I invariably had to wipe away her saliva after each of her angry tirades. She did not like the fact that I often spoke out against the principals of Communist atheism that she was shoving down our throats. After a few months of her constant spouting and spitting, I finally had had enough and decided to send her a message. I arrived early to class and sprinkled a bunch of thumbtacks on her chair. I could barely suppress my glee as she seated her bottom down on her throne, but my joy soon turned to surprise since I witnessed no reaction whatsoever from her. I later discovered that Mrs. Pincus wore a heavy whalebone corset that had protected her from the tacks. The following day I upped the ante. This time I used carpenter's nails, and sure enough, they produced the desired result. Our esteemed professor of official atheism jumped up suddenly and shouted "Oh my G-d!"

Mrs. Pincus angrily strode to the door and locked it as she glared into the impassive faces of each her students. When no one admitted to the heinous crime she opened the door again briefly to send out a student to summon the principal. The Red Giantess arrived in a rage and began interrogating the children one by one. "Who did this!" she bellowed and one by one my fifth-grade classmates began to cry. But when it was my turn under the gun, I did not shed a tear and it was this fact that made both of them suspicious. The teacher and the principal grilled me daily for over six weeks, but I held firm, until finally they threatened to send me to Siberia along with my whole family if I did not admit to this crime. I finally caved in and admitted that I had sprinkled the nails and was ready to take my punishment. But the punishment was never meted out because on the following day the Germans attacked and the war had finally arrived at our doorstep.

As a security officer in the militia, my father came into direct contact with many fleeing Jewish refugees from Germany and occupied Poland who related first-hand accounts of unbelievable Nazi atrocities. It was this knowledge that correctly convinced

13

Tatu we could not sit by and wait for the Germans to overrun our town. We had to flee as soon as we heard that the German armies had attacked Russia and crossed the Polish frontier.

One of my father's good friends, Laibele Lappe, served alongside him as a part of the local militia. Like my father, Lappe accurately recognized the risks, obtained his own team and wagon and, with his wife and infant daughter, joined our ragtag caravan as we trudged eastward towards the neighboring city of Stanislawow.

Once in Stanislawow, my father learned of a military truck that was traveling to our next destination of Chortkow. Tatu conferred with Laibele Lappe and the two men decided to pay the driver to transport their families on to Chortkow by truck. The plan was that Laibele and Tatu, plus the four Friedman boys, would drive the wagons and meet up with us there. Since we would arrive much sooner, Mama, Hetche, and I would have the opportunity to get some rest after our journey.

Reluctantly, my mother agreed. Soon, my brother and I, along with Laibele's wife and baby were bumping down the road in the relative comfort of a military transport vehicle. Somewhere along the way, my mother decided that we had made a mistake by separating. The next town along the road was Buczacz and she decided that this was where we should get off.

"Boys," she told us, "we never should have got on this truck. We're a family and we should stay together. We're getting off right now in Buczacz. Tatu has to pass through here on his way to Chortkow, so we'll just wait for him here."

The driver delivered us to a "refugee house" where we were able to get a little sleep and a bite to eat. Mrs. Lappe decided not to join us, however. She elected to remain on the truck all the way to Chortkow and so we bid her and her baby a good-bye and watched them drive off in a cloud of dust.

After a few hours in the refugee house, Mamma began to fret. How will Tatu ever find us in this *balagan* (great disorder)? She decided that we needed to make ourselves more visible.

"Come on, boys," she instructed, "we're leaving here. Tatu's going to come with the horses and we need to make sure he finds us here in Buczacz." Mamma decided that since Bucacz stood at the crossroads of two major roads, our best bet would be to stand at the intersection and await my father's arrival. No matter from which direction he approached the city, he would need to pass through this crossroads. So we grabbed our single suitcase and posted ourselves at this main intersection. It was a long wait. So long that we took turns manning the lookout while the other two slept by the side of the road.

By the following morning, there was neither hide nor hair of my father or the horses to be found. My mother was going out of her mind with worry. In her hysteria, she was certain that Tatu had been captured by the Germans or the Ukranians. Packing us up and leading us back to the "refugee house," we passed by the now bustling open-air city market.

"Tatu!" I heard my mother scream, "It's Tatu. He's over there!" Sure enough, Tatu was calmly feeding the horses and was quite surprised to see us.

"Why did you get off the truck?" he wanted to know.

"How did you get past us at the crossroads?" we asked. Mamma explained that she decided we had made a mistake by splitting up. "Promise me, Berish," she pleaded, "that we will never split up again." My father complied and explained that he had entered the town the night before, passing through the crossroads only moments before we set up our watch. He had slept in the wagon and had come into the market for supplies and to feed the horses.

Our family once again reunited, we boarded the wagon and pushed on towards Chortkow. Lappe and his family were not so fortunate. Once Laibele saw that we were no longer with his wife and baby, he rushed ahead towards Chortkow to find them. He was unable to do so until after the war, some five years later. The family joined the post-war stream of *olim* (immigrants) bound for Palestine where they settled in Haifa. Laibele, an industrious fellow, set up a small winery and began to take root in the new nation of Eretz Yisroel. Unfortunately, tragedy was to finally overcome him. As he was inspecting the wine vats one day, he slipped and fell into one of them where he was overcome by fumes and perished. Ironically, he had managed to escape the Nazi gas chambers only to meet his end in such a similar fashion.

After Buczacz, our group consisted of only my parents and brother and the four Friedman boys. It was this group that pressed on eastward just ahead of the advancing German troops. Traveling the backcountry roads, never sleeping under a proper roof for weeks at a stretch, we soon became nomadic and began to think of ourselves as gypsies. Riding aboard the wagon was obviously preferable to walking, but if you wanted to ride, you had to work. The oat and wheat harvest was just coming in and we would often pick up bundled oat sheaves from a local farmer for use as feed. Riding onboard the wagon meant you had to keep busy separating the oats from the chaff so that when we stopped for the night they could be fed to our team.

I recall fondly how my father would lovingly groom and feed his beloved horses. He would provide them with whatever comfort he could and even carry on conversations with them.

"Tomorrow, old friend, we need to cover thirty kilometers," he would whisper kindly to into the horse's ear. "Do you think we can do it? Huh?" The horse seemed to understand Tatu as it responded by nodding its huge head up and down and flubbering its lips. One night, as I watched Tatu washing the horses by the river after a long day's trek—looking for all the world like a true gypsy, I ran up beside him and asked, "Tatu. I want to ride the horse. Can I ride him, just once, please?"

"Munjee," he answered, "can't you see the horses are tired. I was just going to help them lie down for a little rest." This was a trick my father had mastered. Not everyone knows that a horse enjoys lying down, but it needs assistance to get down and get back up. My father knew just how to do this and the horses loved him for it. Of course, I didn't care that the horses were tired. I wanted to ride and proceeded to hop onto the darker one in order to ride him barebacked. Tatu grabbed the horse's halter rein and brought his head low enough for him to whisper something into its ear. The horse gave a quick nod and then took off with me at a full gallop. I was screaming with delight as I felt the warm wind whip through my hair. Just as I rode by the encampment, waving proudly to my family, the beast hit the brakes. The horse stopped, but I did not. I sailed through the air and landed with a thump on the ground, my dignity and my rear end both bruised. To this day, I am convinced that it was my father's uncanny ability to communicate with horses that resulted in my downfall.

Although it upset me at the time, we found it in our interest to give up our horses and wagon. I swore that I could see tears falling from each horse's eye as we departed. My father was able to exchange the wagon and team for passage aboard what could be called a private rail car. By our standards, it was quite a luxurious offering, sleeping space and that rarest commodity—privacy. At each station, we would be disconnected and my father would negotiate with the various stationmasters to get our car re-joined to the next train heading east. After several days of this, we found ourselves heading towards the city of Aktubinsk in Kazakhstan. Passing through this regional capitol, our family finally arrived at the primitive town of Alga where Tatu heard that employment opportunities existed for Jews. It was in this remote town of Alga that we were to sit out the war years—years marked by extreme danger and deprivation. But despite the hardships, Alga served as our safe haven from the inferno that consumed the Jews of Europe—an inferno we now call the Holocaust.

CHAPTER TWO

Alga

The town of Alga was divided into two sections by the north-south railroad line that ran from Tashkent to Moscow. The homes on the east side of the tracks were constructed from lime, straw, and brown mud bricks. It was into this area that we found our first shelter. A single room where all eight of us spent our nights sleeping on the mud-packed floor. Our days were spent grubbing for food. Because of the socialist system, no one was permitted to own his own farmland. All food production had been collectivized, and what little food was actually produced in this way was shipped out of the region. Fortunately the authorities permitted the citizens to cultivate small private gardens surrounding their homes. It was the food from these gardens that kept us from starving during those difficult years. We, and our neighbors, raised tomatoes, potatoes, anything that would grow and ripen quickly during the summer months. Of course water was a major issue. The only natural source of fresh water in this arid environment was from the meandering Ilek River so most people relied upon the system of public wells that appeared at the end of each street in Alga.

The west side of the tracks was home to row upon row of wood-frame, two-story tenement houses. Most of the tenement residents worked in the town's major industrial facility, the sulfuric acid factory. Before too long, I succeeded in finding employment at the factory, and this fact qualified our family to move from the Mud Acres area, across the tracks, to the relative luxury of the factory-town barracks.

At about the same time, my father found work at the local labor camp. The camp was a link in the chain of Russian prisons known as the Gulag. Prisoners were housed there for a variety of ostensible offenses against the state and were required to work without pay at the sulfuric acid factory.

Mamma worked harder than any of us. She left early every morning to tend to our neighbors' vegetable gardens. She would water, weed, hoe, plant, and harvest these small plots and succeeded in producing a bounty of fresh food for her employers who would permit her to take home what she could carry in her tired, calloused hands each day. It was by the sweat from my mother's brow that we managed to keep food on our table while watching others around us succumb to starvation.

Before I started at the chemical plant, Mamma would take me along to assist her in the gardens. My job was to man the crank that powered the primitive irrigation system. A jerry-rigged device made of rope, pipe, and rubber flaps cut from old auto tires, the system would deliver water from the river into the irrigation trenches. A day's cranking would result in a payment of a single tomato just for me. I can still savor the sweetness of those hard-earned tomatoes to this day.

Mamma also obtained other needed provisions by trading the clothing we had brought with us from Poland. An old dress would usually fetch a few kilos of freshly milled flour, while a stylish hat might be converted into a chicken. Mamma made me the go-between in these transactions, and as a result, I got to know two industrious young Jewish men. These fellows, both a good ten years my senior, recruited me into their crude business venture which involved hiring out our services to dig water wells. They needed someone with a strong back to share the labor since our equipment consisted only of shovels and sweat. The fellows would contract with a neighborhood that wished to have a well dug nearby. Again, no money changed hands, since no one had any. We were paid in kind by the neighbors who provided room and board as long as we kept digging. We would often have to keep digging forty to fifty feet down before reaching water. The older fellows would lower me down in a bucket and pulley contraption and I would be required to dig the moist earth, piling it into the bucket until it was full and ready to be hauled back up by the other two. When I couldn't go on a minute longer, I would signal the two topsiders and they would pull me up for a few minutes rest before sending me back down into the dank pit once again.

The work was backbreaking and the days seemed endless, but the nights, well, that was a different story. These well-digging junkets were my first experience away from home, albeit not very far from home. I was a young, muscular, red-haired rascal just coming into my manhood and definitely feeling my oats.

I became fascinated with the science of hydrogeology. At a certain point in the digging, I would reach the permafrost, a layer of ice that formed around the sides of the well. I would observe as the water began seeping into the well very slowly, and this was a sign that I was getting close to my destination. Another few shovelfuls and the water began seeping in more quickly and after a few more, a steady flow could be seen. But this water was muddy and brackish and, hence, unusable. The well had only dirt walls, and the muddy water was emerging from the heavy, lime-filled, yellow loam all around me. We knew that this first flush of well water had to be entirely removed before the well could be rendered usable. We filled the buckets with the brackish, muddy stuff and spent the entire night draining our new well. Sure enough, the new water that emerged was sweet and pure and signaled our success as the community well diggers.

Our team soon became known around town as the "Well Digging Crew," and our reputation spread as we completed one successful well after another. Word of our abilities even reached the town's stationmaster who was in charge of the Alga's most important asset, the train depot. After observing us complete a well on his home street, the stationmaster approached us about a somewhat different job.

"You boys sure know how to dig," he started. "Do you think you could dig something besides a well?"

"Like what," I asked.

"I need a potato cellar," he explained, "over next to the train station. A place I can store ice in the summer and potatoes in the winter. I could use it to store fruit, as well." In northern Kazakhstan fruit of any sort was a real rarity. The acidic soil did not permit the cultivation of apples, pears, or similar fruit trees in this part of the world. All fruit had to be imported from Tashkent in the south and, of course, storage was a major problem.

We agreed to do the job and designed a storage cellar built on an angle. The deeper you went in, the steeper the angle and the more space that opened up. The entrance emerged directly next to the stationhouse and was sealed by two wooden doors. Initially, it was to be more of a pit than a cellar. It was dug as an open large hole, and then a thick wood and thatch roof was constructed and placed over the top, providing protection against the elements.

The work was hard, but not really as grueling as well digging, and there was another major attraction. We were permitted access to the rail station. This was a highly restricted area normally limited to military use. The rail line was a major one, thousands of miles long, connecting Tashkent in Uzbekistan with Moscow to the north. We watched as endless trainloads of munitions and newly recruited soldiers were shuttled through our town on their way to the Western front. When the train would stop in Alga, we got a look at these new conscripts on their way to defend the motherland against the fascists, and to us, they looked impressive indeed. Decked out in their newly issued gleaming boots, sturdy topcoats, and uniforms, these were the fresh reinforcements, as yet unscathed by battle. I recall how I admired, even envied, the soldiers with their thick wool caps and their cozy earflaps. How I longed for something to keep my ears warm as I burrowed underground digging the stationmaster's fruit cellar.

As mentioned, Tashkent was the source of fruit and the soldiers brought along plenty of the dried variety to nourish them during their long train ride into Russia. Raisins, dried melon, and apricots filled the pockets of almost every lieutenant who stepped onto the platform at Alga. In the eyes of three enterprising, and shivering, young well-diggers these men were not merely soldiers—to us they were as fresh fruit, ripe for the plucking.

Every night, when the train stopped and the new recruits got out to stretch their legs, we went to work *handling* (negotiating) with them. "How about trading your stiff new boots for these comfortable ones already broken in? I'll even throw in two packs of Ukrainian cigarettes."

"How much for that cap, *tovarisch* (comrade)?" I would offer. "I'll give you three kilos of potatoes if you throw in a packet of raisins. Do we have a deal?" All night long—wheeling and dealing. The soldiers were eager to trade since their army-issued uniforms and boots had cost them nothing. Few of them realized that the quality of your boots, once you reached the front could spell the difference between life and death by frostbite. Each morning, after a busy night of bartering with the troops, we would rush off to the town market where we would convert our booty into needed items such as food and clothing. I'll never forget the day that I managed to put together enough loot to trade for a bolt of fine fabric that I was able to fashion into a stylish suit. I could not have cherished that suit more if it had been made of gold and studded with rubies. Of course what we were doing was called *spekulatzia* and frowned upon by the Soviet authorities that eschewed any form of private enterprise. Our actions might even have been construed as war profiteering since it was really the material provided by the army that fed our little venture. Naturally, this sort of thing could not go on unnoticed, and by the time we had finished digging the storage cellar, things came to a head with the stationmaster. After five weeks, our work was done and we approached him for our agreed payment.

"I'm not going to pay you anything," he proclaimed. "You guys are nothing but a bunch of traffickers and profiteers. I've been watching what's been going on every night with those troop transports. You fellows have gotten plenty rich off of this job already and instead of paying you, I'm going to turn you in to the NKVD!"

Of course, the stationmaster waited until the job was finished before making this threat since he wanted to make sure we wouldn't fly the coop before his storage cellar was completed. He could easily carry out his threat since the railroad station and the police headquarters were part of the same large building and, as a stationmaster, he was in a quasi-military position. His rank brought him certain privileges. For example, his was the only building in town with *key-pee-tauwk* or hot running water.

Whether he was serious about throwing us in jail or whether he was merely bluffing in order to keep from having to pay us for our work, I'll never truly know since as soon as he uttered the words NKVD, the three of us turned tail and took off like a V2 rocket.

The fruits of all my labors were always shared with my family. We realized that in order for us to survive in this desolate place, we had to hang together as a family. Everyone did something. Tatu worked at the labor camp. Mamma tended the neighbor's gardens. My brother, Hetche, became adept at making tin cups and the like from bits and scraps he found here and there. And me. I did everything and anything I could to bring in an extra bite of food to put on our family table.

In addition to the sulfuric acid factory where my father and I both were to work, Alga was also home to a glazed brick factory that was operational only sporadically whenever coal or coke was available to stoke the furnaces. A short-run railroad line connected the two factories that normally remained unused during the winter months. It was near the railroad berm that my father spotted something of interest one day as he trudged homeward through the snow.

"Munjee, I saw a big telephone pole lying on the ground next to the little railroad track by the brickyard," he told me that evening. "We could sure use that pole for firewood." Tatu mentioned that pole for the next several nights, and finally I told Mamma the next evening, "I'm going after that pole and I'm going to bring it home." I packed a strong rope and put on my treasured warm coat that I had hustled from the back of a traveling soldier the month before.

Mamma admonished me, "You be careful out there, Munjee. Look out for wolves. You know there's packs of wolves out there and tonight there's a full moon, too." Heeding her advice, I removed a few bundles of straw from my mattress and bound them up with rope into small sheaves that I could easily stuff into a cloth bag that I slung over my shoulder. If necessary, these straw bundles could be ignited and used as torches to keep away any wolves I might encounter. I brought along my kindling kit that I used mainly for lighting my cigarettes. The kit consisted of a piece of steel, a small flint rock and some dried tree moss. Matches, of course, were more scarce than apples and oranges in those days, so this was my preferred method of starting a flame.

"I'll be careful, Mamma," I said, packing up my rope, my bag of straw bundles, and my fire-starter kit as I made off through the gently falling snow to locate Tatu's pole. I found it right where he said it was, lying on the ground by the tracks. I tied one end of the rope to the pole, wrapped the other end around my torso and shoulders, and began to drag the thing little by little through the snow like a sled. As I marched along, I began to get a bit disoriented as the snow covered my tracks. I pulled the log up the slight berm and positioned it on the rail line itself as I began again to pull it towards home. In this fashion, I knew I would not lose my way since the railroad would steer me to the chemical plant and then it was just a short distance to our nearby barracks. Just then, a sound whipped through the chilly night air that turned my spine into jelly and my guts into water. It was the distant baying of a pack of wolves. I thought of dropping my load and running off, but I was determined to bring home the pole in order to impress my father. The baying and howling got louder with each passing moment as I struggled and tugged against this long wooden anchor holding me back. I thought I could see a few of the beasts edging closer to me.

Finally, I put down the rope and pulled the five or six little straw bundles from my bag and placed them on the ground in a circle all around me. I sat down on the log and got out my kindling kit and struck the stone a few times to generate a spark that ignited the moss. A few puffs on the smoldering moss caused a flame to erupt that I then used to ignite the first straw bundle. By this time, I could see several packs of hungry-looking wolves approaching me from all sides. I quickly lit each bundle from the next as they formed a protective ring of fire all around me. As I huddled inside the ring, it appeared to be a stalemate. The wolves at first did not come any closer, but neither did they retreat. After the bundles had burned down a bit, I could see a few of them inching ever closer until I could make out the reflection of the flames in their feral eyes. I had heard stories of strong young men having their throats ripped out by hordes of Kazahki wolves and I was beginning to feel the icy hand of panic on the back of my neck. I looked behind me and noticed that my towrope had come too close to one of the flaming straw bundles and had burned all the way through. Picking up the piece of rope, I noticed how the smoldering end gave off thousands of red sparks as I moved it through the cold night air. This gave me an idea. I took a longer piece of rope and caught the end of it on fire. I next swung it around my head like a lariat until it came within inches of the wolves' noses. As it swung, the rope gave off sparks like a Fourth of July sparkler and this was enough to frighten the wolves and caused them to take off howling into the night. Sweating and victorious, I trudged home safely lugging my prize and with a story that I realized, even then, that I would be able to someday share with my grandchildren.

That utility pole log would serve to heat our home during the long winter months, but it was not our only source of kindling. All summer, we collected the sagebrush and tumbleweeds that blew across the countryside. We would use them along with dried cow manure to keep the winter fires burning. Sometimes these heat sources led to heated debates between neighbors over rightful title to a particular cow-pie. "That one came from my cow," one neighbor would assert. "Yes, but she dropped it on my yard!"

Another fact of life in Alga was the constant campaign against the bedbug armies. In true military fashion, these little soldiers would invariably first send out a scout before making an appearance. The scout would run back to report, and then three bugs would show their faces, followed next by a dozen and then a battalion of thousands would begin their advance. These were smelly blood-sucking bedbugs that would scamper across your skin as you slept, looking for a tender spot into which they could dip their suckers. When the attacks got too much to handle, we would resort to a counter-attack using DDT, which smelled worse than the bedbugs.

My formal education during those years was virtually non-existent. Our father disapproved of the Soviet educational system and barred both his sons from attending school in Alga. I was learning to play the trumpet before we fled Poland and I wanted to continue my lessons, but my father would not even permit that minimal level of formal education.

I do recall that my parents would, from time-to-time, take in boarders and pick up fellow Jews from the street in need of lodging. One such fellow, from Yassi in Romania, turned out to be an experienced watchmaker. My father made the young fellow an offer, "You come to my house and teach my son the trade of watch making and we'll give you a roof and a little food." For several weeks, he attempted to keep me sitting still long enough to instruct me in the fine art of watch repair, but I was not a good student, either fidgeting or soon falling asleep. He soon grew tired of investing his time in such an inattentive apprentice as me. He packed up his tools and quickly said his good-byes. We later learned that he had joined the Russian Army and was presumed killed in battle.

After a few months, I did succeed in landing a job at the sulfuric acid factory, the town's largest employer. The plant was involved with taking raw sulfur, melting it down, and fabricating the residue into such products as battery acid and kitchen matches. The factory managers eventually learned that they could mix the liquid sulfuric acid with poppy plants to make opium—a medication vitally needed by the frontline troops.

The constant overpowering stench, a mixture of rotten eggs and burning rubber, was something one never fully got used to. On top of the odor, the fall-out from the constantly burning chimneys, with their long yellow plumes of smoke, was unpleasant and unavoidable. Burning chunks of sulfur ash were constantly floating down onto my clothing, face, and hands. When the winds shifted suddenly, it was a horrific sight as everyone scurried for shelter from the flaming acid hail.

My first assignment at the plant was as a metal smith's helper. The smith's job was to fabricate all of the metal tools and equipment needed for the plant operation. Primitive factories such as this one did very little requisitioning or purchasing. All material and supplies, all the workmen's tools, were produced by hand in the factory itself.

The head of the metal smith shop was an enormous Tartar with a droopy handlebar moustache. Most of our time was spent fabricating the huge metal nuts and bolts needed to hold together the manufacturing equipment. One of us would man an enormous bellows used to stoke the hot coke fire and bring it to a temperature high enough to melt the raw steel we used to make the nuts and bolts. Two more helpers, usually I and my buddy, would assist the boss in forging the metal fasteners. The huge Tartar would fashion the square, or sometimes hexagonal, nuts in the flame using a pair of tongs as my partner and I looked on. At just the right moment, the boss would shout, "Whoot," and one of us would strike the piece with our hammer. He would shout it out again, and the other boy swung his hammer. As the pace picked up, a rhythm would develop similar to that used by chain gangs in the southern United States. After a few weeks of life in the forge, I could tell that I was not cut out to swing a hammer like John Henry. From time to time, I would miss my target causing molten steel to fly into my boss's face. After a few such incidents, my boss wisely concluded that this work was not for me and asked the supervisor to move me elsewhere.

My next stop was the electrical shop where all of the factory's electrical gear, with the exception of motors, were manufactured and maintained. I felt a spark of excitement as soon as I began my work there. I loved producing electrical switches out of the wide copper sheets and I became expert at refurbishing worn-out motors with new bearings. The foreman of the electrical shop was impressed with my thoroughness and the overall quality of my work so that when a new directive came through the plant, he called upon me to assist him. He explained that the factory was now going to employ sulfuric acid in the manufacture of opiate-based medicine for the troops fighting in Europe. In order to produce the substance, a bank of metal hot plates was needed to heat the acid-poppy resin mixture contained in large glass beakers. I went to work at once, first designing and then building one hot plate after another. The heating element coil was encased in clay that I glazed to form a ceramic insulator, which was then placed under a circular metal plate about 1 meter in diameter. All day long, women would stand by each hot plate, mixing the black poppy resin with salt and sulfuric acid and slowly stirring it until finally it emerged as a white opium powder.

One of the by-products of the opium production was a constant availability of poppy seeds. They were everywhere. Everyone was munching on them, but if you weren't careful the soporific effects of the poppy seeds would begin to take their toll and you would become very drowsy. This was exactly what happened to me and it spelled the end of my career, after only fourteen months at the sulfuric acid plant. I had worked several night shifts in a row in the electrical shop and was suffering from severe sleep deprivation. Foolishly, I began munching on poppy seeds and climbed up on the roof where I stretched out and soon dozed off. Unfortunately, I was discovered by my boss who gave me my marching papers on the spot.

"Goofing off, I see," he shouted, waking me with a start. "Okay, Mark, I can see that you're too tired to help our troops. Perhaps you should join them at the front. That should keep you awake!" He immediately recommended me for military service and, to tell the truth, I didn't mind. I was sixteen and ready for some adventure. I was sick of the sulfur fumes and the tiring work. My sole image of a soldier's life was provided by the many freshly recruited young men who passed through Alga in their spiffy new uniforms. I had no inkling about the true face of war and the rigors of military life. But I was soon to learn.

While I was paid for my work at the factory—sometimes in food ration coupons and sometimes only in bitter soup—because of my termination, my family would no longer enjoy the many other benefits that accrued from my employment at the plant . . . and the lucrative opportunities that it provided. Like most of the other women and boys who worked there, I became adept at thievery. My thefts were restricted to items that my family could not obtain elsewhere. Light bulbs, for example, were a very rare commodity in our little world. We needed light bulbs because our home was one of the few with electrical service—service that I also stole from the factory. I succeeded in surreptitiously stringing electrical cable from the plant to our door and then wiring our home for electrical service. Of course, we had to keep this fact hidden from our neighbors who would have questioned why light was emanating from our apartment every night. So, we covered the windows with heavy blankets so not a single ray of light could escape.

My father proved to be a ray of light when it came to a different sort of escape. Through his position as a guard at the Alga labor camp, he was able to assist unfairly imprisoned Jewish inmates in making their escapes. He and my mother eventually put together something of an underground railroad that served to liberate prisoners and then smuggle them out of town to anticipated safety. Most of this underground activity took place after I left town to join the military, but the first case, which paved the way for many more to come, occurred during my final days in Alga.

A Jewish mother from Alma Ata, the capital, arrived in Alga seeking her imprisoned son. Somehow she knew that my father was a Jew who worked at the camp and so she approached him for assistance. "Mr. Hasten, you've got to help me get my son out of that place," she pleaded. "He's never done anything wrong. They just locked him up because he's Jewish." My parents were persuaded. They agreed to help, but they needed a plan. They were in no position to mastermind a jailbreak, so they relied upon their intelligence and cunning.

"What about Dr. Krylov?" asked my mother. "He's got a Jewish wife and I know the wife's parents. They came from Leningrad. They have helped me get aspirin and other medications."

"Yeah, Krylov is a good man and I believe he'd help us," mused Tatu, "but the only way that Krylov gets prisoners out of that place is when he pronounces them dead."

A plaintive look came over the mother's face as she narrowed her eyes, turned to my father and asked, "Would he say that my son was dead if he was really alive?" My father picked up the idea and ran with it. "Yes. He might be persuaded to do just that. First, your son would have to be remanded to the infirmary. I could take care of that. Then Dr. Krylov would need to pronounce the boy dead and he would be placed into a shroud like a corpse." Tatu was becoming more animated, pacing back and forth across our one-room apartment as he put the pieces together one by one.

"Every day, we have prisoners who die and two trustees haul the bodies outside the prison grounds in the afternoon to the small cemetery next to the factory. The trustees dig a shallow grave, plant each body, and mark each one with a small cross. I can bribe one of the trustees to bury your son. Your son will be required to remain in the grave until nightfall. We then can go dig him up when no one can see us."

"But how will he survive being buried alive?" questioned the mother. "How will he breathe?" My father had the answer.

"The cross is made of hollow pipe. The trustee will make sure it is carefully positioned over his mouth. By keeping his mouth on one end of it, your son will be able to get plenty of air sucking on the pipe until we're able to dig him up and rescue him."

"That's crazy," exclaimed the prisoner's mother. "What if it rains and the pipe fills with water? What if an animal comes and sits on the end of the pipe blocking the airflow? It's too risky. There's got to be another way." At this point, my mother explained that the grave would be in sight of where she worked each day. She would be able to keep an eye on it and if there were any trouble, she would dig up the boy immediately with her gardening shovel, even if it meant risking her own life.

There was a long silence as the boy's mother considered all of this. Did she come to Alga to rescue her son or to see him die buried alive with a Christian cross at his head? Could she rely upon these people? The Hasten couple seemed trustworthy, but what about this non-Jewish doctor and some unknown trustee?

Could she put her son's life into the hands of so many strange people? In the end, out of desperation and faced with no other options, she reluctantly gave her approval.

The next day, my father sent the prisoner to the infirmary. On the way, he told him,

"Your mother has come to town and she's asked me to help get you out of here. But, you have to do your part. Are you willing?" The young man listened to the plan and quickly agreed to impersonate a cadaver in order to secure his freedom.

Dr. Krylov examined him a few hours later. As the doctor falsified a standard death certificate, he told the prisoner, "You have tuberculosis. A very bad case."

"So, I am going to die from tuberculosis, then," said the prisoner just as Krylov completed his signature on the bottom of the certificate.

"Why are you talking to me?" said the doctor nervously. "You are already dead. Now try not to give us away as they take you out of here or else we'll all wind up dead for real. Understand?"

Shortly thereafter, the two trustees transported the "body" a half-kilometer down the road to the prison cemetery on a cot and there my father's confederate buried the lad in a shallow grave. The trustee placed the pipe into the boy's mouth as the dirt was shoveled over his face and across his prone body. Once he was fully covered, the trustee placed his hand over the exposed end of the pipe and felt the boy's steady breathing. He next affixed a shorter pipe to the vertical one forming a cross to serve as a grave-marker and making it appear just like all the others. The young prisoner lay totally imprisoned in his makeshift grave for over two hours, his chest forced to bear the weight of the dirt with each breath that passed through the iron cross planted in his mouth, until the night finally cloaked the area in darkness.

The boy's mother, along with my mother, stole across the town to the cemetery bearing two of Mama's garden shovels. They dug with a fevered frenzy until they could see movement and were secure that the boy had lived through his ordeal. The two women brought him back to our home where he was cleaned up and given fresh clothing. Mission accomplished, the mother and son said their good-byes and—with much kissing and crying—crept out of town before sunrise.

Once the word got around among Jewish quarters that my parents were able to successfully smuggle prisoners out of Alga labor camp, more and more desperate family members came knocking on our door. My parents aided many of them—often risking their own lives. But by this time, I was already gone to be a soldier.

The only experience that accurately prepared me for the horrors of war was witnessing the fate of the Chechen exiles in Kazakhstan. As the German onslaught that drove my family from Poland swept across the Northern Caucasus, the Nazis managed to form a political alliance with the Quisling government of Chechnya that had been an autonomous Moslem nation. Autonomous in their own eyes only, since Stalin regarded Chechnya as part of the USSR. The Chechens were ready to side with any enemy of their Russian oppressors. In November 1942, German units were approaching Groznyy when they were forced to retreat as the German Sixth Army was cut off at Stalingrad. Although the Germans never actually occupied Chechnya, the Chechen collaboration with the Nazis earned them Stalin's bitter animosity. One and a half years later, after the tides of war had turned in Russia's favor, Stalin ordered an unprecedented act of retribution. The entire nation of Chechnya, along with many ethnic Ingush—some four hundred thousand men, women, and children—were summarily deported from their homeland to remote regions of central Asia, primarily in Kazakhstan in an action known as ethnic transfer. Every man, woman, and child, along with their cattle and livestock, were rounded up from their homes without warning by Red Army troops, placed into boxcars and shipped to the east. Over 30 percent died in transit or during the first year of their exile. Once the freight trains full of human cargo reached Kazakhstan, they would stop at each town along the rail track and disconnect a few boxcars, leaving the Chechens to fend for themselves in the harsh winter climate. I saw that they did not even have overcoats to protect them from the cold, and I watched as frostbite and starvation soon devastated and decimated these unfortunate victims of Stalin's rage. Even though we knew they were German collaborators, my heart had to go out to the starving, homeless children huddled in corridors and doorways against the frigid cold. Our family tried helping a few, but we were barely surviving ourselves so there was very little we could offer in the way of aid or comfort. My father tried to enlist some of the men into work brigades, but it was of little use. They were from a primitive, rural culture and were totally lost and disoriented in the frigid tundra of Kazakhstan. As I watched whole families turn into blackened, frozen corpses on the streets of our town, the Chechens vanished so that by spring it was as though they had never been here.

Soon thereafter, the Chechen-Ingush Soviet Republic was liquidated. A nation was literally erased from the map after its former inhabitants had been "transferred" to the wilderness. According to Solzhenitsyn, the Chechens were the only people "who would not give in, would not acquire the mental habits of submission—and not just individual rebels among them, but the whole nation to a man." After enduring exile and devastation, the surviving Chechens were permitted to return to their homeland after Stalin's death. When I recall the suffering I witnessed in Alga, I am better able to understand the anti-Russian hatred felt by Chechens today and their independent nature that forces them to resist any form of outside domination.

CHAPTER THREE

The Polish Brigade

As instructed by my boss, I reported to the military recruiting station the morning after my termination from the factory. I was accompanied by my father who noticed that I was carrying a tobacco pouch. Since I typically refrained from smoking in his presence, the sight of the pouch surprised him. "So you think you need to smoke to be a soldier?" he prodded.

"Don't worry, Tatu," I shot back, "I don't intend to be a soldier for very long. I'm going to desert the first chance I get." My father stopped in his tracks and turned me by the shoulders to look at him.

"Now listen to me, Mark, whatever you do, don't ever be a deserter," he said solemnly. "If you do it, you'll be sorry and it will haunt you forever." I nodded my agreement and we moved on.

Once we arrived at the recruiting office, I explained that I was a Polish subject, not a Soviet citizen, so I could not be conscripted into the Red Army. I insisted that I be placed into the First Polish Army (FPA) detachment that had been organized by Polish communist colonel Wanda Wasilewska. I had already heard about the First Polish Army and was anxious to join its ranks. The regiment was one of several such groups, organized by Polish communists to work with the Soviets in fighting the fascists. These groups included the People's Guard, a guerrilla warfare detachment, the Kosciuszko Division and the First Polish Army.

Mark Hasten

Wanda Wasilewska had become famous in 1918, as a Catholic high school student in Krakow when she stood up to the nationalists who had gained power and implemented a series of anti-Semitic policies. The students were ordered to separate into groups of Jews and Catholics. Wanda became outraged and stood with the Jews and thereby became known in Jewish circles as an ally. The FPA was organized in 1943 in Poland and originally had over 3,000 Polish men and women under arms. Their first battle against Hitler's forces took place near Lenino in October where the Poles, under Wasilewska, were sorely defeated. Despite my knowledge of this defeat, my sense of Jewish and Polish pride prodded me to tell the recruiting officer that I would only serve in the FPA. He understood and instructed me to report to Aktubinsk, the capitol city of the region, where I would be able to join the FPA forces.

I said good-bye to my family and took the train to Aktubinsk. Once there, I presented myself to the recruiting office and explained that I had come to join the First Polish Army. Unfortunately, I would not be able to join a regiment there in Aktubinsk. It was necessary for me to travel much closer to the front to receive my training and since it was not practical to send recruits off one at a time, I was told to wait until enough others showed up to make up a transport. "How long would that take?" I inquired. "Only a few months," I was told. "And what shall I do in the meanwhile?" "There's a collective farm not far from here that will put you up and put you to work while you're waiting," explained the recruiting sergeant.

Actually, the farm was quite lovely and I really enjoyed being outside in the fresh air and working in the sunny fields by day and carousing with my fellow workers at night. I became something of a country boy while on the farm, letting my beard grow and adopting the ways of a peasant. I recall being on hand for the harvest when all the fruits and vegetables were being collected and stored. I managed to "organize" a wagonload of fresh pro-

ce and spent several days on the road as I delivered the
oceries to my family back at Alga. When I returned home, I
scovered that my brother, Hetche, was recovering from a severe
iess and seeing me, in my full red beard, helped greatly to cheer
n up. The wagonload of foodstuffs naturally thrilled my parents.
most all the farm workers on the collective managed to make
' with at least a wagonload or two of produce to take home with
em. It was this sort of self-interest that led to the eventual
lure of the collective farm system in the Soviet Union.

I once again bid farewell to my family, and this time we all
ew we would not be able to reunite until after the war. By the
ie I arrived back to Aktubinsk, there were already six other
ung recruits ready to attach to the FPA. Our crew was placed
der the supervision of two Russian soldiers who had been
covering from their wounds in Aktubinsk and were now ready to
urn to the front. They were ordered to escort our group a
ousand miles west to the Ukraine, where we were to receive our
sic training.

During the eight-day train ride, our crew of eight grew very
ose to one another. The soldiers instructed us on how to sleep
gether, wash together, and even steal together. Thievery was
cessary if we were to eat since no food provisions had been
ide for our journey. At every stop along the way, our team
iuld hit the little depot bazaar in order to snag something to eat
im one of the food concessions. One of us would distract the
ndor's daughter while another would stuff *katchkies* under his
at while her back was turned. But our group's most notorious
iievement went beyond petty shoplifting. We actually
nvinced our so-called guards to permit us to travel to division
adquarters with-out them. We learned that our train would be
ssing within a few hours of the hometown of our two military
corts. They had not been home for over a year and very much
iged to see their families again. It did not take much persuasion,
d only a few rubles,

39

to convince them to hand over our dossier files to us and hop off the train for a visit home. Once the guards departed, we were on our own. While we were considered to be conscripts, we had not yet received any training, uniforms, or been officially inducted into the military. If we had chosen not to report, we would have technically been AWOL, but it was unlikely that the military would have been able to catch up with any of us until after the war.

The prospect of freedom was tempting, but after talking it over and realizing we had no food, no money, and no contacts, we determined that we'd be forced to live as bandits in order to survive. Judging that a soldier's life was slightly better than a thief's, we elected not to desert and to enter the military as planned. Our group arrived intact at FPA headquarters in the Ukrainian town of Zsitomir. We were put through the standard military induction process; we were given shaves, haircuts, uniforms, and a quickie interview.

"What did you do before?" asked the induction sergeant.

"I worked as an electrician."

"Good. You'll be on the engineering pontoon brigade." End of interview.

Basic training lasted eight weeks during which time we were instructed on how to use a carbine rifle, how to polish our boots, how to shower, how to march in step, and all the usual skills foisted upon a fresh recruit. Both the captain and the lieutenant under whom we served were Russians by birth, but they wore Polish uniforms. While we were called the Free Polish Army, we really were not free of Soviet control, our officers were not Polish and we were not actually an army—more of a division or detachment of the Soviet Red Army.

While I never actually denied my Jewishness while in the army, I did not advertise it either. I was blond, fair-skinned, and spoke perfect Polish with no trace of a Yiddish accent. I'm certain that my fellow recruits assumed I was a Catholic like them, although the subject never really came up. After all, we were part of the Soviet Army and the party ideology demanded strict atheism. I don't believe it was true in the rest of Soviet society, but in the army, religious differences were truly set aside. In fact, I was viewed by my superior officers as a paragon of military perfection. I kept my shoes shined and my uniform was always immaculate. I was often paraded in front of the other troops as a model soldier. "Take a look," shouted the sergeant, pointing at me, "that's what a real soldier is supposed to look like."

Based on my declared skill as an electrician, I was attached to the First Warsaw Pontoon Bridge Brigade *(Pirewszy Warshawsky Pulk Pontonowy Mostowy)* and assigned to keep the electrical motors operational. Our job was to build the pontoon bridges that would allow the infantry to cross a river as part of its advance. Existing bridges were typically destroyed by the retreating German forces. Our crew was responsible for driving a Model T Ford with an onboard DC generator that served as our main power source. The generator was needed to operate all the power tools used in the construction of each bridge. We also looked after the huge pile drivers that were used to plant the pylon footings into the riverbank as the first step of the bridge-building process. These heavy wooden poles would serve as the anchors for the ropes and cables that extended across the river and affixed to the floating pontoons. The pile driver was fueled by high octane, 200 proof alcohol.

Once the pylons were positioned and the cables strung, the first pontoon was put into place. This was a special one known as the shore-hugger. The shore-hugger needed to be secured down tightly since it would sit partially on land and partially in the water. The pontoons used to span the river were actually large wooden boxes, brought into place via truck. The truck would drive out onto the river as far as possible and then drop the next pontoon that would be secured into place by the crews. Next, a series of crossbars would be placed over the pontoon to create a roadway capable of carrying foot as well as armored transport traffic. Once the bridge had been extended by another pontoon length, the truck would return and drop the next one into the water until the river was fully breached. Once on the other side, another shore-hugger was delivered, the pile-driving equipment brought across and fresh pylons were sunk into the opposite shore completing the project. Since we would be expected to construct pontoon bridges often under enemy fire, we were trained in speed and quiet efficiency as officers kept a stopwatch on us, clocking how quickly we could secure each pontoon. Our times dwindled as we became more and more adept at the art of pontoon engineering.

The pontoon brigade headquarters was located in the forest of Lubartov near Lublin. After training was completed, our brigade was stationed for a time in Lublin, near the infamous Nazi death camp at Majdanek where 235,000 Jews were gassed and cremated as part of the Nazi death machine. In July 1944, Lublin, and Majdanek along with it, were liberated by Russian troops under the command of General Bogdanov and Polish militias. Only 1,500 Jews were found barely alive after the Germans fled. Our brigade was instructed to report to Majdanek for billeting, after most of the corpses had been removed or buried. I recall seeing the pitiful survivors receiving medical attention that, sadly, often came too late to save them.

There was a court martial underway as we arrived. A handful of SS guards had been apprehended and charged with mass murder. They were convicted and publicly hung using open flatbed trucks. Five lives in exchange for 235,000 struck me as very poor justice, but I was, nevertheless, glad to see them swing. I recall walking the grounds of the camp on the day I arrived and examining the crematoria ovens. As I placed my hand on one of the doors, I could still feel the heat of the metal which had, at one time, contained temperatures of over 1,000 degrees Fahrenheit required to turn human bone into ash.

As I wandered through the summer fields of Majdanek, I examined the mountains of personal effects. A hill made up of eyeglasses. How many Jews were incinerated to produce such a hill? A mound of shoes many of them belonging to children. I studied a single shoe and thought, "When the mother put this shoe on her baby, did she suspect that it would be for the last time?" Thousands of suitcases, bearing their owners' names in white chalk. Each case packed with the family's most precious belongings and, like their owners, each one ravaged and torn asunder.

Could my family have ended up like this? Shipped to a death center? Processed? Gassed? Burned? As I staggered through this nightmare world, I thought back to a recurring dream that I had experienced the year before in Alga. I dreamed that I had lost all my teeth. I remember sharing the dream with my mother who was adept at dream interpretation. She listened as I described my toothless, gaping mouth to her. Her face then grew ashen and her eyes fell to the floor. "Oh, Munjee. It only means one thing," she said half-moaning. "They're dead. All of our family. All the ones we left behind in Brotchin. They're all dead." At the time, I dismissed her interpretation as so much war hysteria.

I later learned, however, that on June 16, 1942 the remainder of our family, along with all the surviving Jews of our town, were deported from Bohorodczany to the nearby town of Stanislawow where they were butchered by the Ukrainian fascists at a place called Rudolf's Mill. I cannot be 100 percent sure, but I am almost certain that it was the following day, in Kazakhstan, that my mother delivered her frightening dream interpretation to me. Two years later, standing surrounded by the unmistakable evidence of Nazi brutality against the Jews, I thought back to that dream and to my mother's interpretation. "Could she have been correct?" I wondered. "Is everyone really dead?" The thought was too painful to accept. Maybe I was dreaming again. Maybe the ovens, warmed by burning Jewish flesh were a delusion. Perhaps the mountain of artificial limbs ripped from helpless handicapped Jews was a mirage. I wanted badly to wake up but I was not sleeping. I did wake up to many things, however, as the result of my visit to Majdanek, but I still was more or less in denial. "They could not have killed them all." I told myself. "Not Uncle Psachye. Surely, he must have survived." Sadly, I later learned they all were gone.

We received our training in bridge construction along the shores of the Bug River in Soviet-controlled Ukraine, but our first real project was the building of a pontoon bridge across the Vistula in freshly liberated Warsaw in January of 1945—in the midst of a very cold and bitter winter. The Red Army troops needed to cross the river from the east side of the city, known as Praga, which had been taken by the Soviets on September 13, and into the German-occupied western sector known as Czerniakow. The Vistula River, at that point, represented the front.

We were directed to construct the bridge from the Praga side towards beachheads that had been secured on the western side by Polish Home Army troops from the Radom district. It was this army of Polish soldiers under Polish command that sought to liberate the western part of Warsaw from German occupation in a move known as the Warsaw Uprising. During the months of August and September 1944, the encircled Polish Home Army troops staged a mass act of resistance that, had it received support from the Allies, would have succeeded in driving the Germans from the city. But Stalin, always mindful of the post-war political consequences, understood the importance of Warsaw being liberated by Soviet, and not Polish, troops. So assistance, so easily available, was withheld by the Red Army as the Poles were left to fight alone. Some Allied assistance, in the form of airdropped supplies, emanated from the US Army, but since it was based in Italy, some 1,200 miles away across enemy territory, it was of little value. No amount of persuasion by Roosevelt or Churchill could prompt Stalin to extend any form of assistance to the uprising. In fact, indiscriminant Soviet bombing runs throughout the city resulted in its near-total devastation and the loss of more Polish lives than German.

Our first step was to bring in the Model T and set up the generator and begin operating the primitive drop hammers or pile drivers as we forced the wooden pylons into the frozen riverbank. Around us stood war-ravaged Warsaw, with close to 90 percent of her buildings destroyed. The only structure left unscathed was the Royal Palace or Zamek Jaruzelski that our troops rushed to occupy as soon as the Germans were driven out since it was the only spot that offered fresh running water. By January 13, 1945, Warsaw was almost fully liberated, and on that night we hurriedly constructed the bridge that would carry our victorious First Polish Army, under the command of General Poplavsky, into Czerniakow to carry out what was, by this point, merely a clean-up operation against the remaining German rear guard. We encountered very light German resistance and many frozen bodies as we went about our work—merely some ineffective light artillery and cannon fire. Our true enemy was the winter cold that rendered the river partially frozen.

After the pylons were sunk, the next task was to extend two heavy ropes across the frigid water and then link them via a series of bolted crossbars. In order to secure the crossbars, it was necessary for soldiers to get into the water—water whose temperature actually felt warmer than the bitter cold night air. Of course, continued submersion in near-freezing water was resulting in widespread hypothermia among the men. I could see that we would soon begin losing them if something were not done quickly. I was growing more and more concerned when I remembered the 200 proof alcohol spirits we used to power the pile driver. This was potent stuff, highly flammable, but it could be used to keep these fellows warmed up while they finished their work. I quickly grabbed an empty milk can, filled it with the potent stuff and picked up a soup ladle from the mess tent. Venturing out on the floating pontoons, I went man to man instructing each to lift his head and open his mouth as I ladled the fiery stuff into their near-frozen bodies like a mother hen feeding her chicks. It occurred to me that I was carrying out this mission without authorization and that the alcohol I was consuming would surely be missed when it came time to fuel the pile driver. So once the milk can was emptied, I filled it with river water and poured it into the alcohol to cover up my crime. The alcohol served to stave off widespread hypothermia, and after the hour-long job was completed, every man was pulled from the river into the waiting trucks, alive, and slightly intoxicated.

By morning, the bridge was complete and our boys were the first ones to reach the other side. Looking around the ravaged city, still in flames as long plumes of smoke stretched across the red dawn sky, we spotted a building that was nearly intact. It turned out to be a government printing facility used in the production of Polish paper money. Once inside, we discovered vast amounts of paper stock, imprinted on one side only as if the printers were forced to flee before they had a chance to turn the sheets over. We suddenly felt like multi-millionaires. The half-printed currency had enormous value to us as we went about rolling up the paper sheets into log-sized bundles and used them to fuel the fire we used to combat the crippling cold. We joked about having money to burn as we tossed another million or two onto the crackling fire.

After enabling the army to cross the Vistula, we next set to work repairing the bridges and train trestles across the river that the retreating German forces had destroyed or damaged. Our first task was to search each damaged bridge for undetonated mines and disable them. I recall that one rail trestle became a top priority because it was to be used by Stalin's personal coach as he traveled to meet with Truman, Churchill, and Atlee at Potsdam outside of Berlin.

Our next destination was the Oder River that formed the border between Poland and Germany. In April 1945, we were dispatched to Shtetin in Pomerania. Near Shtetin was the village of Greiffenhagen where the Oder branches in two before emptying into the Baltic Sea. The Russian Army had advanced to this point in March and taken heavy losses as they attempted to cross the Oder using its own pontoon bridge. By the time we arrived, the Germans had retreated and we were assigned the job of repairing their damaged bridge. We worked for days fortifying the bridge and rendering it strong enough to support the Soviet advance towards Berlin. It was during this time that we got word that Roosevelt had died and a few weeks later, word spread that Hitler was dead and that the Germans were ready to surrender to the Allies.

On the day the war ended, our brigade was back in Warsaw and joined in the bittersweet celebration. On the next day, we were ordered back to army headquarters in Wloclawek, a little further along the Vistula River, where we received permanent lodging in regular dormitory buildings. The army camp was also being used to house captured prisoners of war—most of them female. Hence, our camp came to be known as the Harem. It was here, at the Harem of Wloclawek, that I would reunite with my family and attempt to rebuild our family structure. An attempt, that ultimately, was doomed to fail.

CHAPTER FOUR

Farewell, Poland

All in all, I had been fortunate. Thanks to my father's far sightedness, we managed to escape the fate of most of the Jews of our community and thanks to good fortune, I was assigned to an engineering brigade that saw very little combat. I emerged from the war with a few medals on my chest and generally grateful to be alive and anxious to get on with my life. As mentioned before, very few of my fellow soldiers knew that I was Jewish. They viewed me as a regular fellow. The fact that I was Jewish never came up during the war years. We shared food, clothing, and vodka. Another thing we shared was lice. Now this was a problem. You didn't mind your own lice, but getting them from someone else was unacceptable.

I became infested with a little white louse variety that managed to get everywhere; in my hair, in my eyelashes, under my skin. And I was a person who prided himself on keeping clean and well scrubbed but no matter what I did, I could not rid myself of these pests. I was referred to a particular woman living in Wloclawek who was reported to hold a power over these vermin, so I made an appointment. Upon arrival, she bid me to get undressed as she produced a straight razor and began to shave every hair off my body. She shaved my head, my chest, my buttocks—she even shaved the pestilence from my testicles! Down on her knees at work, the De-lousing Lady looked up and inquired, *"Ty Zsidik?! [You're a Jew!?]"* I deemed it unwise to lie to someone holding a straight razor so close to my privates. *"Tak. Ya Zsidik,"* I confirmed. Next, she began to cover me from head to toe with naphtha disinfectant. Finally, she began to scrub me with a coarse brush that served to remove the eggs that had been planted all over my body. It was painful and embarrassing, but it worked. I've never been bothered by that particular type of louse since then.

After undergoing the de-lousing treatment, word of my being a Jew began to spread slowly. But after an incident in a local bathhouse, everyone learned the truth. Wloclawek, like many communities in that part of the world, had a central Turkish bathhouse. I was there relaxing and taking my weekly bath in this steamy, tiled sanctuary of sweat, when an entire six-man Polish artillery brigade came in the door. I could see at once that they had been drinking and were becoming steadily louder and more rowdy. After they were undressed, one of their crew pointed to my groin and announced to his mates, "Look, there's a Zsid!" The eagle-eyed Jew-spotter began taunting me, "Zsid, zsid, zsid!" and soon the others joined in. One of the bigger fellows approached me and asked his comrades, "Well, let's see what this fellow can do for us." As I stood there naked, several of them grabbed me, pinned my arms, and held my head under a slowly dripping cold water tap for some Chinese water torture. After they grew bored with this game, they loosened their grip and I slipped from their grasp. By now, I knew what unrestrained Polish anti-Semitism was capable of and I wasn't going to stick around for more of their drunken abuse. Standing there, dripping and naked, I saw that my access to the bathhouse door was blocked, so, without even thinking about my clothes, I decided to make a break for it. I picked up one of the sturdy wooden chairs and swung it hard at the window, shattering it to pieces. I dove through the broken glass unmindful of the scratches and cuts across my unprotected skin. Running like a chicken in the late springtime afternoon, I bolted across a nearby pasture. Standing between two grazing cows stood a young peasant girl, who—if she was at all shocked by the sight of a naked, bleeding, circumcised young man streaking across her meadow—did not show it. She called out to me and indicated that I should come to her. I didn't really know what she had in mind, but, nevertheless, I complied. Once I reached her side, she removed a blanket from one of the cows and helped me use it to wrap myself in. I thanked her, and after making it safely back to my barracks wrapped in the cowgirl's blanket, I later returned it to her along with a gift of army delicacies to express my gratitude for her kindness.

I had just spent two years in the Polish Brigade of the Red Army fighting and risking my life for the liberation of Poland and what was my thanks? Anti-Jewish hatred from these bully young sons of Poland. Outwardly, I did not appear to fit the Nazi racist stereotype of a Jew. My hair was reddish blond and I sported a fair complexion. My German was nearly impeccable and I, in no way, flaunted my Judaism. Since I was easily able to pass for a non-Jew, both in the military and in civilian life, I felt somehow secure and not threatened. On Sunday morning, when my compatriots would head off to church, I would always find a way to wiggle out of it. I would be busy shining my shoes or doing my laundry and tell my friends to go ahead without me. I was the classic closet Jew and I was living in a dream of denial inside that closet. It is safe to say that the bathhouse incident sharply awakened me from my dream state. Like the subject of the old joke: "What is a Conservative? Answer: a Liberal who just got mugged!" I underwent a something of an epiphany. In retrospect, this episode was a true turning point in my life. My naiveté was washed away in the soaking I received that day in the bathhouse. I came away devoid of not only my clothing, but also stripped of any notions that anti-Semitism had died with Hitler. Poles had been hating Jews for centuries before Hitler and are likely to continue doing so for years to come.

Of course, my major priority during this period was reuniting with my family. Before they had left Alga in Kazakhstan, I had written to them, using a secret code, and in this way informed them that I was stationed near Warsaw. The code was needed to get by the military censors that screened all of our outgoing mail. Of course we were strictly instructed never to reveal our position in any of our outgoing letters. Anticipating this situation before I left home, my parents and I devised a simple acrostic code that I would employ to let them know of my whereabouts. My first letter from any new location we found ourselves in would always go out coded. Taking the first letter of every sentence in order would spell out the name of the closest major town to wherever I happened to be. I would write to my parents in both Yiddish and in Russian, but the following example, in English, illustrates how this system worked. I would write:

"We are all enjoying the extra rations we've been given. All of the enlisted men are busy trading cigarettes for food. Remember how Uncle Psachye used to love to eat schnitzel? Someone in my unit talks about schnitzel all the time, too. Are you both doing well? When we meet again I'll give you all a big kiss and hug."

Such an innocuous letter would never arouse the suspicions of the army censors, but by taking the initial letter from each sentence (WARSAW), my parents were able to easily learn my whereabouts. In this way they could determine if I was near the front or out of harms way. I agreed to write at least once per week and as long as one or two of my letters managed to get through each month, my parents knew I was doing all right.

At the conclusion of the war my parents and brother swiftly, and with great difficulty, managed to steal out of Alga and began the long trek back home to Poland. Actually, my father was not too keen to leave and it was only due to my mother's urging and a new danger that surfaced and convinced him to pack up and sneak out of Alga as secret passengers aboard a northbound train.[1] The danger that provided the impetus for their hasty departure was the disappearance of Dr. Krylov, the physician who had assisted my parents in springing prisoners from the local labor camp. One day, shortly after the war ended, Dr. Krylov simply was nowhere to be found. When my mother asked after him, his family said that he had gone to Alma Ata for his health, but when the doctor failed to reappear after eight weeks, my mother correctly feared the worst. We learned much later that he had, in fact, been arrested by the NKVD and taken to the capital for interrogation where he was administered sodium pentothal and questioned about his role in aiding in the escapes of state prisoners. While all of this was not known by my parents at the time, they correctly concluded that if Krylov had been arrested he would undoubtedly be forced to talk. And if he talked, he would implicate my parents as the organizers of many of the jailbreaks. This made it unsafe to stay put and so, by the time that the NKVD agents came looking for my parents shortly thereafter, they and my brother had already hit the road. My father continued to feel the hot breath of the NKVD on his neck the entire time he remained in Russia and Eastern Europe. He was not able to breathe easily again until he finally succeeded in getting the family across the border into Western Europe. I'm certain that this threat hanging over my parents' head contributed to their drive and their desire to get to the West. They simply wanted to get as far away from Stalin as possible.

After many months crossing Russia, my parents and brother finally made their way to Lvov in Poland. Once they arrived in Lvov, I began receiving letters from them addressed to the Polish military base in Wloclawek. The last letter they had received from me in Alga informed them, in code, that I was near Warsaw and they correctly assumed that I was stationed in the nearby military base in Wloclawek. In my responses, I explained my situation and urged them to come to Wloclawek where conditions appeared better than what they were facing in Lvov. My father's letters told of the hardships the family had faced traversing

Russia and further explained that he had tried to return back to Brotchin, but found that to be impossible. None of the family had returned yet, he explained. In fact, no Jews at all had come back to Brotchin and he was unable to learn of their whereabouts after they had all been deported to Stanislawow in 1942. At this point, he was still unable to admit the awful truth to himself that they had all been murdered.

At my urging, my father agreed to pack up my mother and brother and come to meet me in Warsaw. Of course, making connections in this war-ravaged capital was next to impossible. There were no functioning telephones, telegraphs, newspapers, or other means of mass communication available. I visited the spot in Warsaw where I assumed they would arrive—the large bombed-out Jewish central community building where thousands of Jews daily sought to reunite with family members. One of the few remaining walls had been whitewashed and was covered with handwritten messages in every European language creating a huge bulletin board. After much searching, I spotted a message in my father's script. "We are well and will come to meet you in Wloclawek in a few days," was all it said. I responded with another message, "I will wait for you in Wloclawek," and caught a truck back to my army barracks.

Every day from then on, I greeted each train from Warsaw with suitcases stuffed with packages of sugar, butter and other goodies with which to greet my parents and brother—but they did not arrive. In the chaos, they had somehow wound up in Lodz. By questioning many of the Jews getting off the train in Wloclawek, I learned that my family had somehow gotten on the train to Lodz by mistake. I quickly packed up two suitcases full of goodies and caught the next train to Lodz. Once there, locating them was sadly, quite easy. I began inquiring after a couple with a teenage child. Such a family configuration among Jews was a rarity. Very few family units remained intact. Most Jews traveled alone or with a spouse, at most. A family unit composed of a mother, a father, and a child was decidedly unusual and I was soon able to pick up their trail and learn that they had secured shelter inside the old Jewish ghetto. Lugging my suitcases, I hurried off to find them. What greeted me next so shocked and disturbed me that the memory of it still haunts me today.

As I set foot into the dimly lit wooden barracks, I overcame the stench and began scanning the triple-deck bunks searching for a familiar face. The first face I recognized was that of my mother. Her hair had gone to gray under an old *tichel* (scarf). She was wearing a long, ragged *shenel* (military great coat) and a pair of oversized, worn-out army boots. Her feet were covered with *shmates* (rags) that had been stuffed inside her boots. My father was wearing a three-fourth length homemade coat fashioned from an army horse blanket stuffed with cotton for additional warmth. By this point, all of the cotton had sunk to the bottom of the coat, giving him a somewhat outrageous appearance. My little brother, Hetche, wore a small jacket and a pair of dirty *pump hosen* (knickers) over a pair of mismatched shoes. I remembered my parents as being spotlessly and scrupulously clean to the point of mania. To see them in such a state, ripped my heart to shreds. They had all lost weight and even as their sunken eyes began to well with tears, I could not overcome my despair at the thought of how they must have suffered. Ragged, tired, worn-out refugees. Years of being hunted and continuous running had turned them into feral fugitives. They began stuffing the food I had brought into their clothing and under the bed to protect it. I told them not to move from this place until I returned the following day with an army truck I had commandeered. The next morning, I packed them up and brought them back with me to my little duplex soldier's apartment in Wloclawek. To them, it looked like a royal palace. From their viewpoint, indoor running water represented the ultimate in luxury. They marveled at the circular porcelain fireplace providing radiant heat to what had once been German officer's quarters. It was close quarters, but at last, our family was reunited under one roof again.

The apartment was only a few doors away from the administrative office where I worked. I had been assigned to the base's requisitions office. Because of my attractive handwriting, I was called upon to complete purchase orders and carry out other bureaucratic paperwork. I became deft at using an abacus as I helped prepare the camp's bookkeeping ledgers. As mentioned before, all of our officers were Russians including the captain who served as my superior officer. I developed a close relationship with the man and confided in him. "We must get out of Poland, sir. Europe is no longer a fit place for Jews to live," I explained. "We need to get to Palestine."

"You're right," he responded. "And I believe you're going to make it. And when you do, please do one thing."

"What's that?" I asked.

"Take me with you!" I could see that he was only half-joking, so I shot back, "You've got a deal, sir. But meanwhile, you better treat me well." We shook hands and he was as good as his word. He immediately found new, spacious lodging for us in a lovely home next to the base.

Among my duties as requisitions clerk was obtaining provisions for the base. I would complete the paperwork and then travel to one of the large army distribution centers located at either Bydgoszcz or Poznan to retrieve whatever supplies were needed. It was a trusted position, since I could have easily unloaded the goods at any underground flea market for my own gain. For the most part, I managed to resist temptation and carry out my supply runs honestly. The only exceptions were when it came to either tobacco or *svennaya tushonka*. The latter items came from America where they were known as Vienna sausages. These spicy treats were packed in large cans and were highly prized by the local population who like to munch on them when drinking. These snacks, as well as any

Cigarettes that fell into my hands, would seldom make it all the way back to the camp intact.

On one such junket, I was traveling with another soldier in the camp's old Studebaker truck. I carried my pistol and a large leather briefcase, containing all the requisition forms, slung over my shoulder. I found myself at the Poznan railway station standing on a high overpass looking down at the rail yard and platforms below. At this time, I made it a practice, whenever I found myself in a large public crowd, to scan people's faces looking for friends and family whose fate was unknown after the war. For many years, I carried a mental photo album of all the faces I could remember from Brotchin in the hopes that I might find someone alive. As I studied the many hundreds of people moving along the platform some fifty feet below, someone caught my eye. I observed a gentleman walking briskly away from me along the line of boxcars. His back was turned towards me, but looking carefully, I was able to spot something odd. I could tell that the pinkie finger of his right hand remained extended and stiff. This had to be my uncle Hertzl Levy. Hertzl was married to my mother's younger sister, Raizele, and was a friendly fixture of my childhood. How many lazy summers had I spent at his spacious home in the Carpathian countryside, near the idyllic village of Pasechnya, playing with my country cousins skinny-dipping in the Prutt river? The area was marked with lush waterfalls and deep green foliage, and to me, it was a little Garden of Eden to which I was permitted to escape every summer. Uncle Hertzl, known among our family as "Shustak," owned a huge lumberyard that he operated very successfully. In addition, his wealth permitted him to invest into an Italian crude oil distributorship. Shustok enjoyed breeding thoroughbred horses for pleasure. I first learned how to ride on one of Uncle Hertzl's beautiful Arabian stallions.

Shaking off my reverie, I ran down to the platform as quickly as I could to try and catch up with this short stocky man with the stiff finger and the almost oriental, squinty eyes. I scoured each face as I rushed up and down the long platform, but, sadly, I soon realized that I had lost him. I decided that he must have boarded one of the boxcars waiting to pull out of the station. These trains were filled with Russian Poles being returned to Poland as part of the massive repatriation program underway. I hopped into the first boxcar and began shouting in Yiddish, "Hertzl Levy. Hertzl Levy. Has anyone seen a man named Hertzl Levi?!" No response. I went to the next car, and the next and the next—each time repeating my announcement. In desperation, by the time I reached the sixth boxcar I changed my message slightly. "Has anyone here seen a man named Shustak? Shustak. I'm looking for Shustak, also known as Hertzl Levy. Has anyone seen him?" Out from the shadows stepped a stocky, squinty-eyed smiling face that greeted me and said in Yiddish, "You must be a member of my family because you know that my name is Shustak. Who are you?!" I had last seen Uncle Hertzl when I was perhaps twelve years old, and now I was 18. I recognized him, but he, of course, did not recognize me. "I am Berish's son," I told him. The man fell apart. We embraced and were so overcome with emotion, we had to be assisted out of the train onto the platform. Through the gasps and the tears, we recounted our tales of survival. Sadly, I learned, that my dear Aunt Raisele and my childhood, playmate cousins had all been cruelly killed. Hertzl himself had been summarily arrested and packed off to Russia by the Bolsheviks after they had taken over Nadvornya in 1939. He was a successful merchant and considered to be a member of the hated bourgeoisie. One day, he was ordered to report to the newly established NKVD headquarters where he was arrested and shipped off without any word to his family. His wife, my Aunt Raisele traveled the five kilometers to Nadvornya in search of her missing husband. She learned little of his fate from the local *hutzul* (non-Jewish population) who could only tell her that he had been arrested by the authorities. She returned home in despair from where, after the Nazi occupation eighteen months later, she and the children were rounded up, placed into a makeshift ghetto, and murdered by the local Ukrainians one bloody night along with hundreds of their Jewish neighbors.

Meanwhile, Uncle Hertzl was shipped to a remote region of Siberia. Conditions were indescribable, but he managed to survive under several years of confinement. Once Germany invaded Russia, Hertzl was able to convince his captors that he could be of value in the war effort. He convinced the authorities that he was an experienced chemical tanner. He knew how to concoct the formulae needed in the curing and tanning of cowhides for the manufacture of leather. Once they were convinced of his abilities, they constructed a leather production factory somewhere in mid-Russia and placed him in charge of the operation. In this way, Hertzl survived the war and found himself able to return to Poland when it was over. At this point, Hertzl had teamed up with a partner and was heading towards Shtetin, transporting several barrels of chemical compounds, where the two men planned to open a leather tanning facility.

Uncle Hertzl introduced me to an attractive young lady who I just noticed had been standing discreetly by his side during our reunion. "This is my wife," said Uncle Hertzl and I shook the attractive young woman's hand. After learning of the murder of his family, Hertzl had married a Jewish Romanian woman in Russia and was now traveling with her to Shtetin. She held a newborn infant in her arms that I presumed to be my new cousin. Hertzl and I quickly turned to talk of the future. I told him that my father was trying to get the family to the West to Germany and then perhaps to America.

"That's what we're trying to do, too," he told me. "That's why we're going to Shtetin. Because it's on the road to Berlin. Tell your father to write to me and we can make plans together. We can all travel together to America." And, of course, I agreed. At this point, the train began rumbling and we realized that it was time for me to go.

"Come see us in Shtetin," shouted Uncle Hertzl as the train pulled away.

"I'll be there, Uncle Shustak," I yelled back, waving.

When I returned to Wloclawek with the amazing news of my chance encounter, my mother did not appear surprised in the least.

"Don't you remember what I told you about that dream?" she asked me. I thought back and recalled that a few days before my trip I had related a strange dream to her that she had, as was her custom, interpreted for me. In the dream, I saw myself finding a beautifully ornate gold pocket watch on a long golden chain. I remember swinging the watch back and forth and wondering if it was my grandfather's or my uncle's watch. The dream didn't make much sense to me, but my mother explained, "This dream is a very good omen because it means that someone is alive. Someone from our family who we thought was dead is really alive."

Now, Mamma reminded me about the dream. "Don't you remember? I told you then it was a good sign and here it is. This is it." Then I told her the rest of the story. I told her what I learned from Uncle Hertzl of how her beloved sister Raisele had perished along with her three dear children. My mother wept bitter tears at the thought of how these cherished loved ones had been slaughtered for no reason. But what I told her next seemed to mortify her.

"Hertzl has re-married already," I informed her. "He has a young Romanian wife and they've already produced a little baby." My mother was dumbstruck. Even though it had been more than three years since her sister Raisele had been killed, this rapid re-marriage struck her as improper. She never said it plainly, but I could tell that she was thinking, "Couldn't he have waited a bit? Waited until after the war and until after he was sure that she was dead?" In the post-war refugee world, Jewish survivors clung to each other in any way they could. So, it would be unfair to judge Uncle Hertzl too harshly. But, to my mother, what he had done was offensive so she appeared lukewarm as my father and I began to make plans to reach Berlin through Shtetin along with Uncle Hertzl and his family.

Within the next few months, I had arranged to travel to Shtetin several times and invariably stayed with Hertzl and his bride. He and his partner had already set up shop and were working steadily turning cowhides into leather. We formulated a plan that would get both families into nearby Berlin and then on to the USA. But, as things turned out, the plan was never executed and we emigrated out of the Displaced Persons (DP) camps without Uncle Hertzl and his new family. I believe, to this day, that my mother did not wish to face him, much less travel with him. She would have found it heartbreaking to witness her former brother-in-law with his new wife and baby and would have been unable to refrain from giving him a piece of her mind.

During one such trip to Shtetin, I was directed to the large open-air flea market near the center of town. As mentioned, whenever I found myself in proximity of a large crowd of people, I would wander through it searching the faces for lost relatives. I held out hopes of finding more survivors just as I had found Uncle Hertzl. Sometimes I would approach a stranger simply because I believed him to be Jewish. Of course, I had to be discreet, so I would typically brush up close to the suspected co-religionist and mutter either *Sh'ma Yisroel*, or *Amcha?* The first term, which means "Hear, O Israel," contains the opening words of the most well-known prayer in Jewish liturgy. The second term means simply "my people." If the stranger turned around, then I knew I had found a fellow Jew and we could then compare notes about our wartime experiences and perhaps gain some information about a lost family member.

As I was strolling down the lane of vendor booths, scanning each face, looking for—who knows what? Suddenly, I stopped dead in my tracks. On display and being offered for sale were two items that instantly transported me back to our shtetl home during those golden days before the war in Brotchin. I was suddenly in my parents' bedroom that contained two separate straw beds, side-by-side in the manner prescribed by Jewish law in the *Halacha* (Jewish code of law). Over each bed hung a lovely, framed, original oil painting. The paintings depicted pastoral deer hunting scenes. The painting on the left showed the cherub-faced hunting party in traditional German folk garb, lederhosen and feathered caps, as they appeared before the hunt while the right-hand picture showed a scene from after the hunt, as the hunters, smoking cigars and meerschaum pipes, stood around the carcass of the captured quarry. There, before me, on a makeshift display table, among some assorted pots and pans, stood what appeared to be the very same paintings. Were they the same ones? I pondered as I continued strolling by the vendor's booth. They had to be the same ones, I thought to myself. Ours were signed originals—not prints or lithographs. The frames matched exactly. As I walked by, I glanced at the booth owner. She was obviously a *Schwab* (Literally: frog. A German national living in another land). I tried to discern something from her impassive gaze but wound up turning around and walking back to the booth. I looked her in the eye and confronted her in perfect German.

"Where did you get these paintings?" I demanded. She frowned at me with high indignation.

"I'm selling them here," she shot back. "What do you want?"

"I remember these pictures. Where did you get them?" I repeated, becoming more agitated and forceful.

"I have no idea," she said dismissively and began eyeing the crowd over my head, seeking out other buyers. "Now, if you don't mind, I'm trying to do business here."

I knew these were our paintings and I also knew just as well that I could not prove it. So reluctantly, I began to slowly move on. Becoming more upset with each step, I quickly turned around after ten paces, headed back to the booth determined to take back what was rightfully mine. By the time I got there—no more than thirty seconds later—the Schwab and the paintings were nowhere to be seen. The German lady's hasty retreat convinced me completely that these were indeed our paintings stolen from our home in Brotchin by our gentile neighbors. Had I been able to find the vendor and properly question her, I might have discovered exactly which of our neighbors was responsible for raiding our home of its possessions. I related this episode to my parents when I returned home to Wloclawek and they, of course, remembered the paintings fondly. My mother soothed my frustration about not being able to recover them by saying, "Munjee, why are you concerned about some silly paintings when we lost so many people? Who cares about paintings? We'll have many more paintings, don't worry."

Wloclawek was the pre-war home to the Frank Chicory Company, known throughout Poland for their familiar image of a happy coffee grinder under the arching name "Frank." Chicory was a common low-cost alternative to coffee and a staple product in the Polish home. It was a widely held belief that all families who carried the name Frank were either converts or descendants of converts to Christianity from Judaism. This belief may have arisen from an association with a sect founded in eighteenth-century Poland by the Jewish theologian, Jakob Frank. The group was an outgrowth of the Messianic mysticism of Sabbetai Tzvi who headed an antinomian movement in which the authority of Jewish law was held to be superseded by personal freedom. The Frankist sect was discredited by the Jewish leadership of the day and finally found a welcome home in the gentile community with which it finally merged. Evidently, the Nazis also believed that all Franks were biologically Jewish and destroyed the famed Chicory factory after first murdering all the owners.

I soon came to understand that living in Poland would mean confronting anti-Semitism in one form or another every day. We heard reports of vicious anti-Jewish pogroms in neighboring communities and finally it came to roost in Wloclawek. A blood libel began circulating in the gentile community that the finger of a Christian girl was found in the Jewish baker's dough he was preparing for Passover.[2] An unruly crowd of drunken Poles converged on the Jewish butcher shop until they were confronted by the butcher himself, brandishing a large axe and threatening to chop off the head of anyone who crossed his threshold. Intimidated by this surprising show of Jewish strength, the crowd moved away from the butcher shop and headed towards some of the other Jewish-owned businesses on the street. Observing what was going on, I became alarmed because my father's café was in the path of the advancing mob. I turned to one of my fellow soldiers and told him to run to the camp and bring help to quell the crowd. Within fifteen minutes, a military truck arrived at scene with a machine gun mounted in the bed. I jumped into the cab and directed the driver right into the center of the mob that now consisted of about fifty men shouting "Dirty Jews" and other common epithets. They had all but surrounded the next Jewish business on the block and it was clear that their lust for Jewish blood had not yet been slaked. Only a show of real force would get them to cool down and back off. I instructed the gunner to let loose a few rounds, which got the crowd's attention. The soldiers ordered the crowd to disperse and go home and they all complied without further incident. Interestingly, the soldiers that came to the rescue that day were all gentiles. They were friends of mine and I believe that they were not aware that I was Jewish. They complied with my request for aid for two reasons. One, the military, at that time was serving in a quasi-police mode, working to maintain order in the raucous post-war environment. Secondly, like most of the soldiers at the camp, they felt they owed me some allegiance since I was the chief supply officer. They knew that if they took care of me, I would take care of them when it came to cigarettes and other vital goodies.

Despite our relatively comfortable living conditions, we as a family came to the undeniable conclusion that we could no longer remain in our pre-war homeland. Anti-Semitic episodes such as the one described were on the rise and we truly feared for our safety. We also understood that Europe would never again be a place for Jews to find safety and security. The war had changed everything and Hitler had proven that I could never be both a Pole and Jew. I was forced to decide and, without hesitation, I chose to remain a Jew although it meant we had to leave Poland behind.

When the time came to leave, we considered the plans we had made with Uncle Hertzl to travel first to Shtetin where we would join his family and make our way to Berlin. But, due in large part to my mother's strong feelings about Hertzl's rush to re-marry, this was not to be. Years later, in America, I recall asking Mamma, "Why didn't we leave Poland via Shtetin along with Uncle Hertzl? Why did we leave him behind?"

"Freig nischt!" she would reply which, in Yiddish, means "Don't ask!" Till this day, we had no further contact with Uncle Hertzl and I have no idea of what became of him or whether he and his family ever managed to immigrate to the United States.

Instead of going through Shtetin, we decided to leave the country through Lodz. On the night of our departure, our family sneaked away from Wloclawek very quickly. I recall Mamma saying, "Leave the lights burning. The neighbors shouldn't see that we have gone." One, two, three. A little suitcase, a pillow, a cherished photo and *"gegangen!* (let's go!)"* We're going to catch the first train to Lodz on our way to Czechoslovakia, which, we had heard, contained an easy entry point into occupied Austria.

Lodz had a much bigger Jewish community than little Wloclawek. As a "semi-discharged" Polish soldier, I was able to carry a sidearm. This, along with my uniform, earned me a modicum of respect from the local authorities in Lodz who were busily involved in a massive repatriation process. Under the terms of the Yalta agreement, Poland was obliged to turn over all Ukrainians and White Russians to the Soviets and in exchange, the new Polish border would be drawn at the Oder River. Thanks to my military bearing, we were able to board a train in Lodz that steamed through town after deserted town along the new Czech border zone. While passing through the town of Waldbrzech, my father heard that the mayor of one of these deserted towns, Kudawa Zdro'j, was recruiting people for re-population. This suited us perfectly, since Kudawa Zdro'j was very close to the Czech border.

During the dusty train ride, my parents and brother were able to ride in relative style, thanks again to my military affiliation. They enjoyed the trappings of a private coupe while I stood guard at the door to the compartment advising each inquiring official, "They are Polish nationals being repatriated to their homeland," as I flashed the impressive-looking transit documents I had previously made up. As a clerk in the army requisition office, it was my duty to fill out the purchase forms and then submit them to my superior officer for signature and imprinting with the official rubber stamp. In time, we found it easier for the officer to routinely sign and stamp the forms while blank in advance. I would then take a pre-signed and stamped form, and complete it as needed and send it off. Hence, it was a simple matter for me to insert a blank transit visa among the stack of documents offered to my boss for advance signature. Once I had it signed, I filled in the *(phony)* details that identified me as a temporarily discharged soldier free to return to my home in Poland. The papers placed me on inactive duty till I reached age 21 at which time I would be called up again to serve. But by this point, I knew that when I reached 21, I would no longer be on Polish soil.

Getting off the train at Kudawa Zdro'j was a bizarre, other-worldly experience. The entire town was devoid of people. Cows meandered up the main street unperturbed. The town's original German inhabitants had all been shifted across the Oder River to make way for the repatriated Poles, most of whom had been moved from their traditional homes to make way for the repatriated Ukrainians. It was amidst all of this post-war population shuffling, that we hoped to get lost in the shuffle.

Armed with my temporary discharge papers and wearing my spiffy peaked cap, I led my father and several others to the door of the mayor's office. The mayor was actually a military-appointed administrator who had been charged with overseeing the repatriation process. He greeted us warmly and wasted no time in assigning us all new homes. Several families even received a cow or two. In addition to the military presence, the town was also ruled by the local gendarmerie. They were easily distinguishable from the soldiers in their blue policemen's uniforms and metal-trimmed square caps. We immediately made the acquaintance of the chief of police who also happened to be in charge of the one spot we were most interested in—the border crossing. As the sign on his office door proclaimed, this fellow was the head of the *Policia Granichna,* the border police.

Our group of sixteen young Jews quickly settled into our new digs. As we set up our households, we were constantly focused on only one question, "How do we get to this guy—the border police chief?" "How do we convince him to let us cross the border into Czechoslovakia?" These questions consumed us for days on end, and finally, I hit upon the answer. The first step would be to collect as many *lokshen* (literally: noodles) as possible to put together a respectable bribe. Lokshen was the slang term for the old-style American dollars that were used before the introduction of the greenbacks. Lokshen were one of the few hard currencies that still held value in the chaotic post-war European economy. Among our crew we managed to collect a rather respectable booty of lokshen. But there was a problem. As everyone knew, you don't give lokshen to a *goy* (non-Jew) because such an act would raise too many questions. "Where did you get this money? Are you trading in contraband? Are you involved in espionage?" and so on. If you were going to bribe a

Polish official, you needed Polish Z*loties*. Our first mission was to send a trusted member of our group back to the larger city of Waldbrzech to exchange our lokshen for Zloties. Since I looked the most distinguished and officious in my Polish uniform, I was elected to the task. The trip took only a few hours and when I returned my pockets were bulging with over one hundred gold zloty coins.

The money was impressive and was bound to give the police chief something to think about, but we needed more. We needed back up. We were asking him to allow us to sneak across the border—the very border that he was charged with protecting. What if he was a real straight arrow and was not receptive to our financial inducement? After all, we had been brought in to Kudawa Zdro'j for the purpose of populating it. We had been provided with free housing, furniture and other assets to aid in our settlement. How would it look for the police chief to help these new settlers steal across the border? There was honor and principle involved. Money might not do the trick. Fortunately, we found the back up we needed in the holster on my hip. Our plan was a simple one. We approach the police chief en masse and first attempt to reason with him. If he accepts our offer, good and fine. But if he does not, then we show him the gun and make him a better offer—an offer he could not refuse.

The following night, at 3 A.M., our entire group convened at the police chief's front door. Asked to serve as the spokesman, I rapped loudly on the front door until the sleepy prefect arrived—confused at the sight of us as he threw on a shirt.

"What's going on here?" he demanded.

"We know that you can take us across the border," I explained calmly. "We want to get across the border and we want to go right now."

I motioned to his small Dodge truck parked in front of the police station. "We can all fit in your vehicle." He stared into my eyes as he moved his head from side to side trying to assess if I was drunk or not. Once he determined that we were serious, he motioned for me and my father to step inside. "Now tell me again," he said, once inside, "what is it you want?"

"We want to get across the border to Czechoslovakia. You have two choices." At this point I pulled out the cloth bag containing the Zloty coins. "You can let us cross and you take the Zloties, or" — and here I rested my hand on my holstered pistol— "or we take you with us and we keep the money. One way or the other, we are crossing the border tonight." Although he remained stone silent as he pondered his choice, I could see he was taken aback at this utter chutzpah. Looking down at the floor, the police chief said not a word as he reached for his coat with one hand and took the bag of coins with the other.

Two of us sat in the cab of the truck while the rest of our group stood in the truck bed for the ten-minute drive to the border. Once at the checkpoint, the chief jumped out and gave a blast on his whistle. Two border guards, each accompanied by a German shepherd, came running at top speed. The chief motioned for the guards to open the barbed wire gate and to permit us passage. One by one, we jumped from the truck, and clutching our bags, scurried through the crossing and down the hill into the Czech darkness. We hunkered down among the shrubbery and waited for the sunrise of what was truly going to be a new day for all of us. We left Poland—the soil that had stood under our feet for generations—without so much as a backward glance. This soil, I felt, had absorbed enough of our family's blood—it did not need, nor did it deserve, any of our tears.

CHAPTER FIVE

From DP to Irgun Fighter

A few of us tried to sleep among the shrubbery as we awaited the dawn in this "no man's land," but I kept alert for anyone who might spot us. Alas, in the morning light our presence became all too visible and we were soon approached by a contingent of Czech border police. Now what? I wondered. How would this group of huddled refugees, bearing no documents and no money, be received by the Czechs as we tried to steal across their border? We were quite surprised at their reaction. At this point—during these first post-war months—Czechoslovakia had not yet been consumed into the Soviet sphere. The nation, one of the first to fall to Nazi aggression, was still basking in the joy of liberation from tyranny. The Czechs welcomed us warmly. We learned that the US government was funding the Jewish Agency in a program that paid $10 to the Czechs for every Jewish man, woman, or child refugee that was delivered to their protective custody. This policy resulted in a wave of Jewish refugees pouring into Czechoslovakia from all the eastern Baltic states. It was aboard the crest of this wave that we were given food and blankets and directed to waiting trucks bound for the newly established Allied DP camps.

Our first stop was Bratislava where we spent the night and boarded trains bound for Austria the next morning. The trains were cargo boxcars and we definitely felt like human cargo being shipped across the Russian Occupation Zone en route to Vienna. We were instructed not to speak Polish, German, Yiddish, or any language other than Greek while passing through the Russian Zone. The *Sochnut* (Jewish Agency) that was coordinating the transport had evidently identified our group as Greeks undergoing repatriation. We were told to discard any personal items, photos, documents, and the like, that might, in case we were searched, link us to Poland or any Slavic area. We complied and, since we spoke no Greek, we sat mute in the darkness of the rumbling boxcar. Everything having to do with our past lives had now been stripped from us. Even our native tongues had to be wiped from our mouths. We were being reborn into a new life form via a metamorphosis that contained distinct stages of development. This first stage—this larva stage—was perhaps the most difficult as we joined the massive migration of displaced, post-war Jews and became known by the simple title: Refugee.

The next few years saw our family make its way from one Displaced Persons camp to another as we struggled to meet the challenges of daily survival in this series of highly unnatural environments. From Vienna, we were assigned to a camp known as St. Marein in the British Occupation Zone, and after over a year at St. Marein we were moved to a camp in Braunau Am In, the birthplace of Adolph Hitler. Our final camp, Ebelsberg, was located in the American Zone.

At St. Marein, I was recruited by the United Nations Rescue and Relief Association (UNRRA) and put to work distributing food, clothing, bedding, and medical supplies to newly arriving refugees. This job enabled me to provide a few extras for my own family as well, so I was happy to do it. I was assigned to distribute the coupons needed to obtain the CARE *(Cooperative for American Remittances to Europe)* packages that were being shipped into the camp. I became rather adept at CARE-package shenanigans at the Austrian post office. I was able to arrange things so that the best quality goods always got routed through me and wound up in the hands of my family.

My father became friendly with the head of the UNRRA operation at St. Marein, Moshe Friedler. Friedler had emigrated from Poland to Britain before the war where he had joined the British military and was now, under the auspices of the Joint Distribution Committee, in charge of rescuing as many Jewish survivors as possible. In later years, he would emigrate to the United States where he served as the Israel Bonds director in Buffalo, New York.

We attempted to re-establish something of Jewish pre-war cultural life amid the squalor of the camps. I recall how a survivor from Warsaw founded a legitimate Jewish theatre in the St. Marein camp. With his deep black eyes and large bald head, the theatre director was an imposing figure as he rounded up fresh talent from among the newly arrived young refugees. The theatre was a great place to meet young women who flocked there in an effort to inject some normalcy into their disrupted lives. The social climate at St. Marein was a warm one. We would escort our dates to sing-alongs—filled with Jewish and Russian folk songs—or to informal dances, all organized by the camp administration.

Our lodgings were nothing more than straw-bed army barracks that reeked from the DDT disinfectant. Although we were billeted in standard army barracks, men and women were not separated and families were permitted to remain together. To create some level of privacy, blankets and bed sheets were strung up between the bunk beds creating little family alcoves. It was not as luxurious as our little home in Wloclawek, but we were together and besides, it was only temporary. The barracks contained a central washroom that the men and women visited in shifts. My mother could often be found in the central kitchen, making sure that the food was being prepared in a kosher fashion.

Many of the internees had survived Hitler's most demonic extermination camps such as Matthausen and Theresienstadt, and it was through them that we learned the true nature and extent of the Holocaust. It was at this point that I finally became convinced that the family we had left behind back in Brotchin in

1941 had all been murdered along with the other Jews of our shtetl. While I gained an understanding of the Nazi extermination process when I had visited the Majdanek concentration camp, the thought that this nightmare had engulfed the people I knew and loved never fully hit home. It was actually by reading a book that I began to permit the truth to sink in. *The Smoke of Treblinka* (Dymy Treblinka) was a thin volume written by one of the few Polish survivors, Miriam Kuperhand, in which she describes, in great detail, accounts of the gassing and cremation process. She even recounts how the ashes were disposed of. I read this heart-wrenching book in its native Polish and became convinced that these horrors must surely have befallen my own family as well.

While my younger brother sought to pick up the pieces of his war-torn education, I was too old for this. I was, after all, a fully finished soldier and not about to sit in any more classrooms under the thumb of some schoolteacher. I had no desire to further my education or to learn a new trade. My focus was continually on handling. I employed my skills at forgery and my ability to pass as a non-Jew to my full financial advantage. Using forged documents and duplicate passports, I was able to traverse the Russian Occupation Zone and travel into Vienna where I could conduct serious business.

I owned two passports. The first, the real one, stated that I was born in Poland while the second listed my birthplace as Gratz, Austria. Otherwise, both passports were identical. With the Gratz passport, which I had obtained through the regular channels by simply lying about my place of birth, I was able to obtain the necessary transit visas needed to visit Vienna. Vienna's vibrant underground economy lured me to its gates. I knew that once there I could engage in all varieties of black market commerce—be it currency, foodstuffs, cosmetics, or any other attractive commodity. My junkets to Vienna were cut short, however, for a rather simple reason: Fear. Fear of apprehension by the Russians.

Mark My Words!

As I explained, in order to visit Vienna I had to travel by train across the Russian-occupied zone of Austria. This was the most risky leg of the journey as one episode demonstrated. As usual, the train pulled to a stop upon entering the Russian zone as armed border guards went from person to person inspecting each transit visa. "*Ausweiss!,*" they demanded in accented German. "Show us your papers!" As they approached me, each toting a big black Kalatchnikov rifle, I tried as hard as I could to look and act like a genuine Austrian citizen. I carried a rucksack and was dressed in the traditional loden-green feathered cap and lederhosen. I kept silent lest my Polish accent give me away. My German was rather good, but I had not mastered the Austrian dialect that contained many of the more deep guttural sounds. One word from my lips before a true German-speaking Austrian official and I would be exposed and the validity of my documents certainly questioned.

As the first guard eyed my visa, he noted that it was brand new and would not expire for a full year. "This vagabond will be rolling with us for a long time," he commented to his compatriot in Russian, unaware that I understood his words. "I'm going to have to check this character many times," he complained. I was terrified because I had obviously come under the scrutiny of these guards. I was sure to come across them again as I made my way back and forth to Vienna and eventually they would find me out. I knew that once they discovered that I was not Austrian, but a Polish imposter, I was finished. They would arrest me and ship me back to Poland and probably to the Gulag. I began perspiring and silently praying that I would not be forced to speak. Just the sound of the Russian language being spoken by these guards—feeling their breath on the back of my neck—sent shivers down my spine and turned my bowels to water.

Happily, my prayers were answered and the two guards returned my papers without comment. Upon arriving back to St. Marein, I told my father of the incident and his anger erupted. "Why do you take such risks?" he implored. "Do you want to wind up back in Poland after we worked so hard to get out? You could have been arrested and sent to Siberia! You must promise me never to go through the Russian zone again. Is that clear?" I agreed without the slightest reluctance and, after only three visits to Vienna, my career as an international black marketeer was cut short—at least for the time being.

While all of us, my family and our fellow DPs, felt a certain amount of gratitude for having survived the worst bloodbath in Jewish history, we were, nevertheless, constantly focused on the future. As we languished in St. Marein for over a year, our private discussions were always about one thing—emigration. But emigration to where? That was the question. Getting into Palestine through normal channels for a European Jew in 1946 was next to impossible. The British Mandatory Government in Palestine, instead of opening its gates to Europe's hundreds of thousands of homeless Holocaust victims, slammed them shut, allowing only 1,500 Jews per year to enter the region Lord Balfour had identified fifty years earlier as the true Jewish homeland. We knew of the underground immigration known as the Bricha or Aliyah Bet being carried out by the Haganah and the Jewish Agency. But Aliyah Bet was a young man's game and not a suitable option for a family that contained a young boy and a sickly man suffering from emphysema. Also, my family's alignment with Jabotinsky and the right-wing Revisionist movement did not make us suitable candidates for the leftist Bricha. Our talk, most often, turned to immigration to the *Goldeneh Medina,* or America. If not the US, then Canada and if not Canada, then South Africa or Australia. These English-speaking nations were regarded as bastions of political freedom and economic opportunity—the two commodities for which we hungered most deeply.

These emigration discussions most often included my father's friend and UNRRA coordinator, Moshe Friedler, who would stare at Tatu through his thick horn-rimmed eyeglasses as Tatu proclaimed, "If I go to America, I want to wind up in a spot that has four real seasons just like Poland." Friedler nodded his understanding and told my father to wait for a moment. Friedler returned with a large map of the United States that he spread out on the dining room table. He placed his finger somewhere in Kansas and said, "See, Bernard. This is the middle of the country. This area is the North and this is the South," he indicated each region as he spoke. "This is the East Coast and this part is the West Coast. You want four seasons? Go to the North," he stated as his finger came down into Minnesota. It was under that finger, in Minneapolis, that our family would eventually settle. But it was there, in the barracks of St. Marein, on Moshe Friedler's map, that we first discovered Minnesota.

We were very happy when the time came to leave St. Marein and move on to our next camp home in Braunau Am In, still in the British Occupation Zone. Aside from its notoriety as Hitler's birthplace, Braunau was also the site of German wartime aircraft production. The planes were built in huge underground bunkers. Our lodgings became more comfortable at Braunau since instead of converted army barracks, we were put up in residential apartments used by the aircraft workers. But we still were not where we wanted to be. In order to effect our immigration to America, it was important for us to fall under American occupational command. After a few months in Braunau, my father succeeded in having us relocated to Ebelsberg, a suburb of the town of Linz, in the American Occupation Zone.

Our lodgings in Ebelsberg were another step up the scale. We were provided with housing in a high-rise brick apartment building. Each unit provided a small cooking area while we shared a common shower and bathroom facility with the entire floor. The buildings were constructed by the German army for use as officer's quarters.

It was at Ebelsberg that I first became involved with the Irgun Zvai Leumi or Etzel. Etzel was the military wing of the Revisionist Zionist movement founded by Ze'ev Jabotinsky in the 1930s. It was Etzel's goal to regain Jewish sovereignty in all of the land described as ancient Israel in the Bible. They were committed to redeeming the land, on both sides of the Jordan, from Arab and Englishman alike. Etzel's nationalistic sentiments placed it at odds with the mainstream socialist power structure known as the Jewish Agency and led by David Ben-Gurion. After 1943, the Irgun was headed by a fiery Polish soldier, Menachem Begin, who urged all of us to remember that the blood of King David and the Maccabees flowed in our veins. As a member of Begin's Betar youth movement back in Poland, I was a prime candidate for recruitment into the Irgun's ranks. My entry into the Jewish underground came about not so much because of my political ideology, however, but because of a romantic relationship with an attractive young lady by the name of Ashkenazi.

My girlfriend lived in Salzburg, Austria and I would often travel from Ebelsberg to Salzburg just to visit her. Our relationship was becoming more and more serious, but each time I prodded her to take the next step, she resisted. Finally, she revealed the reason. I was not her only suitor. I had a rival and she claimed that she loved him as well as me. "Who is this fellow," I asked warily.

"His name is David Speigel," she confessed.

"David Speigel," I exclaimed. "From Bohorodczany in Poland?" I had known a David Speigel whose father had immigrated to Palestine during the 1930s. The father, a passionate and idealistic Zionist, owned a successful seltzer water bottling business, sold it, and headed off to Palestine to start a new life. He intended to get established and then send for his family. His wife, however, decided not to wait for his return and took off for Argentina along with their little girl, Paula. She left behind David and his brother. Meanwhile, David's father found life unbearable under the left-wing socialist regime that had assigned him to a stone quarry and set him to work building gravel roadbeds. Sadly, the father, disillusioned with the Zionist dream, returned to Brotchin shortly before the war broke out and perished along with David's brother. I later learned how David managed to escape Brotchin before the Russians arrived and had headed towards the West. Was it possible that he had landed here, in Austria? Could this David Speigel be the same fellow? The answer was yes, and naturally, I had to meet him. After all, we were *landsmen* (countrymen), we had both survived the war somehow and now we appeared to be in love with the same girl.

I asked my girlfriend to arrange for a meeting right away, but she explained that it was not that simple. Speigel was a leader in the Jewish underground in Salzburg. He lived in the shadows and trusted no one. Would I be willing to engage in some cloak and dagger in order to meet him? "Of course," I replied, somewhat excited by the intrigue.

My girlfriend gave me the address and the precise appointed time. With some trepidation, I knocked on the door. An odd-looking fellow opened the door and ushered me inside after checking me over for weapons. The doorman escorted me into a very dark, inner room where I was instructed to take a seat. A tall man stepped from the shadows and despite the poor lighting, I could easily make out the distinctive bushy black eyebrows and thin face that told me at once that this was the same David Speigel I knew back in Brotchin. He did not recognize me since I was perhaps ten years old at our last encounter, but he remembered my Zayde and the rest of my family. He recalled that our family was active in the Betar and stated that he considered my father an ally and a fellow Jabotinskyite. I noted that his skin was waxen and pasty as a result of never seeing the light of day. We discussed old times for a bit and never actually got around to the subject of our romantic rivalry. I could tell that his true passion was not Miss Ashkenazi, but rather his deep-rooted, militant brand of Zionism. I told him of my military background in the

Polish Brigade during the war and Speigel wasted no time in attempting to recruit me into the ranks of Etzel.

"We need men like you now more than ever before," he proclaimed. "We need for you to go back to Ebelsberg and recruit as many loyal sons of Zion as possible to our cause. The future of the Jewish people is at stake, Mark. If we don't take matters into our own hands, the British will finish the job the Nazis started. And if we leave it to the socialists, we'll wind up as some quaint religious minority in an Arab Palestine. Jewish history is being written every day. We need men like you to be a part of it."

I did not really need the pep talk. I was sold immediately. I told Speigel that he could count on me to handle recruitment at Ebelsberg and that since I was a trained soldier, I could be useful in other ways as well. Over the next few months, I brought Speigel to Ebelsberg and conducted several clandestine recruitment meetings. Speigel was an eloquent and effective orator. His impassioned words and charismatic leadership style served to swell our ranks very quickly. But shortly thereafter, he mysteriously disappeared without a trace. Years later, I learned that he had been killed and that left-wing followers of Ben Gurion were suspected in the crime.

The Ebelsberg camp was situated atop an intricate series of catacombs and secret tunnels connecting one part of the camp with another. The tunnels were originally built by the Germans to provide shelter and access during air raids. While the occupying American forces were aware of the tunnel system, they only knew the half of it. Our Irgun group managed to discover a second tunnel system in place below the first, and it was using these tunnels that we could move about free from scrutiny by the US Army authorities. In very short order, we became a first-class underground organization in every sense of the word.

Irgun headquarters (HQ) in Europe were located in Paris and communication with HQ was vital at all times. Although the British did not approve, the Irgun was able to operate freely in the wide-open atmosphere of post-war liberated France. The Ebelsberg camp was organized into a pyramid cell network. Each cell contained five agents and each of the five agents belonged to another cell. In this way, each agent knew the identity of, at most, eight other agents. If something went wrong, the network would lose no more than two cells.

Initially, we received our orders via an Irgun representative from Palestine named Yehoshua HaCohen. Cohen, who would later serve as Israel's ambassador to Costa Rica, would visit the camp every few months and meet with the various cells. After we managed to obtain a shortwave radio that permitted Paris to communicate directly with Ebelsberg, it was no longer necessary for Cohen to visit the camp. From then on, it was through this channel that our missions were assigned.

Although our anti-British Irgun activities were highly illegal and kept secret, there was an open face to our group as well. Over time, our contingent became quite vocal and visible in the camp's day-to-day affairs. Although our identities were shielded from each other, I soon deduced who was with us and who was not. Officially, we were organized under the Revisionist banner. It was common knowledge, however, that if a young man called himself a Revisionist, he was, in all likelihood, also a secret Irgunchik. My brother, Hetche, was deeply devoted to our cause, but because of his youth at the time, he could not be enlisted into our ranks. We did employ kids of that age, however, in peripheral assignments such as distributing leaflets, putting up posters, and so on. Hetche, as I recall, was the most industrious, hardworking leafleteer in the camp.

Our group represented the hard-core of the Ebelsberg network. Our leadership sent us guerilla warfare trainers from Palestine who taught us to shoot and how to find our way in the woods at night. These fellows had been trained by the British, and much of that training carried over to what was transmitted to us. We were issued wooden rifles and spent hours in the woods going through marching formations and short arm drills. We became familiar with rifles, pistols, carbines, and all forms of artillery. We also learned about land mines and detonators as we trained in secret almost every night. My military training in the Polish Brigade during the war was put to good use during this period as I trained others in how to read maps and how to clean and maintain their handguns, for example. We were never able to carry out actual mock maneuvers because the noise and the gunfire would have alerted the authorities. Nevertheless, our group was soon honed into a viable fighting force ready to face any enemy, be they English or Arab.

Our biggest obstacle in those days was not the dearth of military training among our ranks—their natural enthusiasm soon overcame this handicap. No, our biggest nemesis was as old as the tower of Babel. We did not enjoy that most basic asset of every fighting force: a common language. Our ranks were filled with Greeks, Poles, Russians, Hungarians, Litwaks, and many who spoke only Yiddish. Our trainers spoke Hebrew and our American overseers spoke only English. Since we were expecting to put our military training to use in Palestine at some point, it was felt that all instructions should be communicated in Hebrew. This sounded good in principal, but in practice, Yiddish still prevailed as the most widely understood tongue among European Jews.

In addition to transforming ourselves into a toughened paramilitary fighting force, our number one priority was the acquisition of firearms by whatever means necessary. We bought guns, we stole guns, we made guns from whatever source we had at hand. I recall burying hundreds of rifles in the woods near Ebelsberg, packed with machine oil in long aluminum canisters. I am certain that not all of them were dug up and sent off to Palestine and if I were to go there today and begin digging, I'm sure I would be able to find many of them still in the ground.

The following example illustrates the type of guerilla activity we engaged in during this period. It was perhaps our most notorious act and was intended to let the British know that Zionist resistance was alive and well in Austria. We wanted to send them a message making it clear that as long as they clung to the occupation of Palestine, they would face renewed resistance throughout the world. We were instructed to blow up a British train carrying troops through Austria. The instructions clearly stated that we were to strive to inflict as few casualties as possible. We were not wanton murdering terrorists even though that's what we were labeled by the British. We were freedom fighters seeking to liberate our ancient homeland from a tyrannical occupier. We regarded ourselves as the zealots, as the Maccabees and, if necessary, as the martyrs of Masada.

Our target was a troop train that ran between the British and American Occupation Zones. As it crossed through the Austrian Alps, the train ran along a steep mountain incline on one side, while on the other, it faced a treacherous drop-off into the ravine below. I was assigned to survey the train's route, and gather intelligence about the best time and place to carry out the bombing. The reason that I was selected for this reconnaissance was because of my ability to easily pass as a native Austrian. My light complexion, reddish blond hair combined with my near-perfect German made me the ideal covert agent—particularly when I dressed in the lederhosen, green jacket, and feathered cap of the traditional Austrian garb. By studying various maps, we had selected a stretch of track between two Alpine hot spring spa resorts, Bad Gastein and Bad Hof Gastein. It was felt that the steepness of the mountain face was minimal at this point and would thereby help us to avoid casualties. It was left up to me, however, to scope out the area in detail and select the precise spot to place the bomb. Our objective was for the bomb to de-rail the train and force it against the mountainside. We did not wish for it to tumble down the ravine and thereby cause unwanted casualties. Our goal was not to kill anyone—we simply wanted to scare the daylights out of the British. I determined that if we detonated the bomb as the train was traveling south at a particular bend in the rail bed, our chances of avoiding casualties would be maximized.

For six weeks before the target date, I conducted detailed espionage, gathering vital data that would be used by our leaders when putting together the tactical logistics of the mission. I noted the location of the train depots, the coming and goings at police stations, scheduled troop deployments, and the like. Posing as an Austrian tourist on holiday, I visited the hot baths and took copious snapshots of the lovely mountain scenery. This cover helped me gain repeated access to the sites I needed to scope out—particularly the train stations where I was often stopped and asked to present my papers. I had to be very cautious. Much of my snooping was done surreptitiously in order to avoid arousing the suspicion of the authorities. If they saw my face around town too frequently, they would question my activities. Finally, after weeks of clandestine reconnaissance, all was in readiness. I returned to Ebelsberg, a few hours away by train, and presented my final report to my superiors. The high command selected two operatives from among our number to accompany two experienced explosives experts brought in from Paris. In mid-June, 1947, this 4-man commando team, armed with maps, photos and other information I had gathered, set off with the explosives, to carry out this daring sabotage raid.

The bomb was carefully placed at the prescribed spot on the train tracks and a fuse run to a standard plunger box some 200 ft. away. The bomb was detonated at the precise moment and succeeded in forcing the train off the tracks to the left, into the face of the mountain as planned. Had the bomb been placed on the opposite rail, the train would have toppled the other way and careened down the ravine. But since our objective was merely to "shake them up" and not to kill anyone—this phase of the mission was deemed a complete success. Our brand of "humane hostility"—directed only at military targets and never at civilians— resulted in no casualties and only a few minor injuries. And the message got through loud and clear. I feel it was because of acts such as this one, targeting British military presence and replicated in every corner of the British Empire, that finally resulted, in

November, 1947, in the ultimate termination of the British Mandate in Palestine.

Unfortunately the mission did not prove to be a total success. After the detonation, the four-man crew scattered and ran off to make their individual getaways. One of the Ebelsberg members of the team, a strapping young blonde chap we dubbed "Ben Yehuda," ran in the wrong direction and found himself heading directly towards the police station at Bad Hof Gastein. Ben Yehuda was quickly spotted by the local Austrian gendarmerie, one of who fired at him as he fled—striking him in the thigh. Our colleague fell to the ground wounded and was quickly apprehended and arrested by the Austrian police. The other three members of the sabotage crew got away cleanly, never returning to Ebelsberg.

Ben Yehuda was treated at a local hospital and then temporarily placed into the local lock-up in Bad Hof Gastein before being turned over to the British military. He was transferred to a basement prison at British Regional Occupational Headquarters in Villach, Austria, near the Czech and Italian borders.

This capture of one of our own necessitated a new objective and a new plan to gain Ben Yehuda's forcible release before he could be tried and sentenced by the British. It took nearly six months, but finally I was once again dispatched to go undercover and carry out clandestine surveillance of the prison and surrounding localities. Villach was, and remains today, a popular Alpine ski resort, so I packed along a pair of skis that I dutifully balanced on my shoulder during my frequent strolls by the British HQ. I never actually did any skiing, but I acted the part of a young Austrian ski bum with convincing accuracy. Enhancing this role was the fake passport mentioned earlier that falsely listed my birthplace as Graz, Austria. I kept my fake passport, plus my actual one showing my true birthplace in Poland, both situated in the inner breast pockets of my jacket—one on either side, with either of them always available for presentation depending upon the situation.

I spent the first few days in Villach taking in the sights, visiting the marketplace, familiarizing myself with the town's layout and major features. I found a perch in the café directly across the street from the British administrative headquarters where I could observe the traffic and note the number of troops at different times of the day in my little notebook. I had to carefully observe the facial features of each British soldier who went in and out to make sure I didn't count the same fellow twice. Most of the data I committed to memory, in case I was apprehended. I would only write down raw numbers plus items that appeared innocuous such as street names and the like. My work received an assist from the weatherman. During January 1948, Villach found itself in the grip of a bitter cold snap. It was actually too cold for anyone to go skiing and hence my hours spent in the café, warming myself on endless cups of coffee, did not arouse any suspicion. I began to look around for a *shiksa* (a gentile woman) whom I could enlist to serve as my escort and thereby enhance my cover. In the evenings, I would retire to my little "pensionne" room, which contained nothing more than a bed and a basin and water jug on a small corner table.

On my third day in Villach, I was awakened by a rough pounding on the door. "Open up immediately! It's the *Gehaims Polizei* (secret police)!" came a shout through the door. I opened up and permitted the three plain-clothed police officers entry into my cramped chamber. My first thought was concerning the two passports—one in the left pocket and one in the right pocket of my jacket which sat draped over the back of the room's solitary chair. If these cops were to search the little room and find both passports, my kosher goose would be cooked.

"Ausweiss!" came the order from the one in charge, asking to see my papers. My flesh seemed to turn frigid from fear as my mind raced to buy myself some time. I definitely did not wish to reach for one of my passports for fear that they would easily spot the other one. I asked them to wait a moment while I got dressed. As I pulled on my trousers, the captain asked me, *"Was machen Sie hier?"* (What are you doing here?).

"I'm a tourist doing a bit of skiing." As I said these words, I quickly developed a plan that, with a bit of luck, might avoid my discovery. I walked over to the pitcher and basin and tried to pour out some water. I knew that the pitcher was empty since it was so cold the night before I had avoided walking out to the courtyard where the faucet was located in a little water closet. Nevertheless, I feigned surprise and asked the police captain if I could go fill up my water pitcher. He agreed, but sent along one of his men to accompany me and make sure I did not try to run off. I hurriedly slipped on my coat, grabbed the pitcher, and walked briskly to the water closet with the cop following on my heels. I opened the door to the closet wide so the officer could see that there was no other way out and that all that it contained was a faucet, a sink, and a wastebasket. There was only room in the closet for one person, so I entered, letting the spring hinge close the door behind me. During the ten seconds it took for me to fill my pitcher, I quickly whipped out my real passport and stuffed it into the wastebasket. As soon as I returned with the filled water pitcher, the captain, who had been inspecting all my belongings during my absence, again forcefully asked for my passport. This time, I had no apprehension. I opened wide my coat, pulled out the fake one and handed it to him with a smile.

After inspecting my passport, the police captain asked me, "Why did you select this hotel?"

"I don't know," I replied honestly. "It looked clean and the price was right. Why do you ask?" He explained that a contingent of Russian diplomats was coming to Villach on an economic mission and they had been booked into this same cheap hotel. For security purposes, the local police were routinely questioning every guest in the place to make sure that there were no suspicious characters staying here. I could see that the captain was trying to determine if I was or was not a suspicious character. Something was troubling him, I could tell.

"Your passport says you were born in Gratz, Mr. Hasten," he pointed out, "yet you don't speak like you come from there?"

My slight accent had betrayed me and raised a question in the cop's mind. "Let's go," he ordered. "You're coming with us."

Seated around a table at the Villach police station, the captain offered me a cigarette. This made me nervous since in the movies, that's what the cops do just before they kick you in the teeth.

"So, if you were born in Graz, how come your German is so poor?" he asked pointedly.

"It's because my family was taken to Matthausen," I lied. "My mother and father were killed there and I was forced to live for four years in a concentration camp for young boys. I never had the chance to go to school and learn proper German, I'm afraid."

"I see," said the captain calmly although his eyes expressed his surprise at learning that I was Jewish. "That's very unfortunate, but I'm afraid I'm going to have to check out your story. Meanwhile, we need to do a complete search of you and your belongings. Please give Sgt. Mueller your full cooperation." I was next ordered to strip after which Sgt. Mueller conducted a complete body cavity search. Whatever contraband they were looking for, they found nothing on me—or in me!

While the search was being conducted, the captain cranked up his ancient telephone and tried to place a call to the police station in Graz in order to check out my story. This again caused me to break out in a nervous sweat. I had presented them with my fake passport because I knew that if they learned I was a Polish national, it would only add to their suspicions. I did not anticipate that they would question it and try to verify my birthplace. Of course, once they got through to the Graz police authorities they would easily discover that no one by my name was born there on the date indicated. I would be exposed as a phony and definitely arrested.

Once again, G-d smiled upon me and arranged for the forces of nature to give me a needed assist. While it was extremely cold in Villach, it was even colder in Graz, which was suffering under blizzard conditions. The roads were impassible and hence even the police station was closed. There was no one in the station to pick up the phone during the repeated attempts by the Villach police captain to call in and verify my identity. After many hours of this futility, he finally gave up and returned my passport to me. He told me to be on my way, never once suspecting that I was indeed on a secret reconnaissance mission against the British. I believe that my Matthausen story got through to them and did the trick. In the current post-war environment, Germans and Austrians were very sensitive about concealing their anti-Jewish sentiments. The Allied occupying forces were still actively tracking down suspected war criminals and I'm certain that this police captain did not wish to be viewed as unnecessarily harassing a Jewish Holocaust survivor. These considerations, coupled with the fact that it was becoming increasingly cold in the police station, prompted the captain to release me and send me on my way.

I immediately went straight to the water closet at the pensionne and retrieved my real passport from the trash bucket. I could not get out of Villach quickly enough. I had collected the information I had been asked to retrieve and so I picked up my belongings and caught the next train heading back to Ebelsberg. My superiors analyzed the information I brought back and rightly concluded that the prison where Ben Yehuda was incarcerated was too well fortified. It was determined that attacking the British installation would be too risky and probably result in the loss of several lives. On top of that, our revolt against the British was pretty much over by this point. They had announced that the British flag would come down over Palestine in May. There was really no longer any reason to worry that Ben Yehuda might reveal sensitive information about our operations while in jail. Hence, Ben Yehudah languished in the Villach prison for nearly a year. By that time, the state of Israel had been established and British rule in Palestine had indeed come to an end. These facts mitigated the severity of Ben Yehuda's crime making it almost a moot issue. The fact that no soldiers were killed and but a few slightly wounded during the attack on the "train to Bad Gastein" helped his case, and Ben Yehuda was ultimately freed by the British and then made his way to Israel where he eventually retired as an officer in the Israeli military.

During the six-month period before Israeli independence, the flow of illegal Jewish immigrants into Palestine picked up dramatically. As explained, the vanguard of this effort was conducted by the Bricha and labeled Aliyah Bet. The Bricha was an arm of the Jewish Agency, headed by David Ben-Gurion and politically reflected the socialist sentiments of its left-wing leadership. As will be described in the following chapter, the Jewish Agency was slated to become the ruling faction of the new Jewish state. Ever mindful of the political consequences of his actions, Ben-Gurion ordered that only those sympathetic to the political outlook of the left were to be transported into pre-independent Israel. This meant no Betar members, no Revisionists, no Jabotinskyites, no Etzelniks were to be afforded passage by the Bricha. Ben-Gurion wanted to limit the numbers of those who would, in all likelihood, join his political opposition once they landed in Israel—despite the fact that as many Jews as possible, regardless of political persuasion, were needed by the fledgling state to combat the overwhelming threat they faced from the monolithic Arab enemy. The fact that Ben-Gurion was freezing us out of our chance to fight for the Jewish state infuriated us and drove our leadership to devise plans like the *Altalena* transport *(see next chapter)* as well as the following mission.

In the spring of 1948, our high command devised a daring raid on the Bremmer Pass, where a clandestine border crossing point near Innsbruck in the French Occupation Zone had been established by the Haganah, the military branch of the Jewish Agency. The Haganah was smuggling large numbers of Jews across the Pass and across the border into Italy from where the refugees could easily be transported across the

Mediterranean and into Palestine. Our objective was to commandeer the Haganah headquarters long enough for us to smuggle a contingent of *Betar* (right-wing) refugees across the border and place them into the underground railway to Palestine via Italy. We simply wanted to boost our side in the numbers war that was being waged by Ben-Gurion against us.

We needed a large contingent to wrest control of the crossing point from the Haganah. We could not merely rely upon a small commando unit. We needed a company of troops. A troop of about thirty young men, including me, from Ebelsberg and other neighboring DP camps was assembled and trained for the mission. On the appointed date, we boarded a train to Innsbruck and from there we traveled via the Bremmer Pass towards the border crossing. Our objective was to take over control of the compound, sequester everyone we encountered long enough for us to smuggle our people across the border—a process we expected would take several days. The refugees we sought to bring to Palestine were concentrated by the Irgun in Innsbruck where they waited for us to do our work. Several of us, including me, carried weapons as we mounted our assault on the compound. Each one of us had a specific assignment to carry out. My job was to locate a top Bricha leader who was known to own a camera. I was to overpower him, place him under house arrest for the duration of our mission, and to confiscate his camera in order to prevent the taking of any incriminating photos of us during the raid.

We easily gained access to the compound in the early twilight hours. I made my way to my target's barracks door that had been identified through excellent advance intelligence. I burst in and ordered him at gunpoint to get up and raise his hands. I could see that he had just awakened as he groggily carried out my demands. I ordered him to give me all his cash, which he did without hesitation. I next asked for his camera, which he located and turned over to me, a bit more reluctantly. After robbing him of his cash and camera, I ordered him to sit down and to be patient because he was going to be my prisoner in this room for the next several days while we, the Irgun, conducted our own border smuggling operation. I had my gun trained on him and I was beginning to introduce myself when a shot rang out nearby. A few minutes later, someone from our crew stuck his head in the door and told me that one of the Haganah guys had just been shot by one of us. He urged me to get the hell out of there right away. I later learned that a young Irgun member from another DP camp—a hot-headed Polish kid who had been a partisan resistance fighter during the war—had fired the shot when his target, a Bricha organizer from Palestine, had put up some resistance. The shot struck his victim in the throat, killing him instantly.

The determination was made, in light of the shooting, to abandon the mission immediately. The refugees at Innsbruck were left behind as we piled aboard our truck and made a hasty getaway. The decision to run was a reaction to the panic of the moment. Had we been a crack military troop, we probably would have completed our mission despite the unfortunate killing. But we were far from that. We were a rag-tag collection of untrained zealots, hailing from different countries, speaking different languages and living in fear and on the run for the past ten years or more. When things started to get hot, we all got out of the kitchen—in a hurry.

The alarm went up as thirty of us barreled out of the compound. We could hear the sirens of the French Sûreté heading our way as we charged down the highway at top speed. We gained a bit of a head start as the police stopped at the camp to gather information about the shooting before taking off again in pursuit. Our truck, burdened with a full load of thirty passengers, had a difficult time negotiating the narrow mountain byways as we sped away from Innsbruck. Not too surprisingly, the truck tumbled down an embankment as the driver swung around a curve a bit too quickly. Although I was not hurt, a few of our number were injured in the crash. Our leader, known only as Buzsik, a heroic Jewish partisan who had led the resistance in Russia during the war, began to shout out orders as we ran from the wreckage.

"Scramble," he shouted. "Everyone's on his own. But first, bring the wounded up to the road." Buzsik managed to convince some passers-by who had stopped to view the accident to transport the injured back to Innsbruck. As for me, I took off at top speed up the mountain slope on foot. About five others decided on a similar route, although we did not stay together.

Before embarking on this mission, I knew that my absence from Ebelsberg would be questioned. I had to make my five-day disappearance appear to be something normal and routine. Hence, like many of my comrades, I arrived to the mission dressed not as a commando, but rather as a dapper gentleman in my finest silk suit. In this way, people who observed me leaving and returning to the camp would not suspect that I was involved in a guerrilla exercise. But now, scrambling through the brush and brambles of the steep mountainside, I was in danger of ripping my wardrobe to shreds. I decided to take off my jacket and re-don it after reversing it inside out. As it turned out, the jacket's lining served as better camouflage and enabled me to conceal myself more easily. This became important as I looked over my shoulder and spied about eight gendarmes, spread out in a row, sweeping their way up the mountainside searching for members of our group. I could see that the police were successfully picking us off one by one. I knew that they would reach me too in very short order. I decided to fall back upon my military training and do my best to camouflage myself. Rolling into a tight ball, I covered myself with leaves and branches and sat stock still as a stone. With my head tucked down behind the branches, I could no longer see the approaching police, but I heard their footsteps as they tramped up the mountainside, literally beating the bushes as they shouted back and forth in French. As they grew closer, I held my breath and prayed silently. One officer came within twenty feet of me and must have looked directly at my position. Fortunately, my camouflage held. After the posse had ascended beyond my position, I could no longer be sure where they were or if they would come back down the same way. So, I remained in my position until nightfall—not moving a muscle and urinating where I sat when nature called.

Finally sticking my head up, I peered out in the moonlight and determined that I was no longer in danger. I rushed back down to the main road and headed towards the far-off lights of what I knew to be a railway station in the distance. I quickly reversed my jacket back and put it on. Arriving at the station, I spotted the stationmaster by the track swinging his lantern.

"Excuse me," I shouted out to him, "can you help me get to Innsbruck?" As I got closer, I could see that he was the switch-man and he had evidently observed that I was not in very good shape after the ordeal of my escape. He invited me to join him at his nearby home and I agreed. When the fellow asked who I was, I replied that I was a businessman from Linz and that I needed to get to Innsbruck. When he questioned my accent, I again explained that my parents had been killed at Matthausen and that I had been interned by the Nazis during the war. He evidently had not heard about the shooting earlier that day at the border and never mentioned it. The switchman, evidently sympathetic towards this young Holocaust survivor, fed me and let me get a few hours sleep before the first train to Innsbruck arrived at 5 A.M. the next morning. With the switch-man's help, I got on the train and soon discovered about twenty more of our crew already on board. We reassembled in Innsbruck where six of us wishing to return back to Ebelsberg, grabbed the next train to Linz. Onboard the Linz train, we were approached by several strangers—all Jews—asking if we had heard about the shooting near Innsbruck and asking if we were involved. Of course, we said nothing since we had previously discussed the fact that if anyone made a move against any of our group, we would join forces and throw the nosy party off the train in a hurry.

Meanwhile, back at Ebelsberg, word had gotten back that there had been a fatal shooting of a Jewish Bricha man at the hands of the Irgun. The camp's population was mostly sympathetic to the left-wing cause and this news spread like a shockwave. Residents approached my father and demanded to know where I was. I had not told him my destination when I left, but he, like everyone else, correctly suspected that I had had a hand in this affair. Ebelsberg was awash in a sea of mourning for the slain Bricha man when I made my way back into the camp. I was repeatedly confronted and asked to explain my absence by suspicious fellow DPs. Thanks to my wardrobe, I could get away with answering them that I had been to Salzburg on business and managed to adopt an air of total innocence regarding the events in Innsbruck. I feel that most did not buy my story, however, including my own father who let me know that he understood that I had been involved. I know that he was saddened by the Jew-on-Jew killing, but I could sense that he was proud of my efforts to get more non-Socialists into Palestine by whatever means necessary.

Our wounded, who had been injured during the truck accident, made it to an Innsbruck hospital where they were all treated and then arrested by the French. None were charged with the murder and were eventually released after a few months. Since, in the eyes of the French authorities, the murder was viewed as an internecine affair—merely a case of one Jewish extremist shooting another one—they did not take the matter too seriously.

Several months later, after arriving in Israel, I again came face-to-face with the fellow I had arrested and briefly held captive during the Innsbruck raid. He was seated on a bus that I had just boarded and we recognized each other at once. Exchanging per-functory greetings, I half-expected him to confront me and demand his camera back, but he did nothing of the sort. He rode on in silence and got off a few blocks later. I never saw him again.

The story of my own eventful emigration to Israel is told in the next chapter. As you will read, I arrived mere days after the birth of the new nation and bore witness to a tragic series of events that almost succeeded in tearing the country in two.

CHAPTER SIX

Aboard the *Altalena*

O n November 29, 1947, we received word in Ebelsberg that the United Nations had voted to partition Palestine into Arab and Jewish states and that the hated British mandate would end in six months. Our feelings of victory were tempered by the prospect of forging a new Jewish state surrounded by 22 million armed Arabs who wished to destroy us before such a state could be proclaimed. Our leadership understood that in order to survive, partisan ideological differences had to be set aside. Left wing, right wing, religious, secular—it did not matter. Any Jew able to hold a rifle was needed to defend the new nation against an ocean of enemies. The need for underground para-military groups now vanished and the Irgun ostensibly joined with the *LEHI* (Lohame Herut Yisrael, a militant Jewish underground organization), the Haganah, and the Palmach in creating the Israeli Defense Forces (IDF). On May 14, 1948, the British flag came down in the *Yeshuv* (the settlement of Palestine) and, as anticipated, the new state of Israel was immediately plunged into its first military conflict known as the War of Independence. The partition arrangement decreed by the UN, and agreed to by the British and by Israel was soundly rejected by all of the Middle East Arab states. They saw the British withdrawal as a golden opportunity to finally drive Western control from the region. The Arab League, under the leadership of Al-Husseini, declared a *jihad* (holy war) to rid Palestine of all Jews. They incorrectly calculated that the Jews would form a much weaker fighting force than the once-mighty British Empire troops and that conquering them would be an easy matter. They failed to consider that the Jews, having endured the crucible of the Holocaust, would now fight like their very existence depended upon it—which, in fact, it did. As the horrors of the camps became more widely exposed, the post-war world came to understand the lengths to which our enemies would go to rid the world of Jews. To the Jews fighting in Israel, the choice was either victory or Auschwitz. This new reality, coupled with an overwhelming desire to demonstrate that Jews were no longer willing to go meekly as sheep to the slaughter, provided the resolve that succeeded in establishing the new Jewish homeland.

From Irgun headquarters in Paris, the order to mobilize went out throughout Europe. We were directed to collect all men and material and report to France for immediate transport to the new nation of Israel. We enthusiastically rushed to join the fighting as Israel fought for her very existence. This was the moment we had trained for over the past two years. My parents did not stand in my way. They expressed their quiet pride in having a son who was to become a soldier for the new Jewish state. Saying good-bye was, of course, difficult, especially for my little brother who desperately wanted to join me but could not because of his age. He also understood that he was needed to help take care of Tatu whose health continued to deteriorate. I recall Hetche's face, white with envy, as we said our final farewells.

Filled with determination, I boarded the train that whisked me, and about twenty-five of my comrades, through Switzerland, across Allied-occupied Germany and into France. We were upbeat and confident about the job we had to do—build a new nation in Palestine. As far as I was concerned, my course was set. I had no intention of ever returning to Europe or moving on to America. In the idealistic view of our youth, our destiny was deeply intertwined with Zion and now we were finally on our way. While we were filled with resolve, we were not hot-headed or in any way fanatical. There was no flag-waving or anthem singing. After years of underground existence, we Etzelniks had learned to behave discreetly. This practice was emphasized repeatedly by our leader, Buzsik *(see previous chapter)*.

As our train approached the French border at Strasbourg, it came to a halt just before crossing the Rhine River. Irgun officers came aboard and shuffled us off onto waiting transport trucks, each bearing US Army license plates. Buzsik ordered us to lay low in the back of the canvas-covered military transports. Evidently, the French border guards were still on the alert for so-called Irgun terrorists attempting to gain entry into France and we could not risk being identified on board the open train cars. When the US military border guards saw us approaching the bridge, they quickly waved us across with no hesitation. Once all the trucks were on the long border bridge, the convoy came to a stop. Irgun operatives quickly appeared and began switching the trucks' license plates and other identifying marks from American to French. The operation took only a few minutes, but by the time we reached the French side of the crossing, we had been transformed to French military and were again quickly waved along by the French border patrol. Once safely across, the trucks were emptied and readied for the next transport. Our journey continued aboard a fleet of "low-boy" moving vans that had been appropriated from G-d-knows-where. In this way, disguised as household furniture, our troupe made its way through the Alsace region of the French countryside heading for Paris.

Once in Paris, we were unloaded, and joined hundreds of other young people assembled by the Irgun from all corners of Europe. Several thousand of us were housed in a small wooded camp facility outside of the city where we were fed and given fresh clothing. The Irgun officers immediately began sifting through our numbers seeking out the most qualified individuals to serve as soldiers. We were informed that, if we qualified, we would be the first to leave for what was now being called Israel—but, for security reasons, we were not told how or when. Based upon my experience in the Polish Brigade and my activities in the Irgun underground at Ebelsberg, I was selected for the voyage. Our group leader, Buzsik, was not picked because of his age and the poor state of his health caused by his extensive war wounds.

Much has been written about the *Altalena* incident that took place during those first days of Israeli independence. Most accounts are colored by political partisanship and often reveal more about the teller than about this controversial and unfortunate chapter in Israeli history. My account is drawn, for the most part, from my own recollections of having been onboard the *Altalena* as well as my first-hand discussions with many of the leaders involved including Menachem Begin, Yigael Yadin, Yechiel Kaddishai, and other principals. I have also read many of the accounts written by scholars and eye-witnesses and have used this information in formulating the account presented here. It should be understood that I was not personally present for many of the events recorded in this retelling of the *Altalena* story. I am relying upon the veracity and accuracy of those whose accounting of events and whose opinions I respect. I was by no means a decision-maker or in any position of authority. I was a twenty-one-year-old Holocaust survivor, caught up in an historic and tragic situation that I did not come to fully understand till many years later. Having said this, I do maintain that my presence and participation aboard the *Altalena* provides me with a better-than-average ability to discern the truth about this controversial episode in Israeli history.

The sequence of events that led to my passage aboard the *Altalena* were set into motion with the UN resolution for the partition of Palestine on November 29, 1947. As a consequence of this act, Irgun members who had been exiled in Kenya and Eritrea by the British were now free to travel. Most made their way to France where the Irgun leadership was headquartered. The Irgun in Europe, under the leadership of Shmuel Katz, Eliahu Lankin, and others mounted a frantic campaign to funnel men and materiel to Palestine in preparation for the inevitable battle with the Arabs as soon as the British departed

There was a second agenda to this campaign—a political one. It was clear that the government of the new Jewish state would be molded in the image of Ben-Gurion and the left-wing socialists. If they were to constitute any sort of political force in the new democratic nation, the Israeli right desperately needed Jews sympathetic to their cause to counter-balance the thousands of Ben-Gurion sympathizers who had been smuggled into the country over the years by the Bricha. So the call was spread throughout Europe for young men and women ready and willing to fight for the new Jewish homeland—and willing to vote for a non-socialist government once the fighting was over. As a result, we found ourselves in a camp, outside of Paris, filled with just such people.

After one week at the Paris camp, those of us who had been selected for service—roughly 1,000 young men and women— were ordered back onto the moving vans and driven first through Paris, down the Champs Elysée, and then on to Marseilles, in the south of France. The convoy was a long one with many of the furniture trucks carrying boxes of munitions as well as men. Most of the weapons had been gathered over the past two years by Irgun units such as ours while some had been purchased from the French. In fact, the entire truck caravan was under the supervision of the French military that often assisted in feeding us and looking after our basic needs. Based in good part on the friendship between Ben-Gurion and Charles DeGaulle, the French served as a vital ally to the fledgling state of Israel, providing much-needed military and economic assistance during the early years of independence.

Once in Marseilles, we were unloaded and billeted in barrack-style housing overnight. The next morning we were assembled and told that a ship called the *Altalena* was coming for us and would transport us, along with the munitions, to Tel Aviv where we would join the newly formed Israeli Defense Forces. We would not sail from Marseilles, however, but from the nearby harbor of Port-du-Bouc a few miles to the south. The vans delivered us to the dock at Port-du-Bouc and we got to work immediately loading the crates of munitions aboard the 4,500-ton freighter.

Security for this part of the operation was tight, forcing us to work mostly at night in a clandestine fashion. Although we had no problem from the French authorities, we had to evade the attention of the many Egyptian, and other Arab agents who populated this international crossroads. The ship bore no flags or identifying markings and we were cautioned not to speak to anyone before getting onboard. Despite these measures, word was beginning to leak out. A small blurb appeared in a French newspaper reporting on rumors of a vessel sailing from France bringing men and weapons to Israel. This exposure, I'm sure, convinced Shmuel Katz that further delay was impossible and it was time to set sail. Irgun leadership in Israel, specifically Menachem Begin, had approved the mission, but had not yet issued a green light to set sail. While Begin expected that he would be the one to order the voyage launched, Shmuel Katz acted unilaterally and okayed the departure on his own.

The *Altalena* (Italian for see-saw) was named for Jabotinsky's pseudonym when he worked as a journalist in Italy. The freighter was originally built as an LST 138 landing craft for the US Army during World War II. It was purchased by Abrasha Stawsky and others via funds collected primarily in the United States by Revisionist sympathizers like author Ben Hecht and Peter Bergson. It had been used for several years to smuggle refugees into Palestine under Aliyah Bet, all the while posing as a commercial freighter. Originally, the ship was to sail on May 15 under the flag of the new Jewish nation that was to be declared as the British departed on the day before, but the purchase of weapons and other organizational matters took longer than expected. Adding to the delay was the fact that the longshoremen at Port du Bouc had decided to stage a strike after one of the boxes of weapons fell and broke open revealing its contents.

Despite these obstacles, the *Altalena* stood ready to set sail on June 10 with its cargo of Irgun-collected weapons and fighters. It was a dispute over the allocation of those weapons that was to lead the ship to tragedy. Between the time the weapons were collected and the time they were placed onboard the *Altalena*, the Irgun in Israel had officially ceased to exist.

On June 1, an agreement merging the Irgun, the LEHI, and the Haganah into the new Israeli Defense Forces was signed by Begin using Ze'ev Jabotinsky's pen. Since the agreement did not encompass Jerusalem, units fighting there maintained their separate identities and command. One of the clauses of the agreement required the Irgun to cease all independent arms acquisition activities. The question of whether this agreement did or did not apply to the *Altalena* was the subject of some dispute since by June 1, the ship's cargo of 5,000 rifles, 250 Bren guns, 5 million bullets, 50 bazookas, 5 tanks, several tractors, and more, had already been acquired and was by now in the pipeline en route to Marseilles.

I boarded the *Altalena*, along with 900 other young, enthusiastic Jewish men and women, just before sundown on June 10. None of us could help but feel a sense of Jewish pride to be a part of this historic expedition. We felt larger than life and were filled with a subdued, yet heartfelt, excitement as the small tugboats assisted our vessel in slipping quietly out of the harbor at dusk. I recall looking down from the deck as the ship inched its way out to sea and observing a small boat skimming alongside of us and attached to its mast was a new blue-and-white Israeli flag. A man, who I recognized as Eli Tavin, the Irgun's overseas intelligence chief, was waving to us enthusiastically from the deck of the small boat and shouting out words of G-dspeed. Tavin, at this point, was coordinating all of the Irgun's weapons procurement efforts. Before Israeli independence, he had been the mastermind behind our campaign against British interests in Europe and had engineered, in 1946, the bombing of the British

Embassy in Rome. Watching one of our top leaders see us off, as the beautiful Israeli flag rippled in the wind behind him, is a memory I still cherish from those moments when the Altalena first set sail. As we stood on her deck, I looked around at this unlikely contingent of new Israeli patriots—singing the Hatikvah as the setting sun soaked their faces in shades of gold. We had been the dregs—the humiliated victims of Europe's greatest bloodbath—but now we were soldiers on an age-old quest to free our beloved homeland. The exhilaration and excitement was palpable.

Our commander was Eliahu Lankin, respected member of the Etzel High Command. He explained that fighting had erupted in the land that was by now being called Israel, and that we were desperately needed to aid in the historic struggle. We did not know, however, that on the day we weighed anchor, June 11, a UN-sponsored cease-fire between Israel and Jordan went into effect that was to last until July 8. British naval vessels were assigned by the UN to patrol the Mediterranean to prevent the shipments of arms or troops to either side in the conflict. By the time the truce went into effect, we were already crossing the Mediterranean. Our departure was kept secret—no cables announcing the event were sent to Israel because of the fear that we might be ordered to stay put by the new Israeli government. We did not learn until later that Ben-Gurion had been informed by Irgun leader, Menachem Begin, about the transport several weeks in advance. Despite the provisions of the IDF agreement of June 1, Ben-Gurion recognized the vital need for these weapons and gave his approval to Begin for the shipment to go on as planned.

Now, with the British naval blockade being put into place under the terms of the UN-sponsored *Hafugah* (ceasefire), Begin, surprised that the Altalena had actually set sail without his direct approval, decided it wise to postpone the arrival, and sent a cable to the ship with instructions to stay put at sea and await further orders. Shmuel Katz received a similar cable. While Katz got the word in Paris—on the morning after we set sail—we, onboard the *Altalena*, did not. As all of us onboard were aware, we were operating under radio silence. This was not due to security, but rather due to a poor-quality radio that functioned only sporadically at best. Throughout our journey, Begin and his radio operator, Ziporeh Kessel-Levi, attempted to reach us by radio and instruct us to avoid arriving into Tel Aviv. After coded transmissions failed to raise a response, Kessel-Levi began open voice communications, repeating over and over, "Keep away. Await Instructions." All to no avail. While many may have felt that our arrival in Tel Aviv harbor on June 20 was an act of defiance, it was not. It was simply due to poor communication, and confusion caused by the faulty radio. Had we received the word from Begin to delay, our leaders would have done so without question. We had adequate supplies and the waters were quite calm. We simply did not get the word and steamed full speed ahead, oblivious of the Hafugah, of the British blockade, and of the internal political machinations our arrival would spark.

As one might expect, a thousand spirited, young people aboard a confined space was, after very little time, certain to lead to social and even romantic encounters. I befriended a group of young French ladies as we cruised the summer Mediterranean and I knew of several couples, such as Yechiel and Bambi Kadishai, who met on board the Altalena and would eventually become husband and wife. A few such shipboard couples were actually married on board during our voyage by the ship's captain, Monroe Fein.

Fein, an American from Chicago, had served as a US naval captain in the Pacific during the war. He had been recruited in New York and had been sailing the Altalena across the Mediterranean for several years posing it as a merchant vessel while actually using it to haul illegal refugees into Palestine.

Fein volunteered to pilot the ship on this mission, but had expressed his qualms to the Irgun High Command about the unknown underwater terrain along the Israeli coast. Ideally, the ship required a steep drop-off so it could navigate square up to the land and drop its huge steel gangplanks onto the shoreline. The Irgun High Command did not have the necessary geological maps and without them, Fein explained that he might risk getting beached and being forced to scuttle the ship. While running ashore was a concern for Fein, running the British blockade was not. He was an experienced WWII naval officer, trained in the South Pacific in the art of evasion at sea and he was convinced that he could outmaneuver any British patrol boat we may encounter. The question of the landing site was complicated by the fact that Katz and the Irgun leadership knew we could not count on Haganah assistance in unloading the boat. A landing site along the Tel Aviv beach across from Frishman Street was selected because it was believed we could easily bring in many Irgunchiks to assist us with the cargo. Fein also had a problem with the coded signals used for visual communication once the ship came within sight of land. Fein revised them and asked Shmuel Katz to get them to Israel by air so they would be in place by the time the ship arrived.

Although the direct journey only took four to five days, because of the evasive zigzag course maintained by Captain Fein, we required a full ten days to cross the Mediterranean to Tel Aviv. Traveling in the open sea, we were always mindful of the risk of air attack. On several occasions, the air raid sirens would sound and we would rush from the deck to the hold and out of sight. Tarpaulins were quickly swept over any visible cargo so, from the air, we would appear as a normal commercial vessel. We were warned that Egyptian air force fighters were on patrol looking for supply ships headed for Israel and since we carried no anti-aircraft equipment, deception was our only defense.

Mark My Words!

We participated in military drills under British-trained officers by day, and sang patriotic songs and socialized at night. When we weren't marching around the deck, we were seated in makeshift classrooms learning conversational Hebrew. Rumors were rampant that the BBC had announced our existence to the world and that rumor, of course, led to apprehension that we would either be attacked by Egyptian fighter bombers or stopped by the British blockade—actually, neither happened. In addition to our hard-core underground European contingent, there were young people on board from Belgium, Mexico, Canada, Cuba, and the US. All of us were there because of our dedication to the Zionist dream and so, despite national and cultural differences, we became bonded as brothers and sisters, thanks to our shared fears and aspirations.

By June 15, it became known to Begin that we were steaming directly towards Tel Aviv and could possibly be intercepted by the British. Begin met with Ben-Gurion and several cabinet ministers and revealed that the ship had sailed without his knowledge and that he wanted to know how best to proceed. On June 16, Ben-Gurion made the decision that he recorded in his diary: "I believe we should not endanger Tel Aviv port. They should not be sent back. They should be disembarked at an unknown shore."

Through his security minister, Galili, Ben-Gurion communicated his consent to the landing of the ship to Begin, adding a request that it be done as fast as possible. At that point, we were instructed by radio to come in to the harbor at full speed. Begin wired the ship with the following message: "Full steam ahead. There are now no internal problems." By now, our communications had improved and we were able to clearly understand the messages. While the Irgun proposed directing the *Altalena* to Tel Aviv, Ben-Gurion's representatives claimed that this was too risky since it would be difficult to evade British blockaders. Begin agreed and we were therefore instructed to head for the Haganah control base just north of Tel Aviv, a deserted stretch of beach known as Kfar Vitkin—named for the nearby village which was a center of animal husbandry and renowned to this day for its pungent odor of horse and cow manure.

Lankin and our other leaders were delighted by this news since it portended well in its implications. As a practical matter, since we were being directed directly into a Haganah stronghold, we would have the assistance of Haganah troops in unloading the cargo. It also was interpreted by our somewhat naïve leaders that this represented a true reconciliation between the left wing, Mapai-controlled Haganah and the right-wing Revisionist Irgun. Perhaps the Zionist vision of a unified Jewish homeland was indeed coming to pass. This, of course, turned out to be a nothing more than a pipe dream.

While there was agreement on the anchoring place of the Altalena, there were major differences about the allocation of the cargo. Ben-Gurion agreed to Begin's initial request that 20 percent of the weapons be dispatched to the Irgun battalions fighting in Jerusalem—fighting units which were not under the control of the Ben-Gurion provisional government. Begin's second request, however, that the remainder of the arms be transferred to the IDF in order to equip us, the newly arrived Irgun troops, was rejected by Ben-Gurion, who interpreted the request as a demand to reinforce an "army within an army." This was not Begin's intention, rather, he saw it as a question of honor that we enlist in the IDF fully equipped. Galili insisted that the balance of the weapons be handed over to the provisional government unconditionally. Begin reportedly tried to reason with Galili by asking him, "Had the boat come several weeks ago, as we had planned, the Irgun would have had all the arms. Wouldn't you agree that our boys should come into the army at least fully armed and equipped? These particular arms were merely late in arriving. Our boys are already in the army or will be within a matter of days. It would only mean that they will be mobilized with the full equipment that we in any case would have given them. What is wrong with that? Why can't you agree?"

But Galili would not agree and reported Begin's intransigence back to Ben-Gurion. Galili further informed Begin that since no agreement had been reached on the distribution of the arms, the government would not help with unloading the ship. Begin, and other Irgun leaders, scrambled to assemble the needed manpower and trucks for the job. Despite the failure to gain government acceptance of the distribution plan, there was an atmosphere made up of frenetic action and high celebration at Kfar Vitkin. At last, all the months of striving and hard work were successfully concluded, and not too late to turn the scales in the battles soon to be renewed once the current cease-fire was concluded. For Begin, it was a great and historic occasion. He understood the significance, after years of underground struggle, of this dramatic and open manifestation of Irgun achievement. Landing the Altalena seemed a fitting last act for the Irgun Zvai Leumi.

As we made our way southward during the night along the Israeli coast from Haifa towards Tel Aviv, I recall seeing the semaphore operators on nearby Israeli frigates, the Wedgewood and the Eilat, attempting to communicate with our vessel. Using Morse code, they instructed us not to approach the shore during daylight and to make our way back out to sea and await further orders. Evidently, there was some confusion about how to interpret the signals. Fein used the revised signaling protocols he had instructed Katz to send ahead. Using this method, Fein took no action and continued moving forward. To the Israeli vessels, it appeared that the Altalena chose to ignore their instructions. Hence, a few marksmen from the Wedgewood fired rifle shots across our bow. Our ship returned fire, directing a machine gun barrage in the direction of the Wedgewood. Finally, in order to avoid further escalation, Captain Fein complied and turned us away from the shoreline back to sea. We dropped anchor and languished in frustration throughout that long day. Finally, in the late afternoon we received our new orders to make our way to the Kfar Vitkin drop-off point.

We reached Kfar Vitkin on the evening of Sunday, June 20. This was our first real glimpse of Eretz Yisroel, of Zion. We were instructed to disembark and not to bother carrying our belongings, just to hurry across the wide steel gangplanks onto the shore and our suitcases would be brought along later. There on the beach stood Begin, who greeted us with out-stretched arms and great emotion. The townsfolk from Kfar Vitkin rowed out to the ship in makeshift rafts and rowboats to assist in the disembarkation. They refused, however, to allow their boats to transport any weapons to the shore. After we had disembarked, tired and hungry, leaving onboard the Irgun leadership and the ship's crew, we were assigned to temporary barracks in Kfar Vitkin where we were able to catch a few hours sleep.

The next morning, volunteers from the nearby fishing village of Michmoret began to unload the ship's cargo. As the arms were being unloaded at Kfar Vitkin, Ben-Gurion, in Tel Aviv, reported to the newly established state council *(Knesset),* meeting in an appropriated movie theatre, about the Altalena's arrival and then publicly demanded that that Begin surrender and hand over of all the weapons. Despite having previously given us the green light, Ben-Gurion ranted as if his authority as head of the government was being challenged. "We must decide whether to hand over power to Begin or to order him to cease his separate activities. If he does not do so, we will open fire! Otherwise, we must decide to dispatch our own army."

Although he would deny it later, Ben-Gurion initially approved the landing of the Altalena. Ever the opportunist, and in his anger over Begin's request to allocate the arms to his own men first, Ben-Gurion seized upon the incident as an excuse to solidify his authority and discredit a political rival—or worse. The landing of the Altalena was by no stretch an effort by the

Irgun, or the Israeli right wing, to undermine the authority of the new government. It was the result, primarily, of poor radio communication. For Ben-Gurion, acting under the influence of his political advisors, to characterize the situation as a near insurrection, requiring an armed response, was perhaps, the most misguided of his many unfortunate decisions. While some have characterized the Altalena incident as a power struggle over who would take the reigns of the nascent nation, I do not view it this way. Begin and his Irgun forces, of which I was a member, never had any intention of usurping control of either the military or the new Israeli government. I believe, as Ben-Gurion later in life hinted, that the situation was misrepresented to him as a potential "putsch" and he then used it as an excuse to solidify his leadership over a political antagonist.

Ben-Gurion's inflamed rhetoric swayed the Knesset and they drafted a resolution to empower the army to use force if necessary to overcome the Irgun and to confiscate the ship and its cargo. Implementation of this decision was assigned to the Alexandroni Brigade, commanded by Dan Even *(Epstien)*, which the following day surrounded the Kfar Vitkin area. Dan Even issued an ultimatum to Begin that stated:

"I am empowered to confiscate the weapons and military materials which have arrived on the Israeli coast in the area of my jur- isdiction in the name of the Israeli Government. I have been authorized to demand that you hand over the weapons to me... You are required to carry out this order immediately. If you do not agree to carry out this order, I shall use all the means at my disposal in order to implement the order... I wish to inform you that the entire area is surrounded by fully armed military units and armored cars, and all the roads are blocked...The immigrants-unarmed-will be permitted to travel to the camps in accordance with your arrangements. You have ten minutes to give me your answer."

The ultimatum, and in particular the demand for an answer within ten minutes, was viewed as insulting and unrealistic by

Begin, who refused to respond to it and all attempts at mediation failed. Begin's failure to respond was a blow to Even's prestige, and a clash was now inevitable. Fighting ensued and because Begin ordered that the Altalena refugees not shoot back, a number of casualties were taken. The army launched its attack from all sides and with a variety of weapons, including rifles, machine guns, and mortars. The Irgun members were unarmed. Begin shouted to the men to scatter, while he and Lankin and a number of others raced to the motorboat waiting at the shore and took off for the Altalena.

Onboard the ship, Captain Fein was startled by the gunfire coming from the shore. He suspected that it was some sort of sneak Arab attack and immediately started the engines in order to put the ship out to sea. He then observed Begin, and about thirty others, speeding his way on the motorboat. As the ship swung around and headed seaward, the starboard side was facing the two Israeli frigates that had been keeping the ship under tight scrutiny. Suddenly, both ships open fired on the Altalena with heavy machine guns. Unprepared and unable to return fire, Captain Fein noticed that the gunners were pointing their weapons at Begin's motorboat. He quickly placed the Altalena between the motorboat and the Israeli frigates in order to serve as a protective barrier. The firing stopped as soon as Begin and his crew were no longer within range. As soon as Begin and the others were safely on board, the Altalena received instructions from one of the frigates to immediately head towards Tel Aviv. Fein complied with the orders and headed south along the coast with both frigates close in tow.

In order to prevent further bloodshed, the Kfar Vitkin settlers initiated negotiations between Yaakov Meridor *(Begin's deputy)* and Dan Even, which ended in a general cease-fire and the transfer of the weapons, which had been partially unloaded on the shore, to the local IDF commander.

Meanwhile, out at sea, the Altalena, bearing its precious cargo of armaments and the top Irgun leadership, was speeding towards the Tel Aviv beach escorted by the two Israeli Corvair frigates. Just before reaching Tel Aviv, one of the Corvairs sent word for the Altalena to follow it out to sea—away from the shoreline. Begin, consulting with other Irgun leaders and Captain Fein, wisely decided to ignore this ominous order and continued his course towards the Frishman Street Beach landing spot. Unfamiliar with the submerged terrain, Fein accidentally ran the Altalena aground and was unable to either approach the shoreline or return back out to sea.

Begin had been originally optimistic about returning to Tel Aviv. Unloading all the weapons at Kfar Vitkin would have taken a week given the available manpower there. Begin foolishly hoped that in Tel Aviv it would be possible to enter into a dialogue with the Ben-Gurion-led provisional government and to unload the remaining weapons there peacefully using manpower from the IDF. But this was not to be the case. Ben-Gurion ordered Yigael Yadin *(acting Chief of Staff)* to concentrate large forces on the Tel Aviv beach and to take the ship by force. Years later, Yadin admitted to me that although he was ordered to do so by Ben-Gurion, he never signed the orders authorizing what happened next. Responding only to Ben-Gurion's verbal directives delivered by his aide, Yitzhak Sdeh, it was left to young Yitzhak Rabin to carry them out. Under Rabin's direction, the artillery cannons were aimed at the vessel and at four in the afternoon, the shelling began. It appeared as though the freshly born Jewish nation—the embodiment of the hopes and dreams of countless dispossessed generations—was only to rise for one month before descending immediately into abyss of civil war.

In the confusion, and within sight of the Tel Aviv harbor, the Altalena was now beached aground and was unable to either approach the shoreline or return back to sea. I believe that had the ship not gotten stuck on the sandbar, what happened next could easily have been avoided. Had it not run aground, it could have continued into Tel Aviv harbor and unloaded the remaining weapons before the IDF forces arrived and had time to take up their positions. Alternately, it could have maneuvered to a different spot along the coast. Even if there had not been sufficient time to avoid the artillery barrage against it, Captain Fein, had he not been beached, could easily have directed the ship back out to sea again and out of range before taking any hits. As it was, the Altalena became a sitting target and an embodiment of defiance of the newly established political and military order. It soon felt the wrath of Ben-Gurion's paranoid rage.

The third shell lobbed at the ship from the shore, and succeeded in hitting the Altalena broadside, and ignited her hull on fire. There was danger that the fire would spread to the holds where the explosives were stored, and Captain Fein ordered all aboard to abandon ship. People jumped into the water, whilst their comrades on shore set out to meet them on rafts. Although Captain Fein flew the white flag of surrender, the shelling continued unabated. Begin, who was on deck, heroically agreed to leave the ship only after the last of the wounded had been evacuated. Fein ordered a reluctant Begin off the ship and nearly forced him to board the small rowboat that was tied off the backside of the hull facing away from the shore and the gunfire. Begin lay down in the floor of the rowboat while others concealed him with a tarpaulin. Evidently, there were those who felt that Begin himself was the target of this attack. Once the rowboat reached the shore and Begin emerged, all the shelling and firing directed at the Altalena were instantly halted.

The evacuees from the ship were forced to make their way to shore aboard rowboats and dinghies while still exposed to gunfire from the IDF battalions on the beach. This, despite the fact that they were unarmed fellow Jews and many were waving white flags of surrender. Once Begin was seen emerging from the rowboat, safely on shore, the order was given, and all firing stopped. The uninjured survivors from the ship were not detained once they landed ashore and were unmolested as they were taken off to Irgun headquarters.

Meanwhile, in Kfar Vitken, we were undergoing induction into the Israeli military when we got word that someone was firing on the Altalena in Tel Aviv harbor. We grabbed bicycles, motor scooters, wagons, whatever we could to propel us quickly to Frishman Street along the Tel Aviv harbor where we observed our burning ship as it was consumed by the flames. There was mass chaos underway in every direction. Former Haganah troops had taken positions along the shore and, under the direction of Rabin, were pumping automatic weapon fire at the unarmed survivors struggling in the water. This continued until we observed Begin emerging from a small rowboat where he had hidden in order to make his escape.

I recall watching Abrasha Stawsky trying to assist the survivors from the dinghies to the shore while attempting to dodge the automatic rifle fire. Stawsky was an Irgun leader of immense proportions, bulging shoulders, heavy hands, bushy brows, and perpetual smile. He was an imposing, flamboyant figure known to always carry a pistol tucked into a shoulder holster and was one of the three men responsible for raising the funds for the purchase of the Altalena. He was called Stawsky, the Rescuer, for his work in smuggling Jews out of Europe during the early 1940s. Stawsky had been arrested in Palestine during the early 1930s in connection with the Arlosoroff affair during which he was unfairly charged with murder. Stawsky was acquitted, and it was just recently uncovered that Arlosoroff was actually the victim of a Nazi plot. As was revealed in his personal diaries, Nazi propaganda minister Joseph Goebbels learned that his wife, Martha, had been romantically involved with Arlosoroff before she wed Goebbels and when both Martha and Arlosoroff lived in Berlin. Goebbels dispatched agents of the ancient Catholic order known as the Knights Templar, who maintained several monasteries in Jerusalem, to carry out a hit against this Jewish rival now living in Palestine. Goebbels, through his minions, not only succeeded in eliminating any evidence that his wife had ever been intimate with a Jew, he also managed to pin the crime on a convenient target, Stawsky.

Abrasha Stawsky, after having survived near hanging for a crime he did not commit, after fighting for years in the underground resistance during the Holocaust, was shot in the knee by Jewish IDF troops and was taken to a nearby hospital for treatment. I became caught up in the effort to get the man to the hospital and stood with him and kept up the pressure on the tourniquet as he lay dying on the front steps while others hurried inside to arrange for his admission. But he was not to be admitted. I was told that they would not or could not permit Stawsky to enter the hospital at this time. While awaiting treatment on the blood-soaked steps of the hospital, Stawsky developed a blood infection and went into shock. For whatever the reason, he did not receive prompt attention and tragically, this great Jewish hero was martyred that day as we stood by helplessly. Of all the shame and disgrace associated with the *Altalena* incident, the tragic and needless death of Stawsky was perhaps the most vile.

For years following the incident, Captain Fein blamed himself for the loss of the *Altalena*—despite the fact that he had foreseen the dangers and warned the leadership of the risk of landing in uncharted waters. He felt that if he had only been able to avoid running aground, the vessel, its cargo, and many lives could have been salvaged. The burden of his guilt tortured Fein for years and eventually drove the poor man towards insanity.

The matter of guilt also plagued the man who today is known as Professor Hillel Dalesky. It fell to Dalesky, at the time a Haganah recruit from South Africa who had been in Israel for only two months, to actually fire the artillery cannon that succeeded in destroying the Altalena. Dalesky today states that he hesitated in carrying out the order, but, in the end, he felt he had no choice but to do as he was told. Today, he finds it difficult to believe that he was able to fire upon fellow Jews in such a wanton manner. He has carried the guilt of his actions with him to this day.

While Fein and Dalesky were branded by their guilt over the Altalena incident, the one figure most responsible for the disaster never expressed the slightest remorse. On the contrary, David Ben-Gurion is remembered as making what became known as the *Totach Hakadosh* or "Holy Cannon" speech to the State Council on June 21. "Blessed be the cannon that bombed that ship!" he proclaimed in reference to Dalesky's gun and Fein's vessel.

The Altalena, with its burned-out hull and charred super-structure, remained on the sandbar in Tel Aviv harbor for several years as a stark reminder of Israeli internecine strife. A graffiti writer at one point emblazoned the rusted hull with the message: "Herut—this will be your fate as well!" referring to the right-wing political party that succeeded the Revisionists and eventually evolved into today's Likud Party. Eventually, Ben-Gurion ordered the ship's carcass, which had become something of an eyesore, towed out to sea and sunk.

While I have expressed my opinion that the events of June 20, 1948 on the beaches of Tel Aviv were the result of an unfortunate series of screw-ups and communication failures, not everyone familiar with the case shares this benign viewpoint. No less a figure than Shmuel Katz firmly believed that the tragic events surrounding the Altalena all point to a single sinister motive. Katz believed that the target that day was not the Altalena, but rather Menachem Begin personally, who represented a palpable threat to Ben-Gurion's control of the Israeli government. In analyzing the events in question, Katz raised a number of provocative points that all seem to support this contention:

1. Why did Ben-Gurion authorize the Altalena's mission and then keep it a secret from his cabinet and the State Council? Why did he later deny doing so?
2. Why was the Altalena really diverted to Kfar Vitkin—a Haganah stronghold out of sight from the general public?

3. Why did Galili at first promise to dispatch Haganah trucks to Kfar Vitkin to assist in unloading the weapons and instead sent Dan Evan with an ultimatum to confiscate the weapons—something sure to elicit a response from Begin and likely result in a firefight?
4. Why did Ben-Gurion employ inflammatory rhetoric before the Knesset when advising them of the Altalena's impending arrival, knowingly distorting the facts to make it appear that the country was about to be invaded by Irgun fanatics bent on seizing power?
5. Why did the Corvair frigates fire on the motorboat as Begin sought to escape the fighting on the shore and board the Altalena? Why did the firing stop once he was out of range?
6. Why was an attempt made to escort the Altalena, with Begin on board, out to sea and out of view of any witnesses on the beach?
7. Why was the order given to fire upon the Altalena, with sufficient firepower to destroy it, thereby knowingly sacrificing a mountain of sorely needed munitions in the process?
8. Why was the order given at Tel Aviv beach to stop shooting once Begin came within view of witnesses on the beach?

According to Katz, the answer to all of these questions is the same one. Ben-Gurion either orchestrated, or intentionally exacerbated, a situation that cast Begin in the role of insurrectionary leader smuggling in a boatload of men and munitions to be used for the overthrow of the new government. Ben-Gurion sought to seize the opportunity, and in so doing, eliminate Begin under the guise of putting down a rebellion and saving the new nation from outright civil war. Of course, none of us was privy to the true motives that drove Ben-Gurion to issue the orders to fire upon the Altalena. I feel that Katz could be correct when he surmises that Ben-Gurion wished to see Begin dead. Ben-Gurion was considered by many to be first and foremost a Bolshevik, and doing in one's adversaries for power, real or imagined, was, by then, a well-established Bolshevik tradition.

It was not only the Altalena that went up in smoke that day, as I stood on the shore watching the flames devour the ill-fated vessel. It was my idealistic notions of a unified Zionist state—the naïve refugee's vision of a Jewish homeland filled with milk and honey once the enemy had been dealt with. But it was not the British, nor was it the Arabs that had fired upon and destroyed the Altalena. It was other Jews. On that sad day, I began to understand what would soon become painfully clear to me in the years ahead—that life was going to be very difficult in this new land for those who did not side with the majority, socialist political power structure. As I stood silently and anonymously amidst the crowd of onlookers that had gathered, I could not comprehend what my eyes beheld. Somehow, the smoke pouring from the doomed ship brought with it images of Treblinka from the book I had read on the subject. Is this the land that I had struggled and prepared for years in which to settle? Where Jews behave like this to other Jews they disagree with politically? This was some sort of nightmare and I found myself numb with disbelief. It was, at that point, the most troubling moment I had yet experienced, and the memory of my frustration and despair has stayed with me from that day to this.

The Battle of the Altalena resulted in nineteen casualties—all of them Jews killed by other Jews. Sixteen Irgun fighters were killed in the confrontation; six were killed in the Kfar Vitkin area and ten on Tel Aviv beach. Three IDF soldiers were killed, two at Kfar Vitkin and one in Tel Aviv. After the shelling of the Altalena, more than 200 members of our group were arrested on Ben-Gurion's orders. Most of them were released several weeks later, with the exception of five senior commanders *(Moshe*

Hason, Eliahu Lankin, Yaakov Meridor, Bezalel Amitzur, and Hillel Kook), who were detained for more than two months. They were finally released, thanks to public pressure, on August 27, 1948 after it had been made abundantly clear that the Irgun did not have any ambitions of toppling the Ben-Gurion government.

Many regard the Altalena incident as evidence of Israel's inherent inability to govern itself without degenerating into civil strife. I look at it somewhat differently. Had the message from Begin for us not to enter the region reached us in time, everything would have been avoided. Had the radio onboard the ship worked properly, all would have been avoided. Had the ship not beached in Tel Aviv harbor, much loss of life and equipment would have been avoided. It was truly a tragic comedy of errors. A series of mishaps and glitches that, in the super-charged atmosphere of that time, gave Ben-Gurion the opportunity to reinforce his total control over the newly established state.

Years later, on the eve of the Six Day War, in June 1967, after Ben-Gurion had retired from political activity and was living in retirement at Sde Boker, Menahem Begin, who had by this point joined the ruling Unity government, participated in a delegation which visited the elderly leader and asked him to return and accept the premiership once again. Ben-Gurion declined, but after the meeting said that if he had then known Begin as he did now, the face of history would have been vastly different. This statement was as close as Ben-Gurion ever came to apologizing in any way for his actions during the Altalena affair.

CHAPTER SEVEN

In the IDF

Many of us did not rush to rejoin our military detachments after witnessing the fate of the Altalena. Who wants to belong to an army like this—one that attacks its own supply ships delivering desperately needed men and munitions? We simply wandered the streets of Tel Aviv for several days trying to make sense out of what had just happened—almost in a state of shock.

Finally, I and my homeless compatriots, wound up living in tents in a rural orange grove for several weeks as we contemplated our fate in long all-day caucuses. We maintained our status as freebooters, and thereby received no compensation or support from the military. We had not yet been discharged, but financially we were on our own. Some of us spoke of returning back to Europe, but this was not for me. Not at this time. I was a trained soldier, and I had come to Israel to fight the enemy, and I was determined to do it. Besides, who had the wherewithal to travel back to Europe? Eventually, we tired of the primitive living conditions and most of us decided to return to our units. Some of the Altalena refugees were absorbed by the Alexandroni Brigade at Kfar Vitken immediately after landing and it was to this detachment—stationed in a Tel Aviv recruiting camp— that my friends and I finally reported once we had decided to return to active duty.

By this time, the first UN-sponsored cease-fire had elapsed. In reality, the cease-fire had turned into an opportunity for our enemies to re-arm themselves. While arms shipments into the region were banned by the blockade, no such blockades were erected in the ports of Tyre and Alexandria that continued receiving massive shipments of armaments throughout the so-called truce. We were sent into combat immediately with no time allotted for training. One of my first tasks after being inducted into the Israeli military was creating my own dog tag. I was handed a small aluminum disc, a piece of rope, and some tools and told to engrave my name and serial number on the tag. I carefully etched, in Hebrew, "Hasten," and then, using Arabic numerals, I scraped in my number, "94721." Today, when I share this fact with a current member of the IDF, they marvel at the sight of a five-digit serial number since today's numbers contain eight digits and are counted in the tens of millions.

Within the Armed Forces, I, and my buddies from the Altalena, were known as MACHAL *(Mitnadwey Chootz L'aretz)* or Foreign Volunteers. As Machalniks, we were not subject to the same regulations upon discharge as Israeli-born soldiers. We held on to our homeland passports and, if we so elected, we were free to return back home after our tour of service was completed. Actually, we had three choices. At the end of our hitch, we could either opt to stay in the military, become a civilian and stay in Israel, or return back to our country of origin. Being a Machalnik was like having an insurance policy. If at any time things got too unpleasant, a member of the MACHAL could pack up and go home with little consequence. Actually, at that time in Israel, it was difficult to discern whether an individual was, or was not, in the military since both soldier and civilian dressed pretty much in the same way. Everyone wore green khaki short shorts, knee socks, and a *Kova Tembul* (dunce cap). These popular hats resembled a sailor's cap with the brim turned down. Originally, we foreign recruits were given French-style foreign legion caps—each bearing a veil in back for sun protection. Eventually, however, these gave way to the more comfortable Kova Tembul caps that are still worn today.

Mark My Words!

All the Machalniks were put up in tents along the beach for a few days awaiting our deportation to the front. My family was sending me messages via new arrivals to Israel and the news was not good. My father's medical condition continued to deteriorate. I recall receiving a letter from my brother describing how Tatu was having great difficulty breathing, sleeping, and doing any sort of work. The doctor had ordered him to stay put and not to go anywhere. He was not permitted to walk to the corner store—much less travel all the way to America, which, of course, was his dream. Tatu correctly felt that in America the medical care he was likely to receive would be much better. But getting him there now became a serious issue in more ways than one.

Ironically, I was assigned to the *Hativat Alexandroni* (Alexandroni Brigade), which was one of the six original territorial infantry brigades taken over at its inception by the IDF from the Haganah. It was centered along the coastal plain north of Tel Aviv and it was this unit that, under the command of Dan Evan, attacked the Altalena on the shores of Kfar Vitkin. The brigade derived its name from the Alexander Brook, which flows into the Mediterranean south of Hadera. Young Ariel Sharon commanded the Brigade's elite 101 Unit during this time. We were stationed near a small village called Kfar Yona at a camp known as Machneh Yehuda not far from Netanya.

At Kfar Yona, we were positioned just behind the front lines of the fighting and continually were assigned into the trenches that looked out upon the plains of Tul-Kerem. Supplies were, naturally, scarce. We were required to double-up and share everything, including rifles. We had, at best, ten Czech carbine rifles for every twenty soldiers. In order to be relieved, an Israeli infantryman shooting at the front would need to run back into the trenches and pass on his weapon to the next soldier who would then take the carbine and run back out to take up the same position. After several weeks of intense combat, a second UN ceasefire was agreed to by the parties, and the army took this opportunity to have us undergo basic combat training back in Kfar Yona. We learned how to use grenades, how to disassemble and clean our weapons, how to curse in Hebrew and slowly we became more of an organized fighting force rather than the sloppy ragtag company we once were.

It was during this time that the malaria which I had contracted back in Russia starting flaring up. As often happened during the summer months, I broke out in a high fever and started experiencing double vision in my astigmatic right eye. In early September, I was placed into a military hospital for treatment. On September 18, lying in my hospital bed, I read the newspaper accounts of the assassination of Count Folk Bernadotte in Jerusalem. Bernadotte was a Swedish diplomat who had headed the Swedish Red Cross during World War II. He was serving as a UN mediator and was responsible for establishing two cease-fires in June and July. He was attempting to negotiate an end to the fighting in Jerusalem when he was assassinated by members of the LEHI, aka Stern Gang. The LEHI regarded Bernadotte as a British agent, a friend of the Nazis and a threat to their goal of an independent Israel with territory on both sides of the Jordan. As a result of this act, reaction against the LEHI by the Ben-Gurion government was very strong and led to the arrest of many LEHI members and the eventual elimination of the organization altogether.

That night, as I tossed and turned in a fever-induced delirium, I began speaking out loud and kept mentioning Count Bernadotte in my rambling incoherency. Lying in the adjacent hospital bed happened to be one of the deputy Tel Aviv police chiefs recovering from some illness. My loud ranting about Count Bernadotte awakened him and he summoned a nurse who administered some more sulfa medication, but not before the police officer instructed her to listen to and remember what I was raving about. A few days later, fully recovered, I was released from the hospital and shortly thereafter received a call from the Tel Aviv police. They wanted to question me and did so in a cramped interrogation room. The questions came at me quickly.

"Were you a member of the Irgun?"

"Yes."

"Did you arrive to Israel aboard the Altalena?"

"Yes."

"Are you a member of the Stern Gang?"

"No."

"What do you know about the shooting of UN envoy Bernadotte?"

"Nothing more than I read in the newspaper."

"Well, we have information that you know more than that. Why were you talking in your sleep about Bernadotte?"

"I was suffering from a high fever. I was delirious. I had just read about his death and maybe it was on my mind. I really didn't know what I was saying at that point."

My interrogator, an older gentleman with strong features, considered this for a moment. I spoke up again, "Look, it's true I was in the Irgun in Europe, but now I'm in the IDF. I was never a big shot. I was always a little shot. Go ahead and ask somebody about me. I was never involved in planning anything. I just did my work." Evidently, they found my story convincing because they released me and marked my file "Case Closed."

In addition to malaria, another problem that plagued me in the infantry—and one that eventually led to my discharge—was my poor eyesight. Although I didn't know it, I was sorely in need of eyeglasses. Because of this, I was unable to shoot my rifle in a normal fashion with the sight up to my right eye. Since I had severe astigmatism in my right eye making my left eye the stronger, I invariably put the weapon up to my left eye in order to better train my sights. I endured a good deal of questioning from my fellow soldiers about the unorthodox method I used to hold my gun. But all concerns were set aside after they marveled at my marksmanship on the shooting range.

After the truce ended, we were next ordered north to the Syrian border to do battle with the armies of the notorious

General Kafkaji. We were assigned to relieve the troops in the trenches. One of our fellow soldiers, Mizrachi, suffered from a form of night blindness known as chicken blindness. I recall returning to the trench one rainy night only to find Mizrachi lying across the sand bag embankments, sound asleep at his post. I shook him awake and scolded him harshly.

"You're supposed to be standing guard," I shouted. "You could have us all killed!"

"It doesn't matter," he explained. "I can't see anything at night anyway. Awake or asleep I'm no good to anyone as a lookout at night." Mizrachi was soon relieved of his duties and reassigned away from the front. As a result, the rest of us foot soldiers had to double up in performing our guard duty. For a short time, our four-hour shifts grew to eight hours.

Our commander at Tul-Kerem was a tough redheaded *sabra* (native-born Israeli) who sported a bushy moustache. He had a curious habit of leaping out of his jeep before it had come to a full stop and letting it continue on without him until it came to a stop by itself. Our commander was a master of decoy and camouflage. He trained us on how to make our forces appear to be better armed than we were. In a maneuver he borrowed from British Field Marshall Montgomery in his celebrated World War II campaigns against Rommel in North Africa, our commander would have us take metal barrels and lay them on their sides. Across each one, we would lay half of a wooden telephone pole and then cover the whole thing with a bit of camouflage. From the air, these decoys appeared to be artillery cannons, particularly when we embellished the effect by placing emptied ammunition boxes next to each one. The boxes actually were empty, but we would put on a show with two of us lugging the ammo boxes as if they were full and heavy in the hopes that our performance would be spotted by the enemy. During the ceasefire, Jordanian reconnaissance planes conducted daily fly-overs of our positions, taking aerial photos. We knew our subterfuge was effective when a newspaper was circulated through the camp showing a photo of our mock cannon emplacements under the headline: "Jordanians Accuse Israel of Cease-Fire Violations. Claim Israelis Reinforcing Positions with New Artillery."

Another deceptive maneuver was conducted using a small fleet of trucks provided to us by the Australians. In order to convince the enemy that our numbers were greater than they actually were, our captain decided to conduct a so-called clandestine troop movement. He instructed the drivers of all seventeen trucks to approach the Jordanian front in the dark of night with their headlights turned off. Once they reached the frontline, they flipped on their headlights and drove along the road heading towards our encampment and in view of the enemy. As each truck pulled away from the front, the driver turned off the headlights and then circled back secretly to the end of the line where he would once again travel down the road with headlights on. As long as the first truck got to the back of the line before the last truck reached the front, the illusion of a continuous flow of trucks was created. The next day, we picked up radio broadcasts from Amman announcing that Israel had once again violated the truce and was deploying thousands of fresh troops near the Tul-Kerem front. We had succeeded in making seventeen trucks seem like 170. While not firing a single shot, our military leaders managed to instill fear into our adversaries through such clever and effective deception.

Sometimes, however, more direct measures were called for. During the truce, soldiers on both sides of the front filled their off time relaxing, visiting cafés, and simply sitting around and waiting. I and seven other privates were summoned from our café tables by our captain who gave us the order to carry out a vital intelligence mission. Our captain informed us that Israeli intelligence needed a *LaShon* (tongue) and we were assigned to pull one in. We were to locate and kidnap a Jordanian soldier and bring him back alive to our camp for interrogation. Our unit immediately went to work crossing the frontline on our bellies to avoid the barricades. We sneaked into Tul-Kerem and immediately came upon a group of Jordanian soldiers doing exactly what we had been doing a few hours earlier—sitting and schmoozing at a sidewalk café. I spotted one fellow who seemed to be the leader and the most relaxed as he rocked back and forth on the back legs of his chair. I pointed him out to my partners and told them that this fellow was the tongue that we wanted. We lurked out of sight on the ground until our man got up and headed for the toilet. "Let him finish and then we'll grab him," I said.

As our prey emerged from the toilet, one of us put a gun to his head while another placed a rope noose around his throat. A blindfold was placed over his eyes and a rag was used to gag him. Our hostage did not put up a fight, but his fear was quite evident as he began shaking and crying. Any attempt at resistance was met with a tightening of the rope that served to cut off his air supply. Once he quieted down, we loosened the rope and let him catch his breath.

It took nearly three hours to get back to camp with our prize crawling on our bellies across an orange grove, tugging our prisoner by the rope around his neck. Evidently, the Jordanians became aware of our mission since we heard gunfire emanating from their side. But by then we were out of range and in no danger. Once in camp, the blindfold was removed and our prisoner looked around and immediately understood where he was. He stared into my face for several silent moments as he assessed me, his kidnapper. He asked me for food and water, which I arranged. Within minutes, a jeep pulled up and the prisoner was blindfolded again and whisked off to headquarters for interrogation. Our job was over and we felt pleased as we returned to our barracks to rest up. We had delivered the goods and fulfilled our assignment perfectly. Nevertheless, I was quite troubled by the prisoner's piercing stare that had succeeded in making me feel uneasy.

Mark My Words!

I soon forgot about the incident until months later, while I was undergoing re-training at Kfar Yona, I was standing in the chow line talking to a fellow soldier, an Egyptian Jew named Avraham. Suddenly, one of the Arabs working in the mess tent approached and grabbed me in a strong bear hug. I wriggled around to see his face only to discover that it was the same Jordanian soldier I had kidnapped months before—only now, instead of a uniform, he was wearing an apron and civilian clothes. Naturally, I tensed and began to call out until I understood what the fellow was saying in his broken Hebrew. *"Todah. Todah Rabah, Adoni!"* (Thank you. Thanks, mister!) As I broke free from his grip, he began speaking excitedly in Arabic as he took my hand and shook it vigorously. Avraham translated his words and I learned that the man was thanking me for kidnapping him and thereby saving his life. After his interrogation, he had been attached to this unit and was now working as a busboy, cleaning tables in the mess hall. He said that being a busboy in the Israeli army was a hundred times better than being a soldier in the Jordanian army. He wanted to live in Israel when the war was over and was sending for his family to join him. He claimed to have no interest in returning to Jordan. I told the story of the kidnapping to my friend and of how I felt some anguish afterwards. This outcome obviously vanquished all such feelings as our former Arab hostage continued to thank me profusely for kidnapping him every time I entered the mess hall.

After almost a year in the trenches, we started to enjoy some R&R and were permitted to go on short leaves from time to time. I was enjoying the first day of my first leave at Hatzor, a resort community in the Galilee near the Golan Heights, when I heard the cannon fire erupting, and was soon called into service along with others from my company and ordered into the trenches to fight the Syrians. These were primarily lookout trenches along mountainous ridges. We spent most of our time peering through binoculars down across the frontier looking for any enemy advances. At the first sign of any commotion from the Syrians,

129

we were to send up warning flares to alert the troops. During the week I was assigned to this "look-out" duty, we observed no troop movements and I was never required to send up any flares. We did endure a good deal of Syrian shelling with howitzers flying over our heads as we hunkered down in the trenches.

Not long after that, in October, the Egyptians invaded Israel from the south and began their advance across the Negev towards Tel Aviv. They soon found themselves surrounded by Israeli forces in what became known as the Al Faluja corridor. We were assigned to a brigade fighting Sudanese Brig. Gen. Taba Bey and whose operation officer Maj. Gamal Abdal Nasser was surrounded with all his main supply lines cut. The Israeli navy also took part in what became known as the Southern Campaign, shelling enemy coastal installations, preventing supplies from reaching Gaza and Majdal by sea, and scoring an outstanding victory on the very eve of yet another truce when its special unit sank the Amir Faruq, flagship of the Egyptian navy, off the shores of Gaza.

Our greatest moment of triumph during the four-month siege came when we received word that Maj. Nasser (who would go on to lead the 1952 Egyptian revolution and become president of Egypt) had been captured along with 3,000 of his men. Isolated in the Faluja corridor, starved of food and supplies, the Egyptians had surrendered en masse to our troops. The Faluja pocket, including the town of Al Faluja, was handed over to the Israelis as part of the February 1949 Egyptian-Israeli armistice. By this time, our regiment had been relieved and it was our successors that handled the capture of the Faluja pocket prisoners.

I was not the only Hasten fighting for Israel in the Southern Campaign. One of my third cousins, Jacques Hasten, who I knew of but had never met, was serving as a mine sapper in a detachment, defending the *moshav* (collective farm) at Yad Mordechai. Jacques, along with his parents, Efraim and Betty, and his grandfather *(my grandfather's cousin),* Moishe, all strong Zionists, had immigrated to Palestine from Vienna, where they had operated a well-known lumberyard before World War II. Now, the Israeli company to which Jacques was attached found itself overrun by the Egyptians. Cousin Jaques was taken prisoner along with five other soldiers. Jacques remained incarcerated for a year and a half. During that time, his family heard tales that filled them with horror. The rumor was that since Jacques was a mine sapper, he was taken by his Egyptian captors and forced to reveal the location of the mines he had placed, and in so doing, had detonated one and blown off both of his legs. Fortunately, all the rumors turned out to be false. In 1950, Israel negotiated a prisoner exchange with Egypt's King Farouk. Cousin Jacques and the five others were exchanged for Nasser and his troops. Farouk may have come to regret this exchange since two years later his regime was toppled by Nasser and the Free Officers Corps that he had organized while in prison in Israel.

Cousin Jacques left Israel after the war and settled in the US. He now lives in Boston and owns an optical boutique. Sadly, the family was marked by tragedy. Jacques's brother was killed in a motorcycle accident in Germany during the 1970s. Tragedy struck the family again more recently when Jacques's other brother, Aryeh, along with Aryeh's son, was driving across the United States from their home in San Jose, California to attend Jacques's daughter's wedding in Boston and both men were killed in a horrific highway accident.

Most of our fighting in the Sinai took place at night. We would visit the front at sunset every evening, shooting a few rounds at the enemy and they fired the obligatory shots back at us in what soon became a protracted battle of attrition. Every morning, our platoon headed back to camp and tried to get some sleep. I don't recall a single casualty on our side during this period although a few men were wounded—including me.

One cool evening, an exploding shell landed a bit too close, and I wound up with some shrapnel wounds in my arm and side.

I bandaged myself with gauze and tape and waited to visit the field infirmary until the next morning where they removed the metal shards and stitched me up. I suppose this would have earned me the Purple Heart in the American army, but in Israel a wound like this was so routine that it was not even noted.

I soon learned the secret of our success in the Israeli military, and this knowledge filled me with the confidence I needed to keep going. The secret was that although the enemy outnumbered us by a factor of eight or ten to one, we still held the advantage. Our advantage was based upon the principle of *Ayne Breyrah* ("We have no choice."). Our troops understood the lessons of recent history. We knew that the only alternative to victory was Auschwitz. In fact, I later learned that Nasser was a great admirer of Hitler and that Haj Amin al-Husseini, the British-appointed grand mufti of Jerusalem, was a close friend of Hitler's and a frequent visitor to Berlin during World War II. During one of these visits, on November 28, 1941, the grand mufti was quoted as saying, "The Arabs were Germany's natural friends because they had the same enemies as had Germany, namely . . . the Jews." Fortunately, the Arabs did not fight like the Germans they admired. One Molotov cocktail thrown to disable a forward position tank was all that was needed for the rest of an Egyptian column to turn tail and flee or surrender. Once I became aware of the fact that I was part of a highly motivated fighting force facing a more-or-less cowardly enemy, any fear I might have had about combat quickly vanished.

The only exception to this general lack of fighting zeal among the Arab forces was among the Jordanian troops, known as the Arab Legion and trained by Sir John Bagot Glubb, aka Glubb Pasha. Despite their small size, the Arab Legion proved to be one of the most effective and toughest fighting forces we faced. This description still holds true today.

In mid-1949, I finally had the opportunity to fulfill not only a life-long dream of my own, but a dream held out by the

Mark My Words!

Diaspora Jews for close to nineteen centuries. Thanks to something called the Burma Road, I was able to visit the holy city of Jerusalem. Under the provisions of the UN partition, Jerusalem was to be an independent city, under its own autonomous rule. Of course, this naïve notion was not accepted by either side once the British departed and the Jew-versus-Arab fighting began. Jerusalem—including the ancient Jewish quarter inside the old city,—home to 70,000 beleaguered Jewish residents, became a city under siege. The quarter was being defended by heroic Irgun fighters, who had not yet been merged into the IDF Jordanian forces. They surrounded and held most of the city. They had managed to cut off all of the normal supply lines over the hills and into Jerusalem. Two days before Israeli independence, a convoy of medical staff and supplies bound for Jerusalem via the main road was attacked and all seventy-two doctors and nurses savagely killed.

In order to gain safe passage, the Israelis, under the leadership of American-Jewish Colonel Mickey Marcus, constructed a new spiraling, serpentine road that circled around several of the seven hills and avoided the Jordanian installations. The new "Burma Road," named after the mountainous highway built by the Chinese in the 1930s and rebuilt by Allied Forces under General Stillwell during World War II, safely connected Tel Aviv and Jerusalem. The road allowed the Israeli forces to break through the Arab siege on June 8, 1948, just days before the first UN-imposed cease-fire.

I had heard stories of the road and I could not wait to use it. Four of us secured a two-day pass and a jeep, mounted a machine gun on its hood, and motored up the narrow mountain passes for my first *Aliyah* or ascension. The one-lane road was only wide enough for one vehicle to pass. If the road curved so you could not view oncoming traffic, there was a pull-off spot constructed so, in case a car was heading straight at you, you could pull onto the spot at the last minute.

We drove by the Latrune monastery, which became a strategic stronghold during the fighting. We arrived in Jerusalem during one of the cease-fires, so I observed no shooting or bombing, but the effects of the siege were everywhere. Naturally, I was only able to visit the Jewish-held portion of the city. The Kotel, or Western Wall, would not become accessible to Jews until 1967. As I strolled the tiny streets and noted the empty market stalls, I stopped to speak to complete strangers. There was a disoriented, dreamlike attitude that they all shared. They did not seem to grasp what the fighting was about and reminded me of the bewildered concentration camp survivors I had seen. These people had lived in this city for generations, and now, there was gunfire and there was no food or fresh water. I distributed what food items I had brought with me and started spreading the good news; "I came on the Burma Road. It is open and safe and soon they'll be bringing you food and supplies."

I had an interest in seeing the King David Hotel that had been the headquarters for the British High Command during the Mandate. At this point, it was sitting partially rebuilt after having been blown up by Irgun freedom fighters. Directly across the street was the YMCA.

Despite the privations and the stark squalor surrounding me, I was, nevertheless, overcome with emotion. Since early childhood, we had spoken about Jerusalem every day. It was our shining beacon of hope of a better world ahead. I was walking the same narrow streets as the heroes of my youth, King David and King Solomon had trod. I experienced a deep sense of pride and fulfillment as I touched the ancient rough-hewn stones, shining golden in the fading sunlight—and they, in turn, touched me. I drove back down the Burma Road that same evening filled with a renewed sense of my place in Jewish history. Sadly, the city fell completely under Jordanian rule where it remained for the next nineteen years—just out of Israel's grasp. The Burma Road was reopened after the 1967 victory, paved, and widened and it still exists today, although it is not widely used.

I was discharged from the IDF in 1950, and in keeping with my options as a Machalnik, I elected to remain in Israel and become an Israeli citizen. I even had the pleasure of voting against Ben-Gurion in the following election.

CHAPTER EIGHT

Hard Times in the Holy Land

The next year was to be one of the most difficult of my life. As a newly discharged soldier, I found myself in an awkward position. On the one hand, I was anxious to begin my new life in the free nation of Israel fulfilling an ambition that my ancestors could only dream about. On the other hand, I was viewed and treated as a pariah because of my party affiliation. Ben-Gurion had succeeded in consolidating the Mapai power structure to the point that it penetrated every aspect of Israeli cultural and economic life. As I sought out suitable work, I faced the same question at every stop.

"To what party do you belong? Do you have a Labor Party *te'udah* (membership card)?" And when I answered truthfully that I did not have such a card since I was member of the Herut Zionist party, the door was slammed in my face.

Although it was of little consolation, I was not alone as I tried to overcome these systematic political obstacles. We wandered the harbors, halls, and alleyways as marked men. We were still looked upon as Irgunchiks . . . even though the Irgun no longer existed. We were viewed as right-wing radicals—outside the mainstream of the Israeli labor movement that held the reins of government and business firmly in its grip. Without the benefit of party membership—Mapai party membership—one could only find the most menial type of employment, if any were to be found at all. Unemployed and penniless, and with no family support to speak of, I wandered Tel Aviv like a homeless vagabond. If I had 50 agurot, I slept in a flophouse and if I did not—the more frequent case—I curled up on the beach. When I could, I worked as a day laborer earning only enough to feed myself, if I was lucky. Occasionally, I found work harvesting crops, much like a migrant worker in the US. But whenever I attempted to gain suitable, permanent employment, I was shunned and rejected because of my politics.

From time to time I would visit my father's brother, Hermann Geller, who had come to Palestine before the war and owned a small grocery. Hermann and my father had operated a delicatessen in Dortmund, Germany in the 1930s *(see chapter 1)* and Uncle Hermann had now set up shop on Ben Yehuda Street near Ben-Gurion's residence. This was no coincidence. Hermann had met the Jewish leader in Germany in the 1930s when Ben-Gurion toured Europe raising money for the Socialist/Zionist movement. Hermann would put Ben-Gurion up at his home and, as a result, Ben-Gurion's wife, Paula, had developed a friendship with Hermann's wife. Although by this point Hermann had become disillusioned about his old friend, the friendship between the two women still continued. Paula was not a particularly sophisticated first lady of Israel—rather simple and down-to-earth. So when she found herself married to a head of state and forced to attend lavish banquets and rub shoulders with foreign dignitaries, she felt understandably out of place. Whenever an important social occasion would arise, the wife of the sitting Israeli prime minister would rush to her neighbor's and borrow some silk stockings from my aunt to wear that evening. The home that David and Paula Ben-Gurion occupied in Tel Aviv is today an historic landmark and museum. I don't know if my aunt's silk stockings are on display there or not . . . but it's possible.

Uncle Hermann would always provide me with a meal and bed and even tried to find me a permanent job. He was aware that I was a trained electrician and he succeeded in getting me a job with a local electrical contractor. I was initially assigned to work at a new apartment construction site installing the electrical wiring. For the sake of expediency, the walls were enclosed before the wiring and plumbing were put in. All the electrical conduits and water pipes ran outside, rather than inside of the walls. This meant that when the wiring had to go from one area to the next, a hole had to be punched through the newly constructed wall material. That was my job. Punching holes in the wall with a chisel and hammer all day long. My hands and knuckles became swollen and scarred from the constant abuse. I went to see the boss to ask about being transferred to a different job assignment to give my hands time to heal. His first question was about my party affiliation. As soon as he saw that I could not produce a party membership card, I was summarily fired and that was the end of that.

Someone suggested that I go to work for the government-owned phone company selling ads in the Yellow Pages. This proved to be very challenging since the entire volume, at that time, was a very slim fourteen pages. Once again, as soon as it was discovered that I was not a member of the *Histadrut* (government-controlled national labor union), I was shown the door.

My next job was on another construction site. A family member had directed me to a company that manufactured pre-fab housing for the new *olim* (immigrants). Every day a truck would pull up at the site and begin to unload its cargo of lumber. My job was to stand below the truck catching the boards and hoisting them up on my shoulders before carrying them in to be slapped together into low-cost housing units. My back became red and raw from the steady barrage of boards all day long. On top of this, the owner was something of a *gannef* (thief). I recall running down to the beach after work to find him relaxing at his hotel. "I'm here to get paid. I just finished ten hours of work and I'd like my money," I said politely. He scrubbed through his pockets and managed to cough up a few Israeli pounds and handed them to me. I could tell from his attitude that he was not used to his workers tracking him down and demanding payment. Sure enough, two days later, I was relieved of my duties as a wood-shlepper, and given my discharge papers. I suppose that after this experience, I could rightly call myself "Board Certified."

Occasionally, my parents, aware of my situation through my correspondence, attempted to send me a few dollars via some of the immigrants arriving to Israel from the DP camps. But even this proved problematic when one such courier proved to be a professional gambler and neither he nor the money ever appeared.

Things continued to go downhill over the next six weeks as my circumstances worsened by the day. Although I had a warm circle of friends, I needed more than moral support in order to survive. What happened next was something that completely disillusioned me about any notions I may have had left about the Ben-Gurion government after the burning of the Altalena.

I shall never forget my shock when I witnessed the destruction of the Irgun Veterans Social Hall. The facility, located on the Mugrabee Plaza in Tel Aviv, was a comfortable spot for former Irgun fighters to gather and enjoy a beer, a free sandwich, and some company. Tsiporah, the wife of Irgun High Command leader, Yaakov Meridor, worked there as a waitress dispensing smiles and snacks for "the boys." Ironically, Tsiporah's father had been the head of the biggest Bundist (socialist sympathizers) movement in pre-war Poland. The social hall was a place of camaraderie and fellowship. But in Ben-Gurion's paranoid mind, it was nothing more than a den of fifth columnists sitting all day and plotting the next coup d'état against him. A few months after my discharge, Ben-Gurion signed the order to bring in the bulldozers in the middle of the night, and by morning, the building was rubble. Every time I witness news reports of Israeli forces dismantling Arab's homes and buildings in the territories these days, I am reminded that the first to feel the Israeli bulldozer's bite were fellow Jews.

Mark My Words!

Eventually, I made the decision that there was no future for me, and others like me, in the new socialist state of Israel. I was raised to believe in free trade and individual initiative. I was a sworn, lifelong enemy of Bolshevism and I had up until now thought of myself as a Zionist. Reconciling these imperatives in light of what I had observed in Israel cause enormous despair. After again receiving word of my father's continually declining health, I concluded that I should return back to Ebelsberg. I went back to the military headquarters and told them that I had changed my mind and now wished to give up my Israeli passport and go back to Europe. They gave me my permanent discharge papers and a few dollars and pointed me towards Haifa. As I departed, I swore an oath to myself never to return to Israel while Ben-Gurion still breathed.

CHAPTER NINE

Homecoming?

In Haifa, I booked passage on the first ship to Italy and disembarked in Venice where I caught a train to Vienna. Returning home to Ebelsberg that winter of 1950 was far from the joyful and triumphant scene I had once imagined. I was returning not with my head held high as the Zionist champion, but more or less as a failure—crushed by circumstance and suffering from what could only be termed post-traumatic depression. I suddenly understood the true price of war. I lay in bed every night, unable to sleep, as I saw only darkness on the road ahead. I was only twenty-three years old, but I felt as though my life was already over.

Everyone wanted to know what was going on in Israel. The questions flowed non-stop in the cafés, on the street corners—everywhere. Most of these people were waiting to gain passage to Israel and they wanted to learn from me what they should expect. Of course, they were curious as well. Why had I left the land of milk and honey to return to a refugee camp when all of them were trying desperately to go in the opposite direction?

I tried to be honest without shattering their dreams too badly. "It's very tough there right now," I would say. "There's little housing, few jobs, and not much food in the shops. And if you want any of it, you'd better tell them you're a Mapainik and love Ben-Gurion. It's a socialist state and if you're not a party member, you could starve to death." One fellow approached me and asked, "Mark, I'm thinking of immigrating to Israel with my wife and two kids. Should I go or not?"

Mark Hasten

"Do you have the strength? Because you'll need it. It's hot and the work is hard."

In Israel, both in the military, and afterwards, I had become used to carrying a gun. So when I arrived back to Ebelsberg, my first stop was to one of the hidden arsenals where, as Irgun underground members, we had buried weapons in the woods. I dug up an old German Luger and took it home with me and stuck it under my pillow. I would carry it around in my pocket although I'm not sure why. I think it's because it gave me a small sense of security in a world that seemed very fragile and unstable at the time. Perhaps it reminded me of the gun I carried when I was in the Polish Army during the war. That old pistol was a poorly made Russian copy of a German Luger. I carried it loosely hanging from my belt wherever I went during the war years. There was a well-known Russian *bubbe meise* (old wives' tale) that stated, "Every gun, at least once in its life, will go off by itself." This proved to be true in the case of my old Russian Luger. As I was bouncing up a stairway in Wloclawek, taking them three steps at a time, the jiggling caused my pistol to discharge and sent a bullet right through my left heel . . . of my shoe.

Even the memories of those Polish Army days could not raise my spirits. As my depression drove me further into decline, I would wander Ebelsberg at night and sleep until late into the day. My social life became non-existent due to my shattered self-esteem.

Finally, my mother discovered the gun. She approached me with it and announced in Yiddish, "Enough is enough. You must stop all this nonsense. Look at yourself. What are you doing? Running around all night. Bringing guns into my house." She made herself plain, "No guns in my house. Get rid of it."

I did as she asked and threw the Luger into the river. The act symbolized a passage of my life. My days as a Polish soldier, an underground freedom fighter, and an Israeli infantryman were now officially over. It was time to move beyond the romance and face life in the real world. I made up my mind to do just that. And that's when things began to change. I made a commitment to myself. I pledged to never again carry a gun under any circumstances and I've never owned a weapon since that day.

Finally, the day came when my parents and brother received the word they had been waiting for—they were authorized to enter the United States as refugees and instructed to report to the Port at Bremenhaven for passage to New York. I had also applied for emigration to the United States and had listed Canada and Australia as my second and third choices. I was pleased that my father received approval first since he needed proper medical attention badly. His emphysema had disabled him to the point that he was nearly unable to board the ship to America. After seeing off my family and assuring them that I would be joining them soon, I decided not to remain in Ebelsberg without them. I had a sweetheart in Salzburg, so I packed up and moved into an apartment in this beautiful, romantic city.

My two closest friends in Salzburg were a husky Russian by the name of Misha Aronson and a short Polish fellow named Eddie Buckner. We were the three musketeers—although at times it was more like the Three Stooges—as we constructed every type of money-making venture we could dream up. We sold watches on street corners, gold coins in the public parks, fake jewelry in the cafés. Buying and selling and always handling or negotiating, trying to scrape together a few dollars. On one occasion, we pooled all of our money and purchased a load of a hundred chickens from a local farmer. Eddie knew a *shochet* (kosher butcher) who slaughtered them after which the three of us got busy plucking and cleaning the birds. Once the chickens were prepared, we each took a third and headed to the various DP camps around Salzburg and Linz and sold them door-to-door to the many observant Jews living there.

In order to turn a profit on these deals, we may have occasionally engaged in *ganvenin* or trafficking in stolen goods. We never ordered anything stolen and, of course, we never actually stole anything, but we never asked questions either about the source of some of the items we were buying.

While wheeling and dealing as an Austrian chicken-plucker held its share of charm, I was, nevertheless, delighted when just four months after my family had sailed for America, word came through from the Joint Distribution Committee that I too had been granted asylum and was eligible to emigrate. But not to the United States, I had been granted approval to travel to my second choice, Canada. This was fine with me. I understood that Canada and the United States were neighbors and they were both rich countries where I had an opportunity of establishing myself anew. I jumped at the chance and was soon packing my bags to report back to Bremenhaven to board the SS *Nellie* bound for Halifax Harbor . . . somewhere near the edge of the world!

I said goodbye to Eddie and Misha and assured them that we would all meet again in America *(which we eventually did)*. The harbor was overrun with thousands of Jews all trying to get to America. I arrived to the appointed dock without a single dollar in my pocket. In spite of all the wheeling and dealing I had been engaged in with my two buddies, I spent it as fast as I made it. But I did come prepared with some American cigarettes, which once on board, proved to be a better currency than cash.

I caught a look at my vessel and it soon became obvious from the smell and from the pens and coops that filled her hold, that the SS *Nellie* had been used to transport cattle. Now she would transport Jews to America. I must say I was quite apprehensive about climbing aboard this floating cattle car, but I overcame my fears and was soon making friends with the others onboard. There was a large contingent of Hungarian refugees and quite a few Chassidic Jews as well. The one thing they all had in common was seasickness. Once we cleared port, most of the passengers began to suffer enormous discomfort from the boat's rocking motion. While this condition never bothered me, the illness of so many others created problems for those of whom were not affected, as well. Finding a vacant toilet stall that was not being used by a passenger as a vomitorium was not easy.

I was approached onboard by some of the Chassidic families. Since I spoke Yiddish and was familiar with Orthodox Jewish customs, they seemed comfortable around me. In fact, a few of the wives asked if I would baby-sit their children so they could spend some time with their husbands. I agreed and spent several days at sea, leading children's games and changing diapers. When it came time for payment, it was clear that they had no money—but they did have cigarettes *(many of which they had purchased from me only a few days earlier!)*. I earned so many cartons of cigarettes that I could not possibly smoke them all. When we made port in Halifax, I came down that gangplank onto Canadian soil carrying my weight in American cigarettes.

CHAPTER TEN

Montreal

The panorama of Halifax harbor was just as I had imagined it. I knew of Ellis Island in New York and assumed that this port would likewise be teeming with refugees—"huddled masses yearning to breathe free." I was not disappointed. The feeling was at once terrifying and exhilarating. I was excited at the prospect of a new beginning—a true fresh start in life, but at the same time I bore no illusions about my situation. I was a stranger in a strange land with no money, no family, no job, and an inability to communicate in either of Canada's two languages. What now? Where do I turn first? Fortunately, as it sometimes does, fate intervened in my behalf.

An immigration officer stood up on a box and began directing the refugees from our boat, "Those with travel documents for Montreal, go to the right. Those without, go to the left." He repeated the instruction in five or six languages. By going to the left, I was placed into quarantine. I was fed during the day and locked up at night until my medical status could be determined and I was pronounced disease-free. I still recall the terror I felt that first night when I heard the door locking us in. We all felt foolish. We had crossed an ocean looking for freedom and here we were sitting in jail. All we could do was wait and pass along the constant flow of rumors that circulated through the quarantine center.

"If you don't have papers to go any further, they'll send you back to Europe."

"If you ever had measles, you won't get in."

"Don't tell them you were in the camps or they'll refuse you." Sadly, several of the rumors proved to be true.

We were fed on something I had never seen before. White bread. Soft white bread that was light as a feather and tasted about the same. First, they lock you up and then they feed you with cardboard bread. I was growing less and less certain about the correctness of my decision to come to Canada. In discussing my problems with another disgruntled inmate, he gave me an idea that seemed worth a try.

"I'm thinking to talk to the warden," he told me. "Maybe he could find me a job here in Halifax on the docks. If I'm working, they won't ship me back."

This seemed to make sense. I went straight to the warden and asked to speak to him. I didn't speak French or English, but fortunately the warden spoke a little German and we were able to communicate.

"How about you get me a job right here on the docks?" I said enthusiastically. "I'm a hard worker and I'm plenty strong." To emphasize the point, I rolled up my sleeves and showed off my biceps. Evidently, I made a good impression because a few hours later the warden called me out from the crowd and instructed me to get onboard a small truck sitting by the curb.

"Go with these guys, Mark. They'll take you to the shipyard and they'll give you a job," he said. I was delighted and hopped aboard the truck after shaking the warden's hand enthusiastically.

The truck drove through the harbor mist to the shipyard where I, and a few others like me, was told to get off and don slick yellow raincoats and high rubber hip boots. "Wait here for the trawler and when it arrives you get up there and start pulling off those fish."

We stood in the mist listening to the incessant knocking of the trawler's motor as it slowly approached the dock. Each of us was given a large wicker basket that attached to our backs with elastic straps. I was able to carry nearly a hundred pounds of raw stinking fish from the trawler's hold into the processing shack on the dock. It was backbreaking and nauseating work, but it paid fifty cents per hour and I desperately needed the money. As a result of this job, I got my fill of fish and have been unable to enjoy eating it ever since.

The shifts were twelve hours long and I worked non-stop, shlepping those fish for the next six days. At the end of the week, I had earned thirty-six dollars. Today, you could offer me thirty-six million dollars, and I would not do this sort of work again. But this thirty-six dollars meant everything to me, since it enabled me to purchase a train ticket to Montreal. And this meant I was no longer exposed to the possibility of deportation back to Europe. That money was my ticket to the future and I was very grateful to receive it.

I quickly ended my career as a marine-life mule, packed my things, and headed to the train station. The warden was happy to see me go. It meant there would be more room available for the next batch of "huddled masses" arriving daily at the pier. The train ticket itself cost eighteen dollars and that left another eighteen dollars in my pocket once I arrived in Montreal.

After about fifteen hours, I got off the train at Queen Elizabeth station and was overwhelmed with the beauty of this grand cathedral-like structure. With a little suitcase in my hand and eighteen dollars in my pocket, I stepped onto the streets of Montreal ready to seek my fortune. Of course, the same question arose as in Halifax: "Where do I go now?" It was a sunny day and the flowers were in bloom as I strolled Montreal's broad avenues. "I had better figure out where I would be spending the night," I thought as I passed a few park benches that seemed to look comfortable enough for this purpose.

As I was taking in the sights, I thought back to how, back in Ebelsberg, we would sit around the family table discussing our future lives in America. I remembered Tatu telling me he had a friend who lived in Montreal. "If you wind up in Montreal," he advised, "look up this family I know by the name of Turner." I immediately headed back to the train station to see if I could locate a telephone directory of some sort. I realized that this was a long shot since I knew only the last name and it was a very common name at that. As I walked about the grand train station trying to plan my next move, I overheard two fellows speaking in Ukrainian. I stepped up to them and asked, in their tongue, "Do you know a family here in Montreal by the name of Turner, by chance?" The first fellow shook his head, but the other chap asked, "Are they immigrants?" I said that they were and I believed them to be Polish Jews.

"There's a family like that over on St. Vyeter Street," he said. "Come on, I'll help you look up their phone number in the directory." With the help of the Ukrainian, I reached Mr. Turner and told him who I was, that my father had given me his name and that I had just arrived in Montreal. Turner insisted that I come over right away and he told me to locate a cab driver outside of the station and to bring him inside and put him on the phone. I did as instructed and Turner gave directions to the cab driver in French and even offered to pay for the taxi.

When I arrived to the Turner residence, I was introduced to the family. Mr. Turner was an unmarried older gentleman who lived with his daughter's family, the Perembas. I met Turner's daughter and son-in-law, Mr. Peremba, who worked in a grocery store sorting potatoes despite the fact that he was highly educated and spoke perfect English. The Perembas agreed to take me in as a tenant and were very kind in directing me as I sought to find employment in my new homeland.

I explained to Mr. Peremba that I was an experienced bench fitter and had worked in various types of machine shops.

"It should be easy to find you work with those skills, Mark," he told me. "Let's check the newspaper." Peremba was referring to the fact that the front pages of the newspaper were filled with news about the newly erupted Korean War and that the demand for skilled industrial workers in Montreal had increased as a result. We spotted a story about a company in Montreal called Canadair, Ltd. Canadair was enjoying a boom as an aeronautic manufacturing company that produced a line of F-86 Sabre Jets used by the US Air Force. The article mentioned that the company would be adding dozens of new jobs over the next few months. But the article gave no information about how to go about applying for one of those jobs.

As I walked up and down the boulevard pondering this problem, I again overheard two fellows in conversation just ahead of me. It sounded as though they were speaking Serbian or perhaps Czech and I heard one of the gentlemen say the word "Canadair." My ears perked up and I immediately concluded from the looks of them, and from the little Slavic language that I was able to make out, that these two were interested in finding jobs at Canadair just like me. I followed them for a few blocks and when they hopped onto a trolley car, I jumped aboard, too. At one point they got off the trolley and transferred to a bus and, of course, I did likewise. At the end of the line, we hopped off and approached a mob of over a thousand men assembled in front of a factory gate bearing a huge sign that read: Canadair, Ltd.

As I mingled through the mob, it was like being back at the immigration dock in Halifax. I heard men speaking German, Polish, Yiddish, Chinese, Spanish, and many other tongues. Every so often, a young clerk would open the factory door and allow about twenty men inside for interviews. Using my crowd management skills developed in the military and at Ebelsberg— and with a bit of elbow power—I succeeded in positioning myself by the entry door. Pretty soon, the door swung open and the fellow allowed another group to enter. I made sure I was among the group, but just as I was about to go in, the doorman began to swing the door shut. I quickly stuck my foot into the doorway. The fellow, apparently impressed with my "foot-in-the-door" initiative, gave me a smile and let me in the door.

I was directed to a chair and given a two-sided application card and a pencil. The form was written in two languages, English and French. Unfortunately, I spoke neither one. I could figure out the basic words, Name / Nom, and was able to complete the front of the form without much difficulty. The back, however, consisted of numerous questions next to little check boxes. This side was more challenging. For example, one question was: "Do you own your own tools? Yes or No." If they had used the word "instruments" instead of "tools," I could have understood the question. But as it was, I was forced to leave the answer blank along with several others before turning the form back in.

After a bit of a wait, my name was finally called and I was brought into a cubicle where an interviewer sat behind a table looking over my application. He asked me to take a chair and appeared to be a dignified French-Canadian gentleman. He began to give me the standard patter speaking in French. I listened politely for a while, but finally had to inform him "Je ne parle pas Francaise, monsieur." He looked up and said simply, "Oh," and immediately began to repeat his opening speech, only this time in English. Once again, I listened intently for a few minutes and then had to give him the bad news once again, "I no speak English, sir."

"Well what do you speak, then," he said with a grimace.

"German, Polish, Hebrew, Yiddish, Russian," I responded but the personnel clerk just shook his head at the mention of each of these foreign tongues. Finally, he noted that I had left the question about tools blank on the entry form. He attempted to explain the meaning of the word "tool" to me by holding up various tools he had at hand. Of course, in a personnel office cubicle the best he could do was to hold up a paper clip, a stapler and letter opener. At this point, I was convinced that the word "tools" must mean office supplies. In desperation, he pulled open his desk drawer and produced a small pocket knife that he opened up, pointed towards me and announced with a flourish, "Voila. Tool!"

I had seen many American gangster movies and had come to believe that most people carried knives and guns with them on the job. From his actions, I assumed that the personnel fellow wished to learn if I carried a weapon. I immediately put up my hands and shook my head as I told him "No, no, no." I patted my pockets in a self-frisking motion to demonstrate that I had no weapons concealed on my person.

The interviewer found my response amusing but had pretty much concluded that we had a serious communication breakdown. He called in one of his associates and instructed him, "Take this fellow to the shop. There's a Polish-speaking guy there who should be of some help."

Once in the shop, I was introduced to a slender machinist who did indeed speak Polish. He laid out some drawings and explained what sort of work he was involved with. I immediately understood the blueprints and began discussing various fabrication techniques with the man. He became quickly convinced of my skills and in fact he said, "You know too much. You're really overqualified for this job." Nevertheless, he got the word back to the front office that I was okay and was soon hired. My new friend explained that the company did not supply machinist tools and that I would have to put together a basic kit, including a micrometer and the like. He gave me a written list of tools and instructed me to assemble my kit at home and report back to work the following day in time for the second shift. I was to be paid the princely sum of $1.52 per hour. This was incredible. I was on cloud nine as I went back and shared my good fortune with the Perembas and then rushed off to buy the tools I needed for my kit.

Sadly, things did not get off to an auspicious start at Canadair, Ltd. Finding my way from my home to the factory without the benefit of the two Czech fellows I had followed the first time proved to be something of a problem. Also, once on the job, I discovered that in order to reach my workbench after punching in on the time clock, I had to walk the full extent of the assembly and the machine shop. Every head in the shop popped up to see the new fish as I made my way, clutching my new toolbox, to my bench. I apologized to the foreman, a burly Hungarian chap, and promised him that I would never ever be late again—a promise I did, in fact, manage to keep. The foreman typically only had three words to say to me in his heavy Hungarian accent, "Vork tomorrow night."

After my first week on the job, I observed my co-workers lining up by the loading dock on Friday afternoon. I watched as an armored payroll truck rolled into the plant from which little brown pay envelopes, containing each man's weekly wages in cash, were distributed. As each man opened his envelope, the next stop was straight to one of the union stewards standing nearby with their hands out collecting the two-dollar weekly dues. We repeated this ritual every week, but I never got used to it. I always bristled at having to fork over my hard-earned two bucks and joined the others in grousing about the union's ability to rob us and provide next to nothing in return.

My work was demanding and challenging. I worked on military airplane components such as landing gear and the fuselage. We were mostly involved with the production of the F-86 Sabre Jet that was being used by US forces in the skies above Korea. These planes would be used in aerial dogfights against the Manchurian-based MiG-15s used by the North Koreans. Both the MiGs and the F-86's were swept-wing aircraft whose designs evolved from the work of German engineers during World War II. Both planes ushered in the era of swept-wing versus straight-wing fighter aircraft.

Canadair, Ltd. was acquired by Bombardier Corporation in 1986. Today, it has evolved into the Bombardier Aerospace division and is primarily involved in the production of LearJet corporate aircraft.

Mark My Words!

I was quickly adapting to my new life in the New World. I was learning both English and French, although this progress was undoubtedly slowed by the fact that amongst ourselves, my friends and I spoke only Yiddish and Polish. One incident convinced me of the need to develop my skills in the languages of my adoptive homeland. I learned this important lesson, thanks to a sponge.

I had ventured into a neighborhood Kresge store because I needed a household sponge. Kresge stores were known as dime stores because they specialized in inexpensive household goods *(the chain later evolved into K-Mart)*. I knew that the Polish word for sponge is *gombka*, which is derived from *gummi*, and that gummi means "rubber"—a word whose English meaning I understood. A pert, young saleslady greeted me as I entered the door.

"May I help you, sir?" she inquired.

"I come to buy a rubber."

The salesgirl stared at me speechless and finally just blinked her eyes. I was familiar with this facial expression by now. It meant that the listener did not understand what I was trying to say. I, naturally, reverted to sign language as I mimed squeezing a sponge repeatedly with my right hand and repeated, "Rubber. You got a rubber?"

The salesgirl's complexion went from florid to crimson and she finally turned and marched quickly towards another sales clerk. I could see her pointing towards me and saying to her co-worker, "That man says he wants to buy a . . . ahem . . . rubber." The two were joined by a few other store employees who soon began chuckling and then laughing openly. The group came back to me and the first salesgirl pointed out the window and said, "There's a drugstore across the street, sir. You need to go over there if you want to buy one of those things." But I would have none of it. I knew that this was the store that sold sponges and I was not going to leave without one.

"I want a rubber. You know, rubber." They all watched me as this time I pretended to wipe down an imaginary tabletop with an imaginary sponge. But when I made as if to wring the water out of the sponge by twisting and turning my joined fists back and forth, some of the women began to scream. Finally, the store manager arrived on the scene and understood that I wanted something from his store that I was unable to articulate. He wisely asked me to accompany him up and down the store aisles scanning all the shelves until I spotted the sponges. I grabbed one and held it up joyously.

"That is called a sponge," the manager explained patiently. "Come over here and I'll write it down for you." I thanked him, paid for the sponge, stuffed the scrap of paper into my pocket, and left Kresge's determined to start improving my English vocabulary . . . before I accidentally started a riot.

In my efforts to become assimilated and shed my refugee image, I also had to change the way I looked. At times this meta-morphosis was more painful than expected. In Europe, I prided myself on my long, lavish pompadour hairstyle. I would spend long minutes before the mirror adjusting each wave and apply-ing just the right amount of "brilliantine" to attain the proper sheen. I took my hair styling very seriously. My regular barber, back in Austria, was once the official barber for the King of Romania . . . or so he claimed. Once I got settled in Montreal, I asked around and was referred to a neighborhood barbershop off Park Avenue. During my first visit, I dozed off in the chair and I awoke horrified to discover that most of my curly locks were being swept off the barbershop floor. "My G-d! I'm bald! What did you do?!" I shrieked.

"What did I do?" exclaimed the barber. "I gave you an American haircut. You're in America now and over here every-one wears crew cuts. Take a look at yourself in the mirror. Now you look like a real American." I could see that he was right and

Mark My Words!

I took comfort in knowing that I was shedding my Old World skin as I watched a part of it being swept away into the trash.

Once I had secured employment, my next objective was to locate some female companionship. My circle of friends consisted mostly of single young men like myself—many of whom were also graduates from the DP camps. At age twenty-four, I viewed myself as a bachelor, although not a confirmed one. I dated a bit here and there, but nothing really took off. Not until, that is, I received a fortuitous letter from my family.

Tatu, Mamma, and my brother Hart *(Hetche's new name)* had settled in Minneapolis and were undergoing the classic American immigrant experience. My father was too ill to work, but fortunately Hart had found a good job at the Bemis Bros. Bag Company and was able to support the family. In one of his letters, Hart wrote to me about a young Jewish lady named Anna Ruth who he believed would be just right for me. How very right he was.

My father, Bernard
Hasten, in Austria.
1946.

My mother, Hannah
Hasten, in Austria.
1946.

At age 17 in the Polish Army Pontoon Brigade. 1944.

In Polish military in Wloclawek. 1945.

Soldiers of my First Polish Pontoon Brigade renovating a
bombed railroad bridge in Warsaw. January, 1945.

My real Austrian
passport. 1946.

In Ebelsberg D.P.
camp, Austria. 1946.

With friends at Ebelsberg D.P. camp in Austria. I am seated fourth from the left. 1947.

Irgun comrades of the Alexandroni Brigade near Tul Kerem.
All were aboard the Altalena. I am reclining on the ground
with a rifle between my legs. 1948.

In the I.D.F. Haifa.
1949.

My IDF Battalion
visiting grave of
Joseph Trumpledore
in the Galilee. 1949.

Exit document issued
by Israeli government to
foreign military volunteers.
1950.

My permit to immigrate to
Canada. Issued in Salzburg,
Austria. May, 1951.

Debonair bachelor in
Montreal, 1952. Photo was
mailed to Anna Ruth with
one of my letters.

Looking sharp in
Montreal. 1951.

With my fiancée, Anna Ruth Robinson, in
Montreal. 1952.

Maytee, Anna Ruth and
Jerome Robinson.
Richmond, Texas. 1935.

Anna Ruth's parents,
Minnie and Ed
Robinson in the 1920's.

Family Photo, 1956.
My brother, Hart; Anna Ruth and me (standing).
Eddie on my mother, Hannah's lap; Michael on my father,
Bernard's lap.

Our first car in Dallas. 1955.

Photo printed in
Dallas Morning
Sun newspaper,
December 14,
1958.
Accompanied story
about my receiving
notice of US
citizenship.

Student I.D. from S.M.U. 1958.

Envelope containing the most important letter of my
life: my acceptance letter from General Mills.
Returned to Sender in error. 1959.

With Anna Ruth, Michael and Eddie at my
graduation from S.M.U. in Dallas. April, 1959.

His First **Free Vote . . .**

BALLOT
BOX

Mark Hasten, Mechanical Engineer at Central Research Laboratories in Minneapolis, will cast his first free vote for President on November 8. Mark, originally from Communist-dominated Poland, came to the United States in 1953 and became a naturalized citizen in 1957. Mark shows how he will cast his free vote in the coming election. Portraying election judges are two other employees of Central Research Laboratories, June H. Whitney, right, secretary to Dr. Harold Wittcoff, Director of Chemical Research, and Charles A. Prange, Senior Machine Designer, Mechanical Engineering Department.

Register, inform yourself and vote!

November 8 is *Election Day*

I was featured in a voter registration advertisement
that appeared in a General Mills internal
publication in 1960.

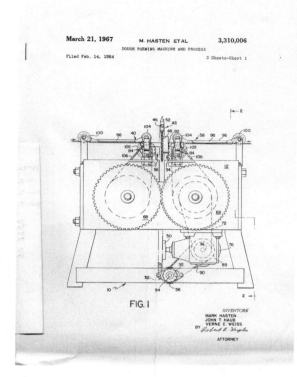

FIG. I

INVENTORS
MARK HASTEN
JOHN T. HAUB
VERNE E. WEISS
BY Robert E. Hugler
ATTORNEY

Illustration for Food Processing apparatus
used to manufacture Bugles snacks. Patent applied
for on Feb. 14, 1964.

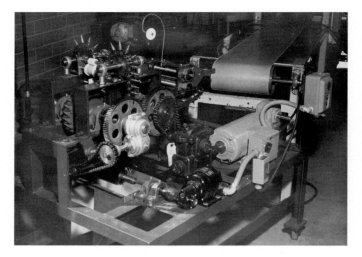

Bugle-making machine prototype. 1965.

Production Bugle-making machines. 1965.

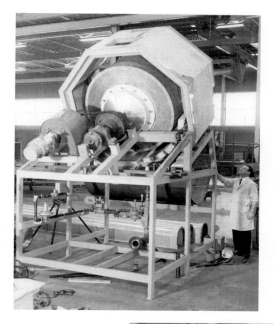

Standing next to a Daisy cooker at General Mills. 1965.

Crouching before my Vertical Vibratory Conveyor used for elevating cereal flakes at General Mills. 1965.

My Beef Jerky
dispenser
developed at
General Mills.
1965.

One of eighteen
$1.00 checks I
received from
General Mills in
consideration of
my assignment of
all rights to one
of my patented
inventions. June,
1968.

Irgun medal. Awarded to me in 1966.

Voucher issued by the Israeli Ministry of Defense identifying me as a veteran of the War of Independence. 1966.

My Irgun identification certificate documenting my resistance work in Austria. Signed by Eliahu Lankin, Menachem Begin, Eli Tavin and Itan Livne. 1966.

Eddie, Anna Ruth and Michael in our second house in Minneapolis. 1960.

Eddie, Judy, Anna Ruth, Monica and Michael at Michael's Bar Mitzvah. 1968.

With Israeli Minister of the Interior, Josef Burg, and my mother,
Hannah Hasten. Jerusalem. 1972.

With Sam Rothbard and Israeli Prime Minister, Golda Meir, during
an Israel Bond mission in Jerusalem. 1974.

Accepting congratulations from Israeli Prime Minister, Menachem Begin, upon my receiving the Jabotinsky Medal. New York. 1980.

With Sen. Birch Bayh in the office of the newly elected Israeli Prime Minister, Menachem Begin. Jerusalem, Israel. 1977.

Receiving an award at an Orthodox Union bi-annual
convention as Menachem Begin (3rd from right), Rabbi
Ronald Gray (far right), and Anna Ruth (3rd from left)
among others look on. Washington, 1976.

Showing Senator Birch Bayh the location of my hometown.
Yad Vashem Holocaust Memorial. Jerusalem, Israel. 1977.

With Sen. Birch Bayh; his wife, Marvella; and his son, Evan on
the Avenue of Righteous Gentiles. Yad Vashem Holocaust
Memorial. Jerusalem, Israel. 1977.

Anna Ruth, Senator Birch Bayh and my
daughter, Judy. 1980.

(standing from left to right) Monica, Eddie, Shulamit,
Michael, Judy (seated) with my mother, Hannah Hasten
and Anna Ruth. Indianapolis, 1978.

My mother, Hannah Hasten, with her first two
great-grandchildren, twins Dovie and Dina. 1980.

With Israeli Foreign Minister, Moshe Dayan.
Indianapolis. 1978.

With my brother, Hart, and Israeli Prime Minister, Yitzhak
Shamir, in New York. 1983.

Groundbreaking ceremony at Hebrew Academy expansion. 1986.

Groundbreaking ceremony at the Hebrew Academy
expansion. 1986.

Monica, Eddie, Michael and Dr. Lander look on as I receive my
honorary Ph.D. degree from Touro College. 1996.

With my brother, Hart; sister-in-law, Simona
and Anna Ruth in New York. 1996.

Addressing the Graduating Class at Touro
College. 1996.

Michael with my mother, Hannah Hasten, at age
100 in 1994.

Family Photo. 1999.

Extended Hasten Family at my grandson, Dovi's wedding to Tali in Jerusalem, Israel. 2000.

Great-grandchildren, clockwise from top left: Yehudit, Yael, Yedidya, Pinchas, and Ari

Standing in front of the road sign on the road into our home town of
Bohorodczany (Brotchin). 2002.

With my brother, Hart, in front of the water well which once stood in our backyard. The site of our former home is now occupied by the Ukrainian Post Office in the background. Bohorodczany, Ukraine. 2002.

Monument standing memory of the 1900 Bohorodczany Jews,
including many members of our family, murdered at Rudolf's
Mill at the hands of the Nazi SS and their Ukrainian cohorts.
Erected on August, 2002 by Mark and Hart Hasten. Ivano-
Frankovsk (former Stanislawow), Ukraine.

CHAPTER ELEVEN

The Story of Anna Ruth

Anna Ruth Robinson was born in Texas and spent the first eleven years of her life in Richmond, a small town thirty miles west of Houston. She was the third child of Ed and Minnie Robinson. Her brother, Jerome, and sister, Maytee, were considerably older than Anna Ruth. Ed Robinson had settled in Texas after immigrating to the United States from a shtetl in Russia, known as Chalabud, before the First World War. After landing in New York, Ed joined family members in Texas who had entered the country via the Port of Galveston during the early years of the twentieth century. In those days, the Jewish population of New York, composed mostly of German immigrants, was not particularly pleased about the growing influx of Ostjuden, or Jews from Eastern Europe, flooding the gates of America. They succeeded in getting many of the shiploads, teeming with mostly Polish Jewish refugees diverted away from New York harbor to Galveston. Shortly after his arrival, Ed Robinson joined the US Army and served with the American Expeditionary Forces fighting the Hun in the trenches of Europe. During his tour, Ed was exposed to mustard gas and carried the effects of that exposure with him for life. After the war, Ed married and began to raise a family in tiny Richmond. He established a dry goods store and oversaw its success though the 1920s. During the economic downturn that began in 1929, Ed managed to thrive by traveling to neighboring towns and buying up the inventory of similar stores that had freshly gone out of business. After disposing of the unwanted merchandise at a closeout sale, he would transport the better quality goods back to Richmond where they would be marked up and sold. Ed parlayed his profits and became a successful stock market investor so that by the early thirties he was already viewed by his neighbors as a wealthy citizen. Motoring about town in his new Packard, Ed Robinson was regarded as a down-to-earth merchant who was anything but ostentatious. The family would never have been accused of "living too high on the hog."

In depression-era Texas, a child would have to have been born illegitimately for it to only be given a single first name. When another baby came along in 1933, Ed, and his wife, Minnie, named the little girl after Ed's late mother, Chanah Raisel or Anna Ruth. Within a year of Anna Ruth's birth, tragedy struck. Her mother contracted pneumonia and, without access to penicillin, she soon succumbed leaving Ed a forty-two-year-old widower with three children to raise.

Ed Robinson needed to find a wife and a mother for his children, and, at just the right time, fate stepped in . . . fate in the form of a man named Moe Strauss. Moe Strauss lived in Minneapolis. Shortly after the death of Anna Ruth's mother, Moe Strauss paid a visit to some family members in nearby Galveston. Moe was married to the former Sophie Colevsky, a native of Chalabud. Sophie had instructed Moe to be sure to extend her warm regards to members of the Shwiff family who had immigrated to Texas from Chalabud via the Port of Galveston and were now living in Galveston. While conversing with the Shwiffs the subject of fellow "landsman" Ed Robinson arose. Moe listened with interest as the Shwiffs explained about Ed's recent loss, and then brought up the name of his wife's niece, Celia Rabutnik Lynchner, who also hailed from Chalabud and who had been widowed the previous year. Moe explained that Celia was twenty-seven years old, and the mother of four-year-old son, Aaron.

The matchmaking wheels began turning. Moe contacted Ed Robinson who greeted the news warmly. The possibility of meeting another Jewish woman from his own *(and his late wife's)* tiny hometown seemed almost too good to be true. Moe returned to his home in Minneapolis and recounted what had transpired to his wife, Sophie. Sophie agreed that Celia should meet Ed and she immediately put the two in touch with each other. Ed and Celia began corresponding and a visit to Texas was soon arranged for Celia and Aaron. In 1935, the young widow and her son were blended into the sprawling Robinson clan of Texas, when Celia became Mrs. Ed Robinson. Celia immediately took to her new two-year-old daughter, Anna Ruth, and Aaron, whom everyone called Sonny, delighted in his new baby sister. Although, for simplicity's sake, Aaron went by the name Sonny Robinson, he was never legally adopted by Ed because his biological father's family, the Lynchners, wished for Aaron to carry on the family name.

Anna Ruth, of course, was too young to possess specific memories of her birth mother and referred to Celia as Mamma as she grew up. In later years, Anna Ruth would employ the term "second mother" when explaining her relationship with Celia.

Despite the swirling dustbowls that drove many families from central Texas seeking the "grapes of wrath" and greener pastures, the Robinson family clung to their home, their business and their way of life with typical immigrant tenacity. Hobos, fresh from riding the rails across the prairies, would often find themselves at the Robinsons' back doorstep asking for a handout. Winnie, the family's maid and nanny, had strict instructions from Mr. Robinson that anyone asking for help in this way was not to be permitted in the house, but was to be afforded a hot meal and allowed to consume it while sitting on the back porch. In this way, Ed Robinson, through his own example, effectively taught his children about the Jewish precept of *tzedakah*, the ordained commandment to extend charitable assistance to those in need without offending the receiver's sense of pride and dignity.

The home in which Anna Ruth grew up was definitely Jewish—although hardly an observant one. It would have been a true challenge for any family to be observant in a small Texas depression-era town. The closest synagogue was in Houston, some thirty miles away, making it impossible to walk to the shul on the Sabbath and on Jewish holidays. Despite these obstacles, Ed took pains to preserve what Jewish traditions he could. Ed, having attended a Yeshiva as a young boy in Chalabud, was considered the most religiously knowledgeable member of Richmond's tiny Jewish community. His father, Anna Ruth's grandfather, Yudel, had been a rabbi back in Chalabud. In fact, some speculated that the reason the family obtained the decidedly non-Jewish sounding Robinson moniker *(their last name was Pentel back in Russia)* was due to an immigration clerk's misunderstanding of the term "rabbi's son."

Each year, during the traditional High Holy Days, Ed, wearing a tall *yarmulke* (skullcap), would conduct Rosh HaShanah and Yom Kippur services in a large room above a neighborhood grocery store where he had installed an ark housing the holy Torah scrolls. Annual trips to Houston to purchase food items for Passover were part of Anna Ruth's upbringing. Although the family was unable to maintain strict adherence to the dietary laws of Kashruth, they refrained from mixing meat and milk products at mealtime and also kept a separate set of Passover dishes. Little Anna Ruth was taught the first line of the *Sh'mah* (Judaism's defining statement of monotheism) by her father. Years before, when Maytee and Jerome, Anna Ruth's older siblings, were younger, Ed had hired a *melamed* (teacher) who drove to Richmond from Houston twice a week to provide the children with some basic Hebrew and Judaic training. The experience had not gone well and the teacher soon packed up and left, unable to relate to the "wild-west" personalities of the two youngsters. Ed would, nevertheless, persevere as he tried to instill positive Jewish values into the hearts of his three children. He once told Anna Ruth that she must be extra nice to a particular classmate of hers because her mother had given birth to her before her mother had gotten married. As a result, the little girl had not been treated well by others and Anna Ruth was instructed to make a point of being especially nice to her.

The other dustbowl that was swirling around swiftly in those days, not just in Texas, but also throughout the world, was the harsh wind of anti-Semitism. Surprisingly, the Robinson family experienced very little overt Jewish hatred. Although Anna Ruth's closest childhood friend was another Jewish girl, Natalie Smith, her world was not limited to the confines of the Jewish community. Before she was even enrolled in first grade, Anna Ruth spent most of her time in the care of a series of African-American nannies. Anna Ruth would often accompany these ladies to some of the local barbecue honky-tonk juke joints where she would interact with some of the town's more colorful citizens. Unbeknownst to her parents, Anna Ruth was even carted to an old-time Southern Baptist tent revival. Ed made certain that the children were very respectful to their housekeeper, Winnie. At one point, he purchased an African-American doll for his young daughter which she immediately named "Little Winnie." Winnie would often take Anna Ruth home with her during long afternoons, giving her young charge a taste of life on the "other side of the tracks." There, amidst the newspaper-lined walls of Winnie's ramshackle home in "Freemantown," Anna Ruth could observe the stark poverty under which others were forced to live. Winnie's little home was meticulously clean, but harshly impoverished—devoid of many of the niceties that Anna Ruth took for granted such as indoor plumbing and electric appliances. These eye-opening experiences proved to have a liberating effect and helped to foster a strongly independent, free-wheeling spirit in the young Jewish girl.

By the time Anna Ruth turned six, Ed Robinson had contracted lung and kidney cancer and his health began a steep decline. The mustard gas exposure Ed had endured fighting in France during World War I, coupled with his heavy smoking, were thought to be responsible for the disease. Because of his condition, he was unable to sleep lying down and could only rest safely while seated upright. In June 1941, after years of suffering, Anna Ruth's father died. Anna Ruth was devastated. She had visited her father during his last week of life in the hospital and had observed him in such pain that he could not even speak to her. On the day of his funeral, Anna Ruth was considered too young to attend and was placed into the care of a housekeeper. Maytee and Jerome were in their teens when their father died and they both soon set off on their own, leaving Anna Ruth under the care of her "second mother." Maytee soon enrolled to the University of Texas while Jerome enlisted in the Army Air Corps.

Celia became increasingly homesick for her family back in Minneapolis, and in 1943 she packed up Anna Ruth and Sonny, gave up the house in Richmond, and headed back up north to rejoin her family in Minneapolis.

The adjustment to life in the north was a tough one for Anna Ruth. The change in schools, in the climate, in the entire way of life created a seismic culture shock for the eleven-year-old Texan. Seeking security, the little family moved in with Celia's parents, Henoch and Chashkeh Rabutnik and Anna Ruth developed a profound affection for her new Minnesota grandparents—an affection that was to run both ways. The Rabutniks, despite the fact that they had their own blood-related grandchildren, took Anna Ruth right to their hearts and always behaved as though it was a privilege to have her in their home. They referred to Anna Ruth as the "Jewel of the Family."

After some time, she became familiar with the old civil-war-era Rabutnik house and made the necessary adjustments from her rural roots to her new urban, predominantly black, neighborhood. It was not always easy. After the loss of her father, the community in Richmond banded together to nurture and embrace the grieving little girl in a way that only a village is able to do effectively. No such crucible of caring existed in big-city Minneapolis and the transplanted eleven year old, so comfortable in the town in which she'd been born, now found herself afloat without a rudder or compass in decidedly choppy waters. Nonetheless, she grew close to her new aunts, uncles, and cousins. Slowly, Anna Ruth developed new friends like Elaine Cohen and her outgoing parents. Celia's brother, Uncle Shepsel, enrolled Anna Ruth in the afternoon "Talmud-Torah" religious school where she was taught to read Hebrew and learn the rudiments of Judaism.

Eventually, Anna Ruth became more and more adjusted and, as a teenager, started to enjoy the freedom that her home life afforded her. Her grandparents, while caring and compassionate people, were kept quite busy, operating their family kosher chicken business. Celia found employment and was out of the house most of the day leaving both Anna Ruth and Sonny to more or less raise themselves.

Shortly after World War II ended in 1945, Celia became friendly with a Holocaust survivor from an area of White Russia, not far from Chalabud. Yoel Meyers had fought with the partisans against the Nazis. During his ghetto imprisonment, he had been beaten and left for dead amid a pile of corpses. Crawling out from under the heap once nightfall arrived, Yoel made it to the edge of the ghetto where fellow partisans pulled him into the forest and relative safety. As a result of his tribulations, he had lost three fingers on his right hand. Yoel recounted eyewitness accounts of Nazi atrocities, opening Anna Ruth's eyes to the unbelievable events of the Holocaust that had just devoured the Jews of Europe.

By the time Anna Ruth turned sixteen, Celia had decided to marry Yoel, who now went by the name Joe Friedman, and the family relocated from the first floor apartment to the second floor of the rambling old Rabutnik house. Joe had never been a father and his background left him ill equipped to handle the role of surrogate. Whereas for years, Anna Ruth had kept house for her family in Texas and Minnesota, Joe now felt it his responsibility to oversee her work.

Despite his shortcomings as a stepfather to Anna Ruth, she always respected Joe Friedman and considered him an honorable and loyal friend. The man with missing fingers worked for many years in a glove factory drawing a minimal hourly wage. Yet he managed to live thriftily and to accumulate substantial savings. Years later, in the sixties, during the final years of Joe's life, he agreed to loan us $7,000 to purchase our first apartment building in Minneapolis, effectively launching our family's future in real estate *(see chapter 14)*. The loan was executed on a handshake, and although Joe did not live long enough for us to totally repay the note to him personally, we did, in fact, pay it off with interest to his widow, Celia.

During Celia's waning years, she was interviewed by her doctor who asked her how many children she had. Celia answered, "I have two. One that is mine and one that is better than mine."

After high school, Anna Ruth followed in her sister's footsteps and enrolled at the University of Texas. Maytee had graduated in 1945 from the School of Pharmacy and urged Anna Ruth to consider her alma mater. Despite the fact that she found the Austin campus to be a delightful environment, Anna Ruth became homesick and left U. of T. after one year. She moved back home and next enrolled at the University of Minnesota's Minneapolis campus. She soon found part-time employment and was able to pay her mother a modest sum for her room and board. One afternoon, Anna Ruth received a phone call.

"May I speak with Anna Ruth Robinson, please," came the confident male voice on the line.

"This is she," she responded. "Who's calling?" It was my younger brother, Hart.

"My name is Hart. Hart Hasten, and I live a few blocks away on Fremont Avenue," he went on. "I believe you know my parents."

"Hmm . . . I'm not sure. Who are your parents?"

Mark My Words!

"My mother is Hannah and she comes over and sits with your grandmother all the time." Anna Ruth wasn't sure to whom he was referring, but she let him go on.

"My dad is Bernard, but they call him Berish and he is a good friend of Mr. Mann's. He's seen you there many times. Do know who I'm talking about?"

"I'm not sure, Mr. Hasten," she replied. "What can I do for you?"

"Well, I'm calling to invite you over to our house for some coffee and cake tomorrow evening. Our family is having a few friends over and I was hoping you could join us."

Anna Ruth was somewhat puzzled by the odd invitation, but she was curious and after obtaining the time and the address, she said simply, "Okay. I'll be there. Thanks."

Hart greeted her at the door and Anna Ruth smiled graciously as she looked over the handsome, athletic young Polish émigré.

After some cake and pleasantries, Anna Ruth was invited to sit in the parlor along with Hart and his parents who began to explain the true reason for having extended this invitation to her. Bernard spoke first in his somewhat decorous, but yet down-to-earth manner.

"Thank you for coming by, Anna Ruth," he said. "I know you're a fine young girl from what your grandmother tells Hannah about you. Also, Mr. Mann says you are a very proper and decent young lady."

"Thank you, Mr. Hasten," she responded, somewhat taken aback.

"That is why I asked Hart to invite you over today. You see, we have another son besides Hart. Hart's brother, Mark is living in Montreal. In Canada. It's not good for him to be there and for us to be here. We can't even visit each other. He should come to live here, in America. But it's not so easy." Hart's mother spoke up next.

"I tried everything to get him into the country," she explained, looking over both shoulders before proceeding. "I even wrote to the senator. That's right, I wrote to Senator Hubert Horatio Humphrey and he wrote me back."

"Tell her what the senator said, Mama," said Hart.

"Okay. Senator Humphrey said that there are 20,000 Poles in line to get immigration visas and if Mark has to get into this line he will be waiting for a long, long time." Bernard took over at this point.

"But, he told us that if Mark should happen to marry an American citizen, well . . ." his voice trailed off. Anna Ruth understood immediately. She had heard of other such "green card" marriages and she knew that some had actually worked out quite well.

"What do you want me to do?" she inquired.

"Is it okay for my brother to write to you?" asked Hart.

"I suppose it is," she said plainly. Anna Ruth was sympathetic to my family's situation. After listening to Joe Friedman's tales of Holocaust horror, she had tremendous sensitivity for Jews who had suffered through that nightmare. Her compassion drove her to be agreeable and try to assist our family. She just did not have the heart to say no them. At the time, Anna Ruth felt that not much would ever come of this . . . so why not be agreeable?

I soon received a letter containing Anna Ruth's mailing address along with a glowing description from my parents who urged me to write to her at once. They advised me that she was American-born and could only speak English and this fact posed something of a problem. My English was getting better, but it still was not adequate to compose letters to a prospective paramour. I asked about and found a friend of friend who spoke perfect English. Unfortunately, his only other language was German. Although I preferred to write in my mother tongue, Polish, I was able to read and write German as well. So I developed a three-stage process. I would first write my thoughts in my native Polish. Next, I translated each letter over to German *(sometimes using a Polish/*

German dictionary) and then deliver the text to my friend who would do an English translation. Finally, I transcribed the English version into my own handwriting before sending it off to Anna Ruth who was unaware of my linguistic gymnastics and assumed I had penned the letters directly. I never informed Anna Ruth that I had employed this assistance and if she was surprised, after meeting me, that my verbal English skills were not up to the level represented by my letters, she never let on.

Our correspondence went on for four months. Each letter increased my level of intimacy and desire to meet face to face. I sent Anna Ruth a rather flattering photo of myself and she responded in kind. We spoke by phone as often as we could afford it. Our conversations would always end the same way.

"I'm sorry that I can't come to visit you, Anna Ruth," I would say. "So I invite you to come and visit me here. You're on summer vacation from school right now. So hurry up. I'm waiting for you."

Anna Ruth was flattered by my oft-repeated invitations, but she really was not all that interested in meeting me. She was dating other fellows at the time and I got the feeling that she was communicating with me in order to satisfy my parents' wishes more than out of any passion she may have held for me. Later, Anna Ruth explained why she finally agreed to accept my invitation.

My family was exerting a good deal of pressure on her on a daily basis. My mother would stop her in the hallway after visiting with her grandmother.

"So, Anna Ruthele, you spoke with my Mark today by telephone?"

"Yes, I did, Mrs. Hasten," she would reply.

"Did he ask you should go visit him in Montreal?"

"He always does."

"So, *nu?* Why don't you go already? He's a sweet boy and very good looking."

This public relations campaign in my behalf was being shouldered by my father and brother as well and eventually, Anna

Ruth gave in. She felt that this was the only way to get the Hastens off of her case and that once she returned from Montreal they would back off and that would be the end of it.

The date was set and the train ticket purchased. I had agreed to meet Anna Ruth at the top of an escalator that delivered passengers from the lower platform to the station. I will always remember my first glimpse of Anna Ruth in the flesh. I don't want to say "love at first sight" but I did tell myself immediately "this is the girl I'm going to marry."

I tried to act the strong and silent type—Gary Cooper-style— but I simply could not control my trembling nervousness. I found out later that she thought I was suffering from some sort of long-term battle fatigue and she was just too polite to mention the fact that I was shaking like a leaf. I told Anna Ruth that I had taken a two-week vacation from my night-shift job at Canadair just to spend the time with her and show her around Montreal.

"This way we'll have the time to get to know each other," I explained. I had arranged for Anna Ruth to stay in a private home owned by an older couple, the Pollacks, and I spent the next few days trying to sweep her off her feet. I wanted to impress her with my generous nature, while not appearing to be too extravagant. We traveled by taxi instead of streetcar as we took in the splendid sights of North America's most European of cities. We visited a different fine restaurant every night and I always brought flowers or perfume. This method of courtship probably sounds pretty corny today, but back then, it was considered proper and, I must say, effective in getting the message across.

For the sake of propriety, the Pollacks acted as our chaperones during the entire two-week period. Mrs. Pollack would remain close by whenever we would sit in her parlor and chat in the evening. They often joined us for meals and made sure that we never were left alone in each other's company. This was considered the proper method of upholding a respectable girl's honor in those days—and despite my urges to take her in my arms and shower her with kisses, I kept my proper distance and remained the perfect gentleman.

Anna Ruth became something of an attraction among my single male friends. An American-born Jewish girl, coming all the way from Minnesota, to hang around with a Polish *greener* (greenhorn) . . . this they had to see. So we were often accompanied during our excursions by a few of my tagalong buddies.

Anna Ruth appeared to be very comfortable among my crowd of European comrades. Among her own family, both natural and adoptive, almost everyone had an accent, so she did not act in any way condescending or patronizing, as other American-born Jews often did. I was impressed by Anna Ruth's sense of independence and her free-spirited nature. She did not seem bound up by social conventions and peer pressure. It did not faze her a bit to be seen in the company of an older man of twenty-five with a heavy Eastern European accent.

I would not describe those two weeks as a whirlwind romance, but as the days melted into each other ever more rapidly, I was becoming increasingly despondent at the thought of giving up this lovely girl's company. From our long conversations, I knew that Anna Ruth's home life was not all that it could be. She never really felt comfortable living under the same roof with her current stepfather and I hoped she would welcome the opportunity of moving up and out.

To put it simply, I did not wish for her to go. I expressed these heart-felt feelings to Anna Ruth with my sincerest conviction.

"Anna Ruth, I don't want you to go back to Minneapolis," I said. "I want you to stay here with me."

"What are you suggesting, Mark?" she asked.

"I say let's get married. Let's not wait. Right now. What do you say?"

"Oh, Mark, I just don't know," she said with some emotion.

"Look, Anna Ruth, I've got a pretty good set up here in Montreal. We'll do fine here. Anyway, what do you have back there that you're giving up? You know you'll be happier here with me than by going back and living with your mother and her husband. Right?" I was making a pretty strong case.

"But what about your parents, Mark?" she asked. "They sent me up here to meet you and bring you back to Minneapolis. Everyone in my family thinks that you're just using me to get an entry visa and green card to the United States."

"I told you before," I said patiently, "I don't care about moving to the US, I like it fine right here. The only thing missing in my life here is you. When we get married, I'll have everything I need. Who needs a green card, anyway?"

I convinced Anna Ruth that I wanted to marry her because I loved her—which I most certainly did. I did not wish to marry her to make my parents happy or to use her as a ticket to America. Anna Ruth, for her part, saw in me the prospect of a brighter future and so she accepted my proposal and we were married as soon as the notarized signature from her mother arrived authorizing the nuptials for her minor daughter. Armed with the document, we dressed in our finest and made our way to the courthouse in downtown Montreal. Both of us presumed that we could undergo a civil marriage officiated by a justice of the peace or similar official. We discovered that since Canada does not practice separation of church and state, the marriage laws were different than in the United States. We were told we needed a government-sanctioned clergyman to carry out the ceremony and sign the marriage license. Returning back to the neighborhood, we greeted my buddies who noted our long, dour expressions. When we explained the situation, one of the guys popped up with, "What about that marriage mill over on Fairmont Avenue?" He was right. We swiftly made our way over to the "chapel" and once there learned that, yes, the rabbi could marry us, but we needed two witnesses and they both had to be married themselves. This qualification posed a bit of problem since my buddies were all single.

"Where do I find a witness?" I asked the rabbi after explaining my lack of married friends.

"Go out to the park and talk to the old men sitting on the benches," he advised me. "They are often called upon for this role and will know what to do."

I did as instructed, taxied to the park and approached an elderly man sitting alone on a bench munching on some sunflower seeds.

"How would you like to be a witness at a wedding ceremony so my bride and I can get married today?" I inquired politely.

"How much?" was his curt reply.

"Well, I'll pay for your cab fare plus a few dollars," I offered, "but you gotta be married."

"Oh, I'm married all right," he assured me waving his ring finger at my face.

"What about him," I asked, pointing to another park bench occupant. "Is he married?"

"Of course," said the man, stuffing his snacking seeds into his pocket, "in this park all the men and women are married. Just not to each other."

Returning swiftly to the marriage factory with our two hired witnesses in tow, we were ready to stand under the well-worn chuppah and recite our vows. The rent-a-rabbi carefully poured some wine from a decanter into a silver Kiddush cup and placed it on a little table positioned before him. He carried out the marriage ceremony, which, at a certain point, called for the rabbi to offer a blessing over the wine and then offer a sip to the bride and another to the groom. He did so, we took our sips, and then he set the cup back onto the table. The rabbi completed the ceremony that concluded with a pop as I stomped on a burned out light bulb wrapped inside a cloth napkin. After accepting the congratulations of the park-bench witnesses, we observed the rabbi return to the chuppah, pick up the wine cup and deftly pour the remaining liquid slowly back in to the decanter—ready for use during the next wedding ceremony. Upon observing this act of rabbinic frugality, Anna Ruth broke out laughing and she still, to this day, wonders aloud about how many other lips may have touched the wine that we consumed on our wedding day.

We were young and we were ecstatically happy, although neither of us had a clue as to what now lay ahead. Despite our accelerated courtship and quickie wedding, we evidently were well matched. Our marriage has been an extraordinary one in every way and in 2002 Anna Ruth and I celebrated our fiftieth wedding anniversary in the company of our children, grandchildren, and great-grandchild.

CHAPTER TWELVE

Move to Minnesota

Our honeymoon in the nearby scenic mountains was unforgettable for two reasons. First, we stayed at a rustic lodge filled mostly with vacationing New Yorkers—many of whom mistakenly presumed from my accent that I was French Canadian. Secondly, we almost wound up washing dishes for our board as my bankroll dwindled down to nothing. Before meeting Anna Ruth, I had managed to set aside about $800 in savings from my weekly salary. I was planning to use this money to purchase a car, but once we met, I decided it would be better used to underwrite my campaign to impress Anna Ruth with my sincerity and devotion. Unfortunately, after our two-day honeymoon, we were required to settle our account at the vacation lodge and my pockets were completely empty. Anna Ruth, resourceful as always, still had thirty dollars of her own. This money *(plus the proceeds of a train ticket we cashed back in)* enabled us to avoid the indignity of becoming honeymoon busboys in the hotel's dining room.

A few days after returning to Montreal, I received notice from the US consulate that, thanks to the newly passed McCarren Act, my visa application for immigration to America, which I had submitted back in Austria, had now been approved. So, despite what Senator Humphrey told my parents, I would have been able to come to America anyway—even if I had not decided to take an American wife. I now had the luxury of having two pathways to rejoin my family in the US. But I faced a dire problem. I truly was happy living in Montreal. The city had a vibrant Jewish community that centered about a cluster of tributary streets off of Park Avenue. These side streets all were named after Christian saints *(Saint Bernard Street, Saint Peter Street, Saint Francis Street, etc.)* but were all populated with Jewish homes, synagogues, kosher butcher shops, and old-fashioned stationery stores with their gleaming, chrome soda fountains. I don't recall experiencing even a trace of anti-Semitism during my one and a half years in Montreal. I had a very good job that paid $1.60 per hour, and I really relished my work. I was able to afford the services of a custom haberdasher who kept me stylishly turned out in fine tailor-made suits. We had sublet a comfortable apartment; we enjoyed a tremendous group of friends, and now I was married to the world's most wonderful Jewish girl. I felt that I had overcome the greener stigma and no longer bore the mark of the refugee. I had found all of life's rewards—things I could only dare dream about in the DP camps and during those difficult, hungry years in Israel. So, instead of bringing me joy, the notice from the US consulate brought me angst and anguish. Should I go or should I stay? I was once again at a difficult crossroads—but this time I was not alone.

Anna Ruth understood my situation completely. She had quickly grown close to my buddies, all of whom were drawn from the Montreal Jewish immigrant community. They all loved and admired Anna Ruth as well. She always managed to bring her levelheaded, common sense wisdom to bear on any problems we faced. I recall discussing our future as we strolled together each morning along Park Avenue beneath majestic Mt. Royale.

"I know how close you are to all your friends here in Montreal, Mark," she counseled me, "and it would be really tough to say good-bye to them and move to the US, but remember one thing: You're different from them. You've got a mother, a father and a brother. How many of them can say that?"

She was right. I was unique among our crowd because I had family. Everyone else's family had been lost in the Holocaust. It was this common human need for family linkage that made our group so tight knit and so intimate. Yes, we were, every one of us, on our own in this world, but I was the only one who received letters from home. This distinction was especially evident after I met Anna Ruth. None of my friends ever overtly let it show, but I could sense that they were deeply envious of me. I could hear them thinking, "Oh, that Hasten is so lucky. If only I had a family in America to send me a pretty young American wife!"

Of course, she was correct. I realized that I should not ignore the fact that fortune had smiled upon me and allowed me to possess the one thing all my friends would never again be able to enjoy—the love of a family. Not a surrogate family, but a real family with a mother, a father, and a brother—people of my own blood. I would be a fool to throw away such a valuable asset by living apart when I was free to join them. On top of this, Anna Ruth wanted to continue her schooling and obtain her college degree from the University of Minnesota.

"Oh, and there's one more thing, Mark" she said with a sideways smile.

"What's that?" I asked.

"We're going to have a baby and I think it should be born in America, don't you?"

I didn't know what to say. I was speechless. After a few kisses and after regaining my composure, I spoke what was in my heart.

"You're so right, darling. We must be in Minneapolis in order to present my parents with their first grandchild . . . born in the USA." My parents sacrificed and endured so much to keep my brother and me alive during the war that I felt that this act would in some way be the most meaningful thing I could do to express my appreciation for all they did for me. We began immediately to plan our move to Minnesota.

In the meanwhile, we had found a lovely apartment in which to set up our first home. I knew an older married couple who were snowbirds. They owned an apartment above a ladies' dress shop on St. Bernard Street, but only lived there during the summer months. They would spend the entire winter in Florida and rent out the apartment while they were gone. Anna Ruth and I spent our first winter together as husband and wife in this tidy and cozy flat, but when springtime rolled around, we were still not ready to leave for the US. The older couple returned to town and we explained our situation. They said that since we were such a nice young couple, and since there was adequate room, why shouldn't we continue to stay and we would all live together. Since this meant a reduction in our rent, we agreed immediately.

Everything was going smoothly until one day I returned home from work and discovered Anna Ruth sitting on the front stoop waiting for me. I could see that she was shaken. I was afraid that something had gone wrong with the pregnancy.

"What's wrong, honey?" I asked.

"I'm not going back up there," she said in a trembling voice, pointing to our apartment.

"Why. What happened?"

"It's that dirty old man," she said referring to our landlord. "I can't even tell you what he did." Finally, with some handholding, I got her to tell me all the facts. Anna Ruth had been in our bedroom getting undressed for bed when she heard a noise outside her door. She quickly swung open the door and discovered the landlord crouched down on his knees. He had obviously been peeping at her through the keyhole. Getting up, he entered the room and tried to explain his actions. He told Anna Ruth that he was attracted to her and that since his wife was too old, he was forced to seek out the affections of younger women such as her. He began moving towards her and as she pulled back, he wound up chasing her around the apartment. She finally had fled outside and had been sitting there on the steps for hours waiting for me to arrive home.

I was dumbfounded, but knew what I had to do. I ran upstairs, packed up all of our belongings into two suitcases and told Anna Ruth, "Let's go. We're never coming back here again." We later learned that this fellow was an established voyeur. He had been caught spying on women customers in the dressing room booths of their boutique as they tried on new dresses.

So now we were homeless—wandering the sainted streets of Montreal's Jewish quarter, carrying everything we owned in the world—refugees once more. On the bulletin board of a little bakery, we spotted a card advertising: "Room To Let." We ran over and were shown a tiny bedroom and informed that we would enjoy bathroom privileges for twenty minutes beginning at 6:10 A.M. in the morning and twenty minutes at 6:10 P.M. in the evening, plus the use of a single gas burner in the kitchen during strictly enforced cooking times. Although it was more regimented than we would have liked, the rent was cheap and we could leave whenever we chose without penalty. "We'll take it," I told the landlady after determining that there was no landlord to worry about here.

We stayed in the rented room only a short time until we were prepared to go south and say good-bye to Montreal. We traveled by train to Windsor, Canada where we caught a ferry to Detroit, Michigan. Several of Anna Ruth's maternal aunts and uncles lived in Detroit and put us up for a few days until we caught the train to Minneapolis.

After a warm family reunion, we began to get our bearings and to settle down in this northern metropolis. We moved in with my parents and Hart into their home on Fremont Avenue. My family had picked up a spare twin bed and mattress at a thrift store and it was assigned to us. The bed sagged so much in the middle that the two of us were forced to sleep in the center of the bed each night. If we hadn't been close to each other before that, we certainly wound up that way as a result.

Hart was, by this time, working his way up at Bemis Packaging and offered to help me find work there. I was hired and assigned to a company machine shop on the outskirts of Minneapolis, far from the Bemis corporate headquarters where Hart worked. As the money began to trickle in, we were able to afford our own apartment and moved into one unit of a quadraplex a few months before the baby arrived. Our little flat was located on Humboldt Avenue, near Plymouth Avenue, just down the street from the Rabutnik home where Anna Ruth's extended family lived.

My father, by this time, had become entrenched in the Jewish community and counted Rabbi Ginzberg as his closest friend. Tatu insisted that we hold a wedding reception in Minneapolis since none of the family or his many cronies had been able to attend our actual wedding in Montreal. I was not opposed to the idea, but asked who would pay for such an extravagant blowout. "Don't worry," Tatu told me, "just make the party. The money will be there." He approached Anna Ruth's mother who was considered affluent, thanks to her inheritance from Anna Ruth's father. Celia was known to be extremely frugal, however, and getting her to agree to underwrite a portion of this bash was an act of supreme salesmanship on the part of my father. Although some might have found it strange that the bride was unmistakably pregnant, the wedding reception was an unforgettable gala event and, in the end, just like Tatu said, everybody got paid.

Our first child, a son we named Edward *(Shlomo Isaac)* in memory of Anna Ruth's father, arrived on October 14, 1953. Our new little home was packed wall-to-wall with dozens of guests to help us celebrate the *Brit Milah* ceremony. The ritual circumcision itself was carried out by Anna Ruth's Uncle Shepsel. The Reverend Shepsel Roberts *(the Americanized version of "Rabutnik")* was the community's foremost *mohel* and had facilitated four generations of Jewish newborns with their induction into the Covenant of Abraham by the time he passed away at age ninety in 2003.

In 1953, the country was coming out of the Korean War and the job market once again became flooded with returning soldiers—most of whom were looking for their old jobs or were given preferential treatment when applying for new ones. This was true at Bemis, as well, and many newly hired workers were laid off to make room for the returning veterans. I was one of them.

I did not really regret losing my job all that much since I did not feel as though I fit in with the working crew at Bemis. I recall how immediately after collecting their paychecks on Friday, my co-workers—mostly Poles and Ukrainians—would make a beeline to the local tavern to cash their checks and immediately invest their pay into liquid assets. I was never attracted to this blue-collar way of life and when I finally discovered a pink slip in my pay envelope, I honestly felt a sense of relief.

A few days after I was laid off, Anna Ruth's older brother, Jerome, arrived to Minneapolis from Texas. Jerome had just been mustered out of the air force and came to town specifically to meet me. After getting to know one another, I explained that I was out of work and was looking for something better than a factory job. Jerome urged me to conduct my job search in Dallas and Houston where the bulk of Anna Ruth's paternal family lived. He would help me get acquainted with all the uncles and cousins and assist me in making the rounds. It wasn't the land of milk and honey, he said, but Texas did hold a lot of opportunity according to Jerome. This all sounded like a good idea. I had always wanted to meet Anna Ruth's sister, Maytee, who was now married to a physician, Ben Fisch, and to meet the many relatives from her original Texas family about whom I'd heard so much.

Anna Ruth had recently received a distribution of $10,000 as part of a final settlement of her late father's estate. I was able to use some of this money to trade-in my broken-down jalopy for a brand new 1953 Chevy as we made plans for our cross-country road trip. It was just after Passover in April, with Anna Ruth and little Eddie in the backseat and with Jerome and me trading driving duties, that we made our own Exodus from Minnesota . . . to the promised land of Texas.

CHAPTER THIRTEEN

Texas Travelers

Arriving in Dallas after a rather arduous, non-stop journey, we checked into an inexpensive, but clean, motel and began making the rounds—showing off Anna Ruth's new baby and new husband to her many Texan relatives. I think the baby probably made the better impression.

Texas certainly made an impression on me. I saw this place as the home of my future. Opportunity was in the air and around every corner. A sharp fellow like me could do all right out here—deep in the heart of Texas. I found Texas beautiful and loved everything about it. After a few days of introduction, I started my job search in earnest.

After reading the want ads and going for a few interviews, I finally landed a solid job offer in my field. The Lone Star Cadillac and Oldsmobile Dealership in Dallas offered me work in the make-ready department. A new car, in those days, required a good deal of service after arriving from the factory and before it could be delivered to the customer. The job paid well and would make use of my talents as a machinist. I deliberated about accepting the position and told the manager I wanted a few days to think it over. I spent the next few days in the dealership's service area, becoming familiar with the work and talking to the other mechanics on staff. I got to know a bright young mechanic named Kahn who introduced me to his co-worker and business partner. Kahn informed me that his partner was the former chief design engineer for the Packard Automobile Company. Packard had gone out of business in 1949 and this fellow had come to work at the Cadillac dealership. Packard had pioneered auto air conditioning and had offered it as a built-in luxury feature in their cars since 1938. At Lone Star, the Packard engineer had met Kahn and the two men put together a business plan for a new company that would mass produce auto air conditioners that could be placed into any type of car after it was already built. They confidentially shared their plan with me and told me they were going to leave Lone Star and start their company as soon as they had assembled enough start-up capital. They showed me blueprints for new manufacturing equipment that would efficiently produce after-market air conditioners that could be installed in all makes and models. I reviewed their drawings and found them to be sound and well designed.

The more I thought about this, the more excited I became. If they could really produce a low-cost auto air conditioner, they could become incredibly successful selling both to car owners and to the auto industry in Detroit. Observing my enthusiasm and recognizing my talents, the two entrepreneurs offered me an opportunity to join them once they launched their company; a company they planned to call FrigiKing. But first, I had to accept the job with Lone Star where I would work until the time arrived for us to break away.

By now, it was time to pack up and head back to Minneapolis to collect our belongings. I told Anna Ruth about my discussions with Kahn and my job offer from Lone Star. I also told her that I had made a decision.

"Anna Ruth," I said. "We're not going back. Right here in Texas is where we belong." She was surprised, but did not try to dissuade me. Her schooling was not an issue since she had put her education on hold after Eddie was born. Her common sense kicked in, of course, as she began asking practical questions.

"Well, that's fine, Mark, but what about your parents? Won't they be upset if you take away their only grandchild?"

"I'll take care of all that," I reassured her. "I'm going to drive back to Minneapolis myself, while you move in for a while with

Maytee and Ben in Gainesville. I'll explain everything to my parents. I'll take care of our stuff, too. What I can't sell, I'll bring back with me in the car. You'll see, I'll get it all smoothed out."

And I did. I drove back to Minneapolis, collected, and sold off all of our belongings at the local pawnshops. I gave my family the news that we were moving to Texas, and while they weren't happy about being separated from their only grandchild, they did not to try stand in my way. My mother was simply pleased that I was married, settled down with a family, and living in the US. She did not seem too upset that I was picking up and moving to the Wild West. After a few weeks of tying up loose ends, I headed back to Texas with our car stuffed with personal items plus a new rug I had purchased for Anna Ruth, along with a Kirby vacuum cleaner, all lashed to the roof of the Chevy. I had informed the Lone Star Cadillac dealership that I would accept the mechanic's position and so I hurried across the highways to get back in time for my first day on the job.

While I was busy closing doors in Minneapolis, Anna Ruth was involved in opening them in Texas. She took little Eddie and began shopping for a house around Dallas. Anna Ruth was rightly concerned that we would burn through the inheritance money and not have anything to show for it. So, while I was in Minneapolis, she began her quest for home equity. She quickly located a modest 900-square-foot frame bungalow with a one-car garage on a large attractive lot. She showed it to me as soon as I got back and we made an offer and closed the deal for $7,000. The down payment on our bungalow came to $1,400 and the mortgage payments were $50 per month. We couldn't move in right away, however, and were required to wait for the current owners to vacate. During this period, we were put up by Maytee's in-laws, Hyman and Rosie Fisch who lived in a suburb of Dallas, Oak Cliff, where they operated a good-sized grocery store.

After a few weeks, we were able to move out of the Fisch home and into our new residence. It wasn't much by today's standards, but to us it truly was our "Blue Heaven." Today, this same neighborhood is lined with expensive homes, but back then it was just one vacant lot after another interrupted by the occasional new GI Bill pre-fab special. We had no furniture so we outfitted our nest with a few wooden crates and boxes, our new rug and low-cost bedroom and dining room suites picked up from "Railroad Salvage," a local emporium of discounted and slightly damaged goods that had purportedly fallen off of railway cars. We even had a pay telephone installed. It was a residential model and we were required to deposit a nickel into the attached box before receiving a dial tone.

Once we got settled into our new digs, I started working at Lone Star and in a matter of weeks, the break came and I joined the two founders of the FrigiKing Auto Air Conditioning Company. The founders had secured venture capital financing from a wealthy Dallas investor, a member of the Samuels family. It was exciting work, but it did not pay very much. The company was just getting on its feet and did not have a very big bankroll. Besides, I soon realized that I was merely an employee and that no matter how hard I worked and how successful the company became, without any ownership interest, I would remain what I was—an hourly mechanic. FrigiKing gained some success as an after-market vendor of auto air conditioners, but, as Detroit moved to include A/C as a factory-installed option for passenger cars, FrigiKing shifted its focus to mobile refrigeration systems. Today, FrigiKing, part of the Carrier organization, provides refrigeration units for millions of trucks and rail cars around the world.

It wasn't too long before I began looking around for other opportunities. Opportunities of ownership. My search took me to the community of Tyler, Texas where I had learned that a small hardware store was being offered for sale. I visited the establishment and it looked as though it might be successful if managed properly. I made the seller an offer—50 cents on the dollar for all of his inventory and I would take over his lease. The owner rejected my offer and came back with a counter-offer, which I was considering as we sat around Ben and Maytee's kitchen table discussing the deal.

"It's a pretty little store," said Anna Ruth, "and I know Mark would do a great job of running it."

"If I can buy it for the right price," I added. "But if I pay too much, I'll have to borrow the money and then all the profits will go towards paying back the loan."

"Can I ask you something, Mark?" asked Maytee.

"Of course," I answered. Maytee was older than Anna Ruth and we both looked up to her. She was very bright and very generous with her consistently sound advice.

"Do you really want your children spending their lives behind the counter of a hardware store?" she asked me in dead earnest. "That's how Anna Ruth, Jerome, and I spent our childhoods, you know. We spent our days and nights in the store waiting on customers. We were the Jewish kids that worked at the store. I think you want something better than that for your kids. Am I right?"

Of course, she was absolutely right. I let the hardware store opportunity pass me by. Anna Ruth and I quickly concluded that there was something we sorely needed in order to achieve financial success. One of us had to undergo some education or training. Without a degree, I would never find work as anything more than a laborer. Likewise, Anna Ruth would not be able to find work as a teacher unless she finished her education. After spending some time with Maytee and Ben, a highly successful physician, I soon came to realize the outstanding benefits America had to offer to its educated citizens.

From time to time, Anna Ruth and I had discussed continuing our education when we were back in Minneapolis, before moving to Texas. But now, correcting this deficiency took on a new priority and we discussed it daily.

"One of us has to get educated, Mark, if we ever hope to make a decent living," Anna Ruth opined. "And it can't be me, because I'm tied up all day with the baby. So that leaves you."

"Why me?" I protested. "I barely can speak English and I only had a fifth grade education. How can I get into college?"

"Well, it can't be me, darling, since I just received some more news today from the doctor." This time I saw it coming. With the stork on the way with another delivery, I realized that Anna Ruth was not going to become our family's breadwinner. The inheritance money was great, but it was going to run out eventually. The best thing we could do with it was to invest it—but not into risky ventures, not into new business start-ups but into ourselves. We would use the money to live on while I acquired a higher education degree. A degree that I could use to support our family for the rest of my life. The only problem was—how would I get one?

CHAPTER FOURTEEN

College Bound

Anna Ruth had read a piece in the local newspaper about a co-op engineering program at nearby Southern Methodist University (SMU) that allowed a student to take classes for two months and then join the workforce for another two months. Alternating in this way, between the A Section and the B Section, over a five-year period, the student could obtain an engineering degree while working and earning enough to support himself and pay for his education. It sounded like just what we were looking for. Tuition and books alone cost $1,000 per year and would quickly deplete our remaining savings, unless I could find a way to keep earning while I was learning.

The problem I faced was that I did not even have a high school diploma. This fact made enrolling into any college next to impossible.

"The article says that SMU also operates a GED program," said Anna Ruth. "That's a Graduate Equivalency Diploma for adults who want to get a high school degree. Why don't I call them?" I agreed, and Anna Ruth put a nickel in the phone. The university promised to send out an information packet about both the GED and Co-op programs.

When the literature arrived by mail, Anna Ruth and I pored over every word in close scrutiny.

"The GED program looks pretty good," she said. "You could attend night classes and get your diploma in two years."

"That's too long, honey," I responded. "I don't want to wait for two years before I can even start. Why don't I apply directly to SMU and forget the high school classes?"

"That's going to be tough, but I guess it's worth a try," said Anna Ruth. "I'll call them and see if we can get an appointment." And that's just what she did.

A few days later, Anna Ruth and I, along with little Eddie, were seated in the office of the dean of students at the SMU School of Industrial Engineering. The dean, a professor Schumacher, was an imposing figure who had lost an arm during World War II. The dean looked up from my application form and addressed us both bluntly.

"Thank you for your interest in our school, Mr. Hasten, but there's not much I can do for you unless you've got a high school diploma."

"Is there someone higher up we can talk to?" asked Anna Ruth.

"Well, yes," he admitted. "You could go see Dean Fleck. He's the head of the entire SMU School of Engineering." Somehow, Anna Ruth managed to get us in and in a few short hours we were again seated opposite a desk in the office of Dean Fleck.

"Mr. Hasten, I don't see how we can possibly enroll you at SMU. First, you never even attended high school. Secondly, you have not completed any of the entrance exams." He paused while Anna Ruth helped me understand his words by translating from English to Hebrew and Yiddish.

"And third," Fleck continued, "you won't be able to bring your wife with you to class to translate your professor's lectures. And finally, you indicate that you will need financial assistance in order to make the tuition payments. I'm not sure you qualify for a scholarship and if you don't get one, where will you get the money?" The dean shook his head and finally said, "These are very formidable obstacles indeed, Mr. Hasten."

Anna Ruth translated his negative message and I offered responses for each objection he raised.

"You're dealing with one very stubborn Pole here," said Anna Ruth with a hopeful smile, but it was not going to work. Fleck pressed his intercom button summoning his secretary. When she arrived, he nodded towards us and said to her, "Please show them out. I'm sorry."

As we passed back through the waiting room, Anna Ruth and I chatted about what we could do next. Our words were overheard by Professor's Fleck's secretary, an older unmarried woman who evidently took pity on us. She approached us and began speaking in hushed tones.

"Look, you folks seem like nice people. Why don't you come back in a few days for the School of Engineering orientation session? I'll make sure that there will be a packet for you there." We thanked her abundantly and left the building with renewed hope.

On the appointed day, I arrived at the campus and approached the School of Engineering main lecture hall where the student orientation was being held. I located my packet and as I reached the opening that led into the hall, I spied a familiar figure. Right in the entryway stood Dean Fleck. He spotted me at once.

"What are you doing here?" he queried. I just stood there looking at him. I could not put my foot in the door, as I had done at Canadair, since there was no door—only an open entryway. I finally got out, "I come here for orientation," and held up my packet bearing my name for him to see.

Dean Fleck pondered this for a moment as a look of consternation came over his face. Finally . . . and oddly . . . he simply turned his back on me and walked slowly away, saying nothing. "Well," I thought, "he didn't say 'yes' and he didn't say 'no.' I guess that means I can go in." And that's exactly what I did. Why didn't Fleck stop me from entering the hall? I'm not exactly certain, but I suspect that it was because of his secretary. She had overheard our conversation in the waiting room at which time Anna Ruth had mentioned that although it would be very tough, we would be able to come up with the $800 per year tuition fee if we had to. Evidently, this message of financial ability prompted Fleck to drop his misgivings about accepting me once he learned we were able to pay the ticket price.

I took my seat up front among the 450 other students who had been accepted into the School of Engineering. We were addressed by a Professor Jack Harkey who gave us a general overview of the school and described the co-op program in detail.

Finally, he made the following announcement: "Look to your right and look to your left. Of the three of you, only one will actually graduate from this program." I did as he said. I looked to the young man on my left, pointed at him and said "You!" and then did the same with the man on my right. Sure enough, Professor Harkey was correct in his prediction. Of the 450 who entered the orientation hall that day, only 153 graduated. I was determined to be among them.

The next five years was a period of intense study and struggle for both Anna Ruth and me. The co-op program did not begin until my third year. During my freshman and sophomore years, I was required to be a full-time student enrolled in a full compliment of classes. During my first year, I took nineteen credits—a next-to-impossible class load. I was not able to squeeze in a much-needed English class until my third year. I could not keep my job at FrigiKing and wound up taking part-time odd jobs to help make ends meet. I found work as a gas station attendant, a grocery carryout boy, and other positions that would allow me to keep my books with me on the job. The grocery job was the most lucrative since I developed a good relationship with the store manager. Each night, after closing the store, he would give me some cash and ask me to go into the nearby liquor store and purchase a fifth of whiskey for him. I, of course, obliged and then watched as my boss drained the entire bottle in a single sitting every night. I soon realized that he needed my services as a beard because the liquor store clerks, aware of my boss's rampant alcoholism, had years ago stopped selling him booze. My willingness to be his delivery agent soon earned me a 25-cent raise to $1.25 per hour.

My college classes included Physics, Trigonometry, Chemistry, Biology, and Algebra taught by Dr. Paul Minton—a particularly charismatic and dynamic instructor. By my fifth year at SMU, Dr. Minton was seriously attempting to recruit me for the faculty at the university and wished for me to join his department. I told him I wasn't really interested in teaching and besides, my English skills were too limited. With all the math and science classes I was taking, I was unable to fit English classes into my curriculum until I reached my third year.

My English deficiency created some serious problems for me. One, in particular, almost resulted in my flunking out of Dr. Minton's Algebra class. In mid-December, as the first term was about to end, Dr. Minton asked me to stay after class for a moment for a chat.

"Mr. Hasten," he began, "I don't know how your other teachers do it, but here is how I calculate your final grade in this class. One fourth of your grade is the total of your weekly quizzes, another fourth consists of your test results, and one fourth is your final exam score." I nodded my understanding. "As a good math student, you quickly realize that one fourth is missing . . . and that's the problem. One fourth of your total grade is based upon your homework performance, and so far, you have not turned in a single homework assignment!" I was shocked.

"Even if you earn the highest possible score in all three of the other categories," he explained, "and that's a possibility in your case, Mr. Hasten . . . your total score would only be 75 percent and that would get you a C."

"What are you talking about?" I asked in astonishment. "What homework assignments?!"

"Do you recall what I write on the blackboard every day just before the dismissal bell rings?" he asked. I responded that I had often wondered why he would go to the board and write the letter P followed by a number, and, below it, another P followed by another number.

"That stands for page number and problem number in your Algebra textbook," he went on. "I explained on the first day of class that I would assign a different problem at the end of every class and that you were required to work on it at home and turn in the completed solution on the following day. I take it that you did not understand this instruction."

"You are right," I told him, "I did not know about this and I apologize. Let me ask you, Professor, is it too late? Can I make it up?" Minton said he would permit me to turn in all of the missed homework problems as long as I did so before the semester ended in a few weeks.

I went home and explained the situation to Anna Ruth and she took the news calmly.

"Well, do you want to flunk out?" she asked me. "And waste all that tuition money?"

"Of course not," I protested, "why should I flunk out? Algebra is my best subject. I should get an A. I'm just going to have to do three months worth of homework in two weeks. And on top of that, I'm going to have to start doing the daily homework problem from now on."

"Well, if you're determined to do it, then I'll help," she offered. "You take some time off work and I'll start baby-sitting again. It's only fifty cents an hour, but every little bit counts."

Anna Ruth got busy caring for three children during the day, whose parents both worked, and caring for an elderly couple in the evenings. With Anna Ruth's assistance, I stayed up every night and got through as many problems as I could before I either fell asleep or the sun came up. I managed to get all the problems turned in and got almost all of them correct, allowing me to pass the course and continue my education. This experience—you might call it my initiation—taught me what it really meant to be a student and opened my eyes to how tough it really was going to be from now on.

Mark My Words!

It was also becoming increasingly tough to make ends meet. Anna Ruth would sometimes call the mortgage holder on our house, a very decent Jewish businessman, and explain that we just did not have the money for this month's $50 payment. He was very understanding and instructed her to send it in next month after tacking on a two-dollar penalty.

Once the inheritance proceeds ran out, and with only a trickle of money coming in, we found ourselves precariously close to the poverty level. Whenever I would observe Anna Ruth's spirits sagging under the burden of economic hardship, I would try to buoy them with something like:

"We're not poor! We're rich. We have a beautiful home, a great car, and free medical care from Ben. As long as we have food in the refrigerator, we're rich!" I proclaimed defiantly. I even made a few attempts to cut down on our grocery expenses through some shenanigans. I had heard that SMU football players received free meals from the university. If I could only get onto that team, I was sure I could round up enough food to feed myself and to bring some home for my family. I met with Coach Forest Greg and informed him that I was an experienced soccer player, and tried to convince him that I would surely make a great place kicker (*although I wasn't too sure what a place kicker was*). Coach Forest explained that first-year students were not allowed to play on the school's varsity football team, but he would grant me a tryout for the Freshman team. While my bravado managed to earn me an audition, I evidently did not have what it took to play college football in the mid-1950s and did not make the team.

While at the football training area, however, I did manage to make friends with one of the black chefs that ran the team dining room. His specialty was a dish he dubbed "Cadillac Chicken." I'm not sure why he called it that other than the fact that it was deep-fried in about as much oil as you'd find in the crankcase of a Coupe DeVille. Our family had not yet made the move to keeping kosher, and so, on many evenings I could be seen walking homeward lugging a bucket of leftover Cadillac Chicken for our family dinner.

Throughout my college career, and especially during those first few years, Anna Ruth provided critical assistance that made all the difference in the world. I was better able to understand spoken English than written English and so Anna Ruth would read my homework assignments to me out loud. She did the typing, on a one-hundred-year-old Royal elite collector's item, and helped me get through the language found in complex math and physics problems. Without her help, I am quite certain I would have wound up among the two thirds who failed to earn a degree. At times, I know it was very hard for her to keep on dispensing her help. I recall when Anna Ruth was about to deliver our second son, Michael, she had been placed under observation at a Gainesville sanitarium by her brother-in-law, Dr. Ben Fisch. Every night after my classes at SMU, I would make the drive from Dallas to be with her. One night, I became stuck on an advanced Algebra problem and I reluctantly woke up Anna Ruth about midnight for help. Although she was nine months pregnant, she grabbed a cup of coffee and looked the problem over.

"Why don't you try $x^2 = b^2 / c^2$?" she said with a yawn and returned to bed. I turned in her answer the next day and I was the only student in Dr. Minton's class to get the problem right. I will be forever in her debt for her devotion and unwavering dedication to our future.

With Anna Ruth's help, I managed to survive my first two years at SMU and was finally ready to participate in the co-op program. I attended classes for two months and then I reported for work for the next two months. I was assigned to engineering jobs at several large-area companies. One of the finest was the Atlantic Refinery Company *(later to become part of Atlantic Richfield)*. It was my job to prepare engineering drawings of their many Texas oilfields, laying out the oilrigs, pipelines, etc.

Mark My Words!

I finally had the opportunity to enroll in English class and was amazed at how much I enjoyed it. As a final thesis for this class, I submitted, with Anna Ruth's assistance, a paper about the works of Mark Twain. I was familiar with Twain's writing since I had read much of it, translated into Polish, as a young boy. The paper earned me an A along with a very flattering note from the professor who commented that he had never seen a paper like this from a third year foreign-born student. With my English improving dramatically, I felt sufficiently confident to apply for US citizenship. I was proudly sworn in as a US citizen in December of 1958.

During my final year at SMU, Anna Ruth got a job with Texas Instruments where she worked for about one year. Our second son, Michael, had arrived during my freshman year and was now a bouncing two-year-old. In order to keep up the tuition payments, we were required to go into debt. I took out a student loan and also borrowed $500 from each of Anna Ruth's uncles in Houston. I'm proud to say that every penny was paid back. But I am even prouder to report that I succeeded in obtaining my engineering degree in 1959 graduating 8th in my class of 153. Not only did SMU leave its mark on me, I also managed to leave my mark on the campus. For my final thesis, I had designed a new theoretical air conditioning system for Dallas Hall, the school's oldest lecture facility. I later heard that years after my graduation, the school located my designs and implemented them when upgrading the building's heating and cooling systems.

Now that my schooling was near completion, we took another hard look at our family's financial situation. While opportunities for a trained engineer abounded in Texas, as our family grew, we became increasingly more interested in moving back to Minneapolis. And not only for economic reasons. Anna Ruth's mother was getting older as were my parents. My father wrote and explained that his health was steadily getting worse and he really wanted to spend what time he had left with his grandchildren. I also believed that I could find a higher paying job in the North. I had been approached by campus recruiters during my final year and received a very tempting offer to work at the US Jet Propulsion Laboratory on the Redstone rocket program. I declined this and similar offers because I had no wish to work at a job that required government clearance. At this point, I wished to have nothing to do with the military and so I avoided job offers that might have any sort of military connection.

During my final spring break from classes in April, I traveled to Minneapolis for some serious job searching. I began knocking on doors as soon as I arrived, starting at the town's biggest employers, the 3M Company and Honeywell Instruments. This time, with an imminent engineering degree on my résumé, I was shown a much warmer welcome than when I was forced to stick my foot in the door at Canadair ten years before. Perhaps I was even a bit too cocky.

I recall that during the interview process at Honeywell I was escorted into a cubicle and given fifteen minutes to complete a psychological profile exam. The attractive young personnel clerk put a kitchen timer down in front of me and set it to click off the quarter hour. The multiple-choice questions consisted of inane inquiries into my psyche and personal life. There were intimate questions about my bathroom habits, my sexual preferences and others that just seemed bizarre and nonsensical. I decided that I really did not have the time or inclination for this sort of Mickey Mouse. I asked to see the personnel director.

"Yes? You asked to see me? Have you finished the test?" he asked as he entered my cubicle.

"No, I have not. I would actually like to meet the weirdo who wrote this test," I pronounced.

"I take it you have a problem with this test?" he said.

"I do and I don't care to waste my time on a ridiculous exercise like this one," I told him bluntly. "If you want give me any type of exam to measure my engineering skills, that's fine, but this is pure nonsense and I won't do it. If you have a job for me, give it to me. If not . . . thank you very much."

"It's just part of our standard screening process," said the director somewhat apologetically, "we all have to take it, I'm afraid."

"Well, I don't," I proclaimed, standing to walk out.

I turned in my unfinished test paper and left the building. I was quite surprised, therefore, to receive a job offer in the mail from Honeywell a few weeks later. I guess they agreed that they were more interested in my engineering skills than in my psychological profile. Who knows? Perhaps they were impressed by my chutzpah.

I did not respond immediately to the Honeywell offer because I was still awaiting word from the company that was my first choice, General Mills. I had gone through the interview process at their research and development division and came away very impressed. This seemed like the perfect place for me to exploit my newly acquired engineering skills. General Mills had a very advanced R&D department *(Research and Development)* that clearly encouraged innovation and inventiveness. Evidently, I also made a good impression on General Mills because, before I left, I received a verbal job offer at $500 per month from a Dr. Paul, the personnel director. Dr. Paul told me that I would be getting a formal written offer in the mail within a few days and that would spell out all the details. I gave him my address in Dallas and promised to respond as soon as I received the formal offer.

I returned back home to Dallas in high spirits to finish out my final weeks as a college student. I shared the good news about the General Mills job offer with Anna Ruth and she was delighted and very supportive. At this point, I was working as an activities coordinator at the campus student union building. I was well-known around the campus and looking back, those final college days were some of the most wonderful days of my life.

Ironically, my workplace was directly next door to the campus mailroom where all the student mail was processed and sorted. I would often assist the older lady who ran the mailroom in sorting the incoming mail.

Each day I would return home from class or from work and ask Anna Ruth if the letter from General Mills had arrived. This went on for weeks and weeks. Finally, at Anna Ruth's urging, I telephoned Dr. Paul and asked him about the job offer.

"I'm so glad you called," Paul said. "We thought we had lost you. The letter we sent you was returned by the school and stamped 'No Such Student at SMU.'"

I could not believe it. It turned out that Dr. Paul had given my address to his secretary and instructed her to mail me a standard job offer letter. She had mislaid my address and labeled the envelope: Mark Hasten c/o S.M.U. Student Union Building, Dallas, Texas. Instead of coming to my home, the letter arrived to the Union—to the office right next door to where I worked every day! The postal clerk went to look up my street address in the student directory. Unfortunately, there had been a printing error in that year's student directory. All B Section students from the school's engineering program had inadvertently been omitted from the directory. Since my name could not be found, the clerk stamped the envelope "No Such Student" and returned the most important letter of my life back to the sender. Ironically, the editor of the student directory that year, and the one responsible for leaving out my name, happened to be Anna Ruth's cousin, Annette Robinson. I've teased her about it ever since.

After everything was straightened out, we accepted the offer from General Mills and told them I would be available to start my new job as soon as I received my degree in June. On the day after graduation, we were packed and ready to go. We had sold the house for $9,000 and netted a profit of $2,000 on the sale. This, our first real estate transaction, made a deep impression on me. We had invested only $1,400 *(our down payment)* and five years later gotten back $2,000. This worked out to over 8.5% per year return at a time when savings accounts were offering only 2 percent interest. We concluded that real estate was definitely something worth looking in to.

And so, as we had done before, in Poland, in Kazakhstan, in Austria, in Montreal, and in Minneapolis, and as we would do again, we packed up our dreams and set out to seek a sweeter life a little further down the road.

CHAPTER FIFTEEN

A Passion For Property

Before leaving Texas, I was able to sell my beloved 1953 Chevy with the straight 6-cylinder engine to my friend, a Korean-born fellow student. The four of us, Anna Ruth, Eddie, Michael, and I actually wound up flying back to Minnesota where I soon was able to purchase another car. Hart and my parents, at this point, were living on Newton Avenue. Anna Ruth and I decided to rent a nearby place as we searched for just the right house for ourselves. The rental apartment we found was an old rambling frame house that served as our residence during our first year back in Minneapolis.

As we searched for a permanent home we could purchase, we made education the number one priority. We wanted a place that would permit the kids to walk to both their public school and to the afternoon Hebrew School. This was in an era before day schools, and the Talmud-Torah after-school program in Minneapolis was regarded as one of the finest of its kind in America.

I went scouring the appropriate neighborhoods for available homes—going door to door and asking the owners if they were interested in selling. I came upon a fifty-year old, two-story brick house on Russell Street that looked like it might work. I walked up the stoop, knocked on the front door, and introduced myself to the lady who answered, a Mrs. Landy. We began to chat and she informed me that her late husband had owned a large *(non-kosher)* slaughterhouse. She explained that her sons were now running the business and she asked me how I knew that she wanted to sell the house.

"I did not know, Mrs. Landy," I replied honestly. "I just liked the looks of your house and its location . . . and I had a hunch it might be for sale."

As Mrs. Landy showed me around, I found the interior even more attractive than the outside. The home featured a large formal parlor and a half bath on the main floor. I made her an offer of $11,200 on the spot and she accepted, agreeing to take $2,000 as a down payment and I was able to mortgage the balance with a local bank.

We lived at the house on Russell Street over the next two years as our fortunes began to climb and our family expanded. Our daughter, Monica, was born and brought home to this house and, in 1961, it was there that we first welcomed my brother Hart and his new bride, Simona. Sadly, it was during these years that our family also became smaller—by one. After valiantly struggling against emphysema for most of his adult life, my father, Bernard, finally succumbed[3].

We left the house on Russell Street much in the same way as we arrived. One day, in early 1964, a knock came at the door. A gentleman introduced himself as a real estate developer and explained that he had recently built a custom home for a client in an area known as Golden Valley. The client was unable to keep up the payments and he, the developer, was forced to foreclose. He now owned the home, but he did not wish to live in it. He was, however, very attracted to our home for many of the same reasons that had attracted me to it several years earlier. He wanted to know if I would be interested in a swap, my old home for his new one. I was intrigued and told him I would be happy to drive out to the suburbs and have a look at it. By now, many Jewish families had resettled to the suburbs and there was bus service available to transport the children to afternoon Hebrew classes.

Mark My Words!

I surveyed the home and found the exterior very run-down with weeds growing up to my waist. Once inside, however, it was a different story. I discovered a luxurious three-bedroom ranch house with an enormous basement and I decided that I should give the home serious consideration. Anna Ruth, while a bit reluctant at first about leaving the old neighborhood, finally agreed that the area was better suited for our growing brood and gave the place her blessing. I was able to execute the swap without going out of pocket at all. While the new home was worth considerably more than our old one *(about $19,000)*, I was able to put together a deal whereby I paid off my old mortgage, transferred the title to the builder and took on a new longer-term loan with the same lender. The only economic change for me was a modest increase in our monthly mortgage payment. With this transaction, I became even more impressed with the extraordinary money-making opportunities available via real estate. Through effective leveraging, we were able to start with a $1,400 investment in 1954 and, ten years later, were now living in a $19,000 home without ever having kicked in an additional dime. I decided that I had to learn more about this amazing business and began reading and talking to everyone I could, in order to educate myself about how to make money in real estate. I recall discussing my dreams with my brother in 1967. Hart had moved to Indianapolis, where he had been transferred by Bemis Corporation, his employer, to manage one of their large production facilities.

"If I ever own an eight-plex, I'll be the richest man in the world," I told Hart, referring to a multifamily housing unit that would accommodate eight households under one roof. It was not long after that conversation that my dream began forming itself into reality. I learned of a builder who had constructed two adjoining twelve-unit apartment buildings in a Minneapolis suburb known as Fridley. All of the apartments were 900 sq. foot two-bedroom units. Situated near one of the new interstate exits, the buildings were sitting nearly vacant because the builder had been unable to find any interested tenants. After looking over the property, I decided to make the owner an offer. Following a bit of negotiation, we agreed upon a purchase price of $2,000 per unit, or $48,000 for the entire property.

In order to finance the project, I needed capital and I began scrambling. I first had our home reappraised and was delighted to discover that the valuation had risen from 19 to 27 thousand dollars in the four short years we had lived there. I immediately took out a second mortgage with the Golden Valley Bank which, when coupled with some additional collateral *(a diamond ring inherited by Anna Ruth, three $500 Israel Bonds, and anything else of value I could lay my hands on)* succeeded in putting $9,000 in my pocket. Turning to my family, I borrowed another $7,000 from Anna Ruth's stepfather, Joe Friedman. Accepting the $16,000 I had in hand as a down payment, the seller agreed to take back a note for the $32,000 difference. But the only way he would agree is if the note carried a one-year term. In other words, I would have to make regular payments to him for twelve months after which, if I could not refinance or pay off the balloon payment, he would have the right to foreclose, and I would lose everything I had put in to date.

I retained the services of an attorney, Chuck Rubinstein, who sat at the closing, biting his nails as he watched me sign a purchase agreement—against his advice—that he was sure would lead to my ruination. Anna Ruth was also very nervous about my gambling everything we had on this white elephant.

"Are you sure you know what you're doing, Mark?" she asked me at the closing.

"You bet I am. This guy doesn't know what he's got," I confided, referring to the seller.

"I know what he's got," she replied. "He's got everything in the world that we used to have. Plus everything we're going to have for the next year. And what have we got? A big empty apartment building by the side of the highway that nobody wants to live in."

"Look, Anna Ruth," I explained, "these units are brand new and we can rent them out for a high price—once people learn about them. If we can get even a seventy-five percent occupancy, this place would turn into a gold mine. It's just going to take a little work."

And we did get to work right away. I hired an onsite property manager who was given free rent in exchange for his services. He was an industrious fellow from Wisconsin with a large family. He told me that he would be glad to work for me in exchange for free rent, but he had to have a three-bedroom apartment—I had to permit him to add on an additional bedroom. I agreed to his terms and his first assignment was to convert his own apartment from a two-bedroom to a three-bedroom unit. He liked this idea immensely and enthusiastically went to work annexing a bedroom from a neighboring two-bedroom apartment.

Next, I had determined that approximately twenty-five thousand cars whizzed by our apartment complex daily on the nearby interstate highway. Why not put up a sign that would direct drivers to come have a look *(this was possible in the days before Lady Bird Johnson's 'Beautify America' campaign got underway)?* I decided to make the sign myself, but this was not to be any ordinary sign. This sign was going to be sixteen feet long and eight feet high. I visited the lumberyard and bought plywood sections, letter stencils, paint, and brushes and brought them all into our basement and started working on the sign. I had the entire thing put together when I sheepishly realized that the sign was now too big to haul out the basement door. Thanks to the fact that I now held a degree in mechanical engineering, I was quickly able to figure out how to take the sign apart and then reassemble it once I had gotten it outside. As it turned out, my marketing efforts—giant highway sign and all—were unneeded.

Within two months, my industrious property manager had succeeded in filling up the entire complex with tenants . . . before I even had a chance to erect my nearly completed mega-sign! He understood that in order to ensure his own job security, the property would have to become a moneymaker. He was also wise enough to understand that once the place was completely full, his primary job of rounding up new tenants, became a breeze. He went to nearby churches and spoke to the congregations and posted ads. He visited nearby factories and convinced employees that they would save money by living close to their workplace. He printed up promotional leaflets and plastered them everywhere. In other words, he pounded the pavement aggressively day and night and delivered over twenty signed leases to me in record time. As for "the mother of all road signs"—it never saw the light of day and went back into my basement. The plywood was later salvaged for some home improvement projects.

One of the attractions that we were able to offer prospective tenants was the availability of laundry washer and dryer units in each building. I did not have the money to buy this equipment, so I wound up leasing it. Residents were required to pay 25 cents per wash load. Every week, Anna Ruth and I would visit the machines and empty the coin boxes. In the evening, back home, we would sit around the kitchen table and count out the quarters and carefully stuff forty of them into yellow tubular paper wrappers we got from the bank. There were always enough filled $10-tubes to make the equipment lease payment, plus a little left over.

Once the property was filled, we were generating sufficient cash flow to make the mortgage payments, pay all the bills, and generate a small profit. This situation would be ideal were it not for the looming balloon payment that we were to face at the end of the first year. If I was unable to refinance the project—and come up with a corresponding down payment—we could lose everything we had invested to date if the note-holder were to foreclose. Where would we get the money to avoid this situation? Anna Ruth and I prayed for an answer and our prayers were received. We were saved by an "act of G-d" . . . although G-d often works in mysterious ways.

Mark My Words!

In the spring of 1966, devastating tornadoes ripped through Fridley. Our apartment complex was seriously affected. There was extensive damage to the roofs of both buildings and an exterior wall section had partially collapsed. Fortunately, the damage did not force any of the tenants to re-locate. I contacted our insurance carrier's claims adjuster and, after some haggling, we settled for the princely sum of $39,000. I determined that I could save money by doing much of the repair work myself. I personally repaired the exterior walls—fastening the brick veneer to the building's wooden frame. With Anna Ruth carrying the bricks and with a pair of helpers from the nearby Indian reservation, I was able to complete the work over the summer months. I was never too fond of working at great heights, so I trained my helpers in the proper way of laying shingles and oversaw them as they carried out the roof repairs. The instruction took place on the ground, using sheets of plywood laid out on the grass. Once I was convinced that they understood the procedure, they ascended to the second story roof and nailed down the shingles.

I managed to do most of the work during my regularly scheduled vacation time off from General Mills. In addition to my efforts, I spent roughly $10,000 on materials and payments to my helpers. This left $29,000 in my pocket from the insurance proceeds. In essence, I had paid this amount to myself, in consideration of the work I had performed, rather than paying it out to third-party carpenters and roofing contractors. This money proved to be a godsend—a literal "windfall"—enabling me to accomplish two important objectives.

First, I was able to pay off the $18,000 balloon payment on the apartment buildings—effectively launching my career as a real estate developer. Secondly, in October of that year, I was able to silently invest the remaining insurance proceeds, $10,000 with my brother, Hart, who was assembling the capital needed to purchase a small nursing home business in Indianapolis. Both the real estate and the nursing home businesses flourished and they can both directly trace their earliest origins to the "mighty winds" of Minnesota back in the spring of 1965.

As time went by, I was starting to become well known in the local real estate business and, as a result, other developers would contact me about new projects. One such fellow—a Jewish builder who I had met socially—told me about a piece of vacant land that had highway frontage and was available at a decent price. The parcel was located at the intersection of Highway 100 and Interstate 495, off of France Avenue, and could, according to the builder, nicely accommodate a new one-hundred-unit garden apartment community. I visited the site and agreed that it was an ideal location. We set up a partnership, each putting in $500, and negotiated a purchase price with the Italian-born owner. Once we had a sales contract put together, we next needed to locate financing. This process took several months and during that time, a strange thing happened. The value of the property began rising dramatically. We soon realized that we could turn a quick profit by putting the lot back on the market once we had title to it. At the same time, I was having difficulty securing financing. I was already fully leveraged and the banks did not think it prudent to add to my debt burden. When I told my partner about this, he immediately seized the opportunity and offered to buy out my interest in the partnership for $5,000 and I accepted. Although my partner came out even better on the deal, I had turned $500 into $5,000 within a matter of months.

This episode only served to further fuel my passion for real estate investment. It seemed to offer amazing and incomparable opportunities. Plus, I was gaining an appreciation for the fundamental realities of real estate investment. The key to understanding real estate in a free market economy is all embodied in the law of supply and demand. Land is a commodity that enjoys a limited supply ("G-d ain't makin' any more of it!*"—Tony Soprano*) and an unlimited demand. The key to successful real estate investment is understanding the dynamics of that demand. And the key to very successful real estate investment is knowing how to benefit from that demand through patience and good timing.

CHAPTER SIXTEEN

Bac-O's, Bugles and Bendable Straws

As mentioned, I went to work for General Mills as a research engineer at the starting salary of $500 per month. My primary responsibility was the design and construction of proprietary equipment used in the production of food products. I was only involved in the creation of machines that could not be acquired from outside sources. For example, I was not involved with packaging equipment since it could be easily obtained through a third party vendor. The machine that made Cheerios breakfast cereal, on the other hand, was a one-of-a kind unit and had to be built in-house. Taking it a step further, I was only involved with the research side of the equation and not the development side. In other words, our department would be provided with specifications for a new product from the company's marketing gurus and then asked to come up with designs for new equipment that could efficiently produce such a new product. If the designs were approved, we would then be asked to create a prototype before handing the building specs over to the development team who would then physically produce the actual machinery. The following story illustrates this process.

The marketing division determined that there was an emerging demand for a new type of food product: precooked chicken. Chicken meat was inexpensive, and the convenience of not having to actually prepare the chicken before serving was determined to be attractive to busy consumers. A research team was assembled consisting of a chemical engineer, a processing engineer, and me, the mechanical engineer. Our team determined that a canned product made the most sense and then set out to design an assembly line process that would produce the product with the highest degree of efficiency.

The challenge we faced was how to de-bone the chicken quickly and effectively. Finding a way to do so fell to me and I considered various strategies until I hit upon the right one. I was familiar with the puffing-gun production method used to create our leading breakfast cereal, Cheerios, and this inspired me to come up with a solution to the chicken problem. In order to make Cheerios, baked dough made from raw oat flour was sent through a proprietary James cooker where it would be extruded through a shaping die and sliced and then dried into individual pellets. The pellets were next loaded into the barrel of a machine that resembled a cannon where they were pressurized and heated. The moisture in the pellets would expand rapidly creating an explosive "shooting" effect and thereby puff up the pellets into the familiar Cherrios torus shape. "Why not apply the same technology to chicken?" I surmised. I thought back to the immense power provided by the alcohol-powered pile drivers our pontoon brigade employed during World War II *(see chapter 5)* and came up with what seemed a workable solution.

My theory was that if we could place chickens into a sealed space and apply heat and steam pressure, everything would fall apart quickly. On top of that, the freshly de-boned chicken meat would emerge already cooked. To test this concept, I built a small experimental prototype that would accommodate just one chicken. It consisted of a wire cage surrounding a tubular chamber. The chamber containing the chicken was heated until the pressure reached a fixed level. At this point, the chicken gun would be fired as the door to the chamber was freed and the chicken meat would be flung from the bone and against the wire cage surrounding the chamber. The bottom of the cage emptied onto an conveyor belt that carried the meat and the bone, now separated, on to the cannery. The prototype worked flawlessly, but the bones, unfortunately, would still have to be plucked and removed by hand and it was this obstacle that I was seeking to overcome when General Mills pulled the plug on the project. Had our research been successful, I would have obtained a patent for the "Chicken Cannon" and then turned the specs over to the development crew to actually build the equipment capable of deploying this newly created technology for the mass production of canned, boned chicken meat. As it turned out, the world will never enjoy the benefits of my "poultry pulverizer" device. Many of my other inventions, however, were implemented by General Mills and several are still in use today in the production of familiar consumer food products such as Bac-O's, Bugles, and bendable plastic straws. My first big success was *(not surprisingly for an enterprising Jewish engineer)* a means of producing bacon that even the most orthodox rabbi in the world could fully enjoy.

In the mid-1960s, the wonders of the versatile and low-cost soybean were just beginning to be understood by American industry. Used for some time in the manufacture of plastics and other industrial products, the eating of soybeans was heretofore restricted to oriental diets. General Mills was interested in employing this high-protein vegetable in the creation of new consumer foodstuffs and turned to its research division to come up with new ideas on how to create such soy-based products. I was put on this project and shown how the soybean is converted through cooking into a heavy molasses-like paste. I was asked to devise methods of converting this paste into simulated meat products. One property of soy paste was that it easily retained whatever flavoring was added to it over a long shelf life period. So obtaining a meat-like taste was a relatively simple matter and it involved merely coming up with the right recipe of spices and flavorings to accurately simulate the meat you were trying to imitate. The greater challenge, however, was converting the substance into something with meatlike fiber and texture. In this way, the finished product would not only carry a meatlike flavor, but would actually taste like the real McCoy when consumed.

After pondering the problem for a while, I had a brainstorm. I needed to make artificial fiber. "Well, what else has artificial fiber?" I asked myself. "Fabric, of course!" I rushed to the library to educate myself on the manufacture of nylon, rayon, and other man-made clothing materials. While there, I learned that most such materials were fabricated using something called a spinneret. A spinneret is an extrusion die containing very tiny holes. As the raw material was forced through, it would be fashioned into fine threads. The die head would rotate at a fixed speed and in so doing, twisted the strands into a strong fiber thread that could then be woven into stockings and other clothing items. I decided to apply this same technology to the soy molasses paste as soon as I could lay my hands on a spinneret.

I set up the prototype using an unmodified spinneret obtained from a nylon production plant. Before entering the spinning die head, however, the soy paste had to be immersed into a soaking chemical bath to rid it of all impurities. The prototype proved to be 100 percent successful. The soy paste was fashioned into fibrous, taste-free, rope-like strands, about one half inch in diameter, ready for the addition of flavorings and further processing.

Next, the soybean ropes were immersed in a flavoring bath composed of a liquid designed by the chemical engineers to impart a "bacon-y" flavor to the substance. The problem was that the ropes were not very absorbent and the flavoring failed to penetrate beyond the exterior. So I came up with an emulsifying device that sent the strands between the teeth of several gears thereby forcing the flavoring into the material evenly. The next step in the process was to mash the flavored strands into thin flat sheets that were then sliced into little cubes. Once dried, the little cubes resembled crumbled pieces of pork bacon. More importantly, they tasted like real bacon bits in terms of both flavor and texture. As an added bonus, the product was one hundred percent kosher *(NOTE: In 1966, I personally obtained a kosher certification, or hekshur, for Bac-O's from Rabbi Rosenberg of the Orthodox Union in New York, the nation's leading provider of Kashruth certification).* Today, Bac-O's are produced by the Betty Crocker division of General Mills and they are the number one salad-topping product in the world.

I was also instrumental in the production of a breakthrough new baking product, Wondra Flour. Back in the late 1950s, General Mills introduced a new approach to baking with the announcement that the sifting of their Gold Medal brand flour was no longer necessary. The sifting of flour dated back to an attempt to make the measurement of flour as consistent from recipe to recipe as possible in order to help ensure successful outcomes. Based upon their research, it was found that sifting was not required with Gold Medal and more consistent results could be achieved by dipping the measuring cup into the flour and leveling it off.

In 1963, I became part of the team that developed Gold Medal Wondra Instantized Flour. It was an all-purpose flour in a revolutionary new granular form. It was made by a process of agglomeration of small flour particles to make a more uniform instantized product. The process involved taking regular flour and forcing water bubbles through it. When the bubbles burst, the flour became wet and I was called upon to devise machinery that would dry out the product. There were no chemical additions in the processing and the baking characteristics of all-purpose flour were not changed. Wondra had the same nutritional food value as any other enriched flour and was made of a specially selected blend of wheat to make it suitable for all types of baking. Wondra was particularly useful for making lump-free sauces and gravies because it dispersed instantly and evenly in cold liquids. It poured freely and measured the same, cup after cup, because of its controlled uniformity. Wondra was also dust-free.

Mark Hasten

The General Mills Research Division operated its own machine shop where the equipment we designed was fabricated. I loved to spend time there because it took me back to my days as a machinist and even reminded me of my boyhood days at the sulfuric acid factory in Alga. Just as in Alga, we were required to fabricate much of the equipment we used everyday. Back then, it was because there was nothing else available, but now it was because of the proprietary nature of the equipment. We did enjoy the use of highly qualified manufacturing consultants at General Mills such as Don Craighead. Don was a manufacturer's representative for companies that provided machinery components. He sold me gear drives, servo-mechanisms, motors, chains, and other parts needed in the creation of new equipment. Don was highly knowledgeable and our families soon became good friends. I would rely heavily on Don's equipment and his considerable expertise as I embarked on my next project—perhaps the most challenging of my career at General Mills.

One day in mid-1965, I was routinely eating lunch with some of my colleagues at the company cafeteria in our new facilities in Golden Valley where General Mills had recently moved from the eastside of Minneapolis. The meal concluded with that day's dessert special: ice cream cones. We were discussing the company's recently announced intention of entering the snack food business that, at that time, was dominated by potato chips, corn chips, and some popcorn products. At that point, the company was focusing on corn-based products. We all agreed that the corn chip arena would be a difficult market for General Mills to enter without some sort of novel or unique product. Simply coming out with a new brand of "me-too" Fritos was not going to get us very far. I was listening to the conversation as I nearly finished eating my ice cream cone. For some reason—perhaps because of my fetish for cleanliness—I never ate the last pointed tip of the cone where my fingers came into contact with it. I would always discard the final inch of the cone instead of popping it into my mouth. Today, I fiddled with it in my fingers as the others spoke of their desire to come up with a totally original snack food item. On impulse, I tossed the ice cream cone tip onto the lunch table.

"There you are, my friend," I proclaimed, addressing the chief product engineer. "There's your new snack food. If you guys can design it, I'll make a machine that can produce it." This was said half-jokingly as I got up to return to work, but evidently the others decided to take my words seriously. Six days later, the product engineer walked into my office and laid six little corn-based mini-ice cream cones down across my desk. I was stunned and very impressed. They had taken my off-hand remark and turned it into a product that would, in very short order, revolutionize the snack food industry.

"These look great," I remarked. "I don't think there's anything like this on the market."

"It's all corn-based," said the product engineer. "Can you whip together a machine that would crank these babies out?"

"I think so, but I can't just start a project on my own. We've got to get the okay from the higher-ups."

"You said if we designed it, you'd build the machinery. Don't worry about project approval—just get started. I've already shown these prototypes around and marketing can't wait to get something produced and test marketed. Consider this your green light, Mark."

The product engineers told me they wanted a machine that could process between two and three thousand pounds of corn product per hour. I returned to my drawing board and immediately got to work trying to figure out how in the world to make a machine that would generate a ton and a half of miniature corn ice cream cones every hour around the clock. Me and my big mouth!

Fortunately, I had a very wise and supportive boss at the time. A brilliant Japanese-American engineer, Tak Tushiya was not only my supervisor but also my mentor, guide, and friend. In an effort to strengthen our relationship, I once invited Tak and his family to our home for dinner. At the time, we had three youngsters in the house, all under the age of ten. All through dinner, my kids could not take their eyes off of Tak and his family. I'm sure it was making our guests very uncomfortable. Finally, one of the boys spoke up. "Poppa," he said, "why do they look different? Aren't they Jewish?" It was obvious that my children had never encountered oriental people before and were naturally curious—just as Tak's kids would have been if we were in Japan and the situation had been reversed. Little Eddie's comment broke the ice, however, and we all had a good laugh and a delightful evening.

Tak was incredibly enthusiastic about the ice cream cone project and ordered me to work on nothing else until I had the necessary equipment designed. The challenge of devising the original equipment specs that would effectively and rapidly produce the product we were looking for consumed my waking thoughts day and night for the next several weeks. During dinner with my family, I would sketch machine components on the paper napkins. I was driven to come up with something that would do what no machine had ever done before. Finally, after some inspiration and a lot of perspiration, the manufacturing process became clear in my mind's eye.

I would design an entirely new cooking device—a sort of continuous autoclave that cooked the dough evenly using steam pressure. The challenge was figuring out how to get the dough in and out of the cooker without losing pressure and without having to ever shut it down. In order to solve the problem, I designed a huge circular chamber onto which were mounted two opposing rotary valves. The valves permitted the raw corn flour and other ingredients to be fed into the chamber from an overhead hopper. As the first flour-filled valve rotated, it continuously emptied its cargo into the autoclave steam cooker. After cooking, the second valve brought the dough out of the chamber the same way.

The machine produced tough lumps of cooked dough which would then be pressed out into 8-inch wide, paper-thin sheets using specially designed "calendar" rollers. The surface of these rollers was serrated and served to imprint grooves into one side of the dough sheets. This created what appeared to be a basket-weave pattern that was strictly cosmetic and was thought to make the snack more closely resemble the texture of an ice cream cone. The sheets would then be sliced into 1-inch wide strips by passing them through a series of blades mounted on another roller in a manner similar to the way paper was cut into sheets.

Now came the tricky part. The strips would next pass between two vertically mounted cutting wheels. Embedded on the edge of each wheel was a zigzag blade that would cut the dough strips into triangular shapes. The ingenious part of this arrangement was that there was no waste. When you cut a series of triangles from a strip that is exactly as wide as the height of the triangle, you are left with another series of triangles. In this way, every molecule was used with no dough left over.

In between the teeth of the two cutting wheels, I inserted a mandrel. A mandrel is a tapered shaft to which you attach the product you're working on during machine tooling or when using a lathe. In this case, the triangular piece of dough would come off the cutting wheel and adhere to the cone-shaped tip of the rotating mandrel. The rotation of the mandrel, opposite to the direction of the cutting wheels, would then cause the triangle to seal upon itself. Finally, the mandrel gave a quick thrust against a spinning brush that would knock the newly formed cone down onto a waiting assembly belt. The belt delivered the mini-cones into a drying and seasoning chamber after which they were ready for deep-frying, further seasoning, and packaging.

It was an amazing process that required clockwork precision and great durability. The machine, after it was built, had a sort of pulsating rhythm all its own. Visitors, as well as General Mills executives, became mesmerized watching the elegant machinery churning out the new little snack goodies.

Those little snacks, dubbed Bugles by the boys in marketing, would soon make an enormous impact on the entire food industry *(I thought they looked more like little ram's horns than bugles, but I guess the name "Shofars" was not considered suitable)*. Bugles were introduced nationally, along with two other similarly produced products, Whistles and Daisys, in 1966 and became an immediate success creating a whole new category of puffed, shaped snacks. Each of the three products had a different shape, texture, and color—and, of course, required a different piece of production machinery.

Before launching these products, General Mills had conducted extensive market testing in six test cities. When the test was concluded, and the products withdrawn from stores, retailers faced a storm of protest from consumers who wished to continue munching on the tasty snacks. Their three dimensional shape made this new snack food ideal for dipping into cream cheese dips and the like. In response, General Mills was finally forced to run full-page newspaper ads in all the test cities apologizing to customers for the fact that they had not properly gauged the overwhelming demand for these new products and had not produced enough of them. The ads promised that Bugles, Whistles, and Daisys would be back on store shelves very soon. The ads were a marketing breakthrough generating national news coverage to the tune of "General Mills Apologizes For Not Making Enough Bugles." When the products finally went out nationally, they were an instant phenomenon. Whistles and Daisys were eventually dropped some years later, but Bugles remain today as one of America's most popular snack items.

Our next big challenge, inspired by the success of the Bugles trio, also resulted in a breakthrough product that has endured to the present day as the sole inhabitant of its own product category: the pre-formed potato chip known as Pringles. As mentioned, General Mills wanted to enter the highly lucrative potato chip market but was faced with some unique challenges in bringing such a product to a national audience. At the time, potato chips were mostly manufactured and distributed by local producers. The reason was perishability. Potato chips did not enjoy a very long shelf life—in a day or two, they would become rancid as the oil in which they were prepared would break down and become stale. Hence, most potato chips reached grocer's shelves through what are known as rack jobbers or independent route drivers who would pick up a truckload of freshly made chips at the factory every morning and then distribute the product to their customers while picking up yesterday's unsold inventory for credit. This procedure is common for all highly perishable grocery items such as milk, bread, eggs, doughnuts, etc.

General Mills, however, did not work that way. It sold boxcar and trailer loads full of product to large grocery wholesalers who then, in turn, re-sold their product to retailers. General Mills products, like those produced by Procter & Gamble and others, had to be rendered suitable for large-scale centralized distribution. For this type of distribution to work, you needed an item that would hold up and remain fresh during all of that shipping, warehousing, and handling. You also needed a product that was not sold on a guaranteed basis. Once the retailer bought a case of Wheaties, for example, he had to be allotted enough time to sell it before it became outdated and stale . . . because there was no way for the grocer to return a stale item for credit. No one had ever sold potato chips in this way before—as a standard grocery shelf item. To do so would require enormous innovation and a complete re-invention of the venerable potato chip itself.

Our starting point was a look at the existing potato chip production process. I headed a team of engineers that were sent to observe the production facilities of the Morton Potato Chip Company in Dallas, Texas. The Morton Company was founded by C.G. Morton and had recently been acquired by General Mills.

We learned all we could about standard potato chip creation and came away convinced that very little of what we saw could be used by us. Potato chips were being produced there as they always had been for years. A machine peeled and sliced the potatoes *(creating a great deal of waste)*, and the resulting thin slices were soaked in water and then dropped into a vat of boiling vegetable oil till they were cooked. The chips were then fished out of the oil using wire mesh baskets. The finished chips were salted and placed into a sealed paper bag that was inflated with air to cushion the product in transit. One problem with this method was the disappointment experienced by the consumer who would get the bag home, open it, releasing the air, and find only a half bag or less of actual chips. General Mills believed that consumers preferred buying packages filled to capacity with product and that they resented paying money for a bag filled mostly with air.

The two challenges we faced in creating a mass-produced potato chip were consistency and perishability. We learned that potatoes from different parts of the country had different molecular characteristics in terms of starch content, moisture content, trace minerals, etc. If we were going to produce a uniform chip, we needed a uniform potato. Even more formidable was the problem of storage. Potatoes defied standard storage methods. No matter how you stored them, you only had so long before they began to break down and lose their nutritional value. We needed a way to stockpile vast quantities of potatoes in the same way that we were able to store corn, wheat and other grains. We hit upon the idea of using reconstituted potatoes made from potato flour. If we could control the moisture and starch levels in the flour, we would be able to maintain a high level of product consistency. And of course, once the potatoes were converted to potato flour, they could be stored indefinitely under controlled conditions.

Our next stop took us to Idaho in the heart of the potato-growing industry. We met with a leading potato farmer and asked him to help us with an experimental food-processing program. If he would agree, our team would set up a facility on his property to convert his fresh potatoes to potato flour that we would then agree to purchase from him in bulk. The equipment consisted of a crusher and a heated rotary drum dryer that separated the potato starch from the potato's moisture content and produced a fine potato flour under controlled conditions. These conditions allowed the farmer to set the degree of moisture remaining in each batch of potato flour while it was being further dried as it awaited shipment back to our laboratory. With this set-up in place, we returned home and began ordering potato flour, specifying various degrees of moisture, for our experiments. Simply bringing the potatoes into our lab would have worked for our experimentation purposes but that would not have been possible for ongoing mass production. Through rigorous experimentation, we had licked the issue of how to get the potatoes from the field to our production facility while maintaining freshness. Our next objective was learning how to reconstitute those potatoes from their powdered flour state into a viable pre-fabricated potato chip.

Our research concluded that in order to produce uniformly identical potato chips, our first choice was to engage in extrusion of the reconstituted potato dough. This presented several key problems. First off, extrusion had never before been used in the production of potato chips. We were going to have to literally reinvent the wheel here. The reason for this is that in order to get a substance to go through an extruder's diehead, it must be pushed through under pressure—pressure that would invariably begin to break down the chemical structure of the potato. The machines we designed had to handle the potato dough very gently so as not to harm its fragile molecular structure. At the same time, the machinery had to move the product through the production cycle quickly and efficiently.

As our testing progressed we relied upon a team of food and chemical engineers who would analyze our output and provide us with ongoing feedback. Too much moisture. Too little moisture. Too much pressure. Too little heat. Knead the dough more gently so as not to break down the molecular structure . . . and so on. When we finally got the extrusion process down just right through laborious trial and error, we were ready to move on to the next phase. At this point, the production process was as follows: The potato flour, shipped in from Idaho, was reconstituted with water and formed into a potato dough that was kneaded and gently extruded into a long roll of about 2.5 inches in diameter. The roll was then run through a slicer that produced perfectly uniform round, flat discs that were then fried, seasoned and packaged into a bag.

The name for our new product was Chippos and, once approved, production commenced under the Betty Crocker banner providing sufficient product for several test market cities. The product was shipped in a cardboard box containing a sealed foil bag and came in various flavors such as barbecue and sour cream and onion. Interestingly, the artwork on the back of the Chippos box depicted, in comic strip format, the revolutionary production process used to create Chippos. A cartoon chef walked the consumer through the various production stages in order to clearly illustrate that the customer was not merely eating a lowly potato chip, but rather a modern, advanced technology snack food. TV commercials of the day, featuring a live Betty Crocker character leading housewives through her kitchen and explaining the wonders of Chippos, were used to flog the product in the selected test markets. All to no avail, I'm afraid.

The market tests failed for two important reasons. First, we were unsuccessful in sufficiently extending the product's effective shelf life. To avoid handling stale product, grocers were forced to pull Chippos off the shelf before they had adequate time to sell it. Secondly, and most importantly, consumers saw no benefit in consuming a mass-produced potato chip sold in a cereal box—no matter how many cute cartoons and TV commercials tried to convince them otherwise. The fact remained that Chippos did not taste any better than regular potato chips and were priced about the same. There simply was no compelling reason for potato chip eaters to switch their traditional snacking habits. Besides, a stamped out, mass-produced product did not have as high a degree of perceived freshness as did a standard potato chip. About the only thing Chippos did better than regular potato chips—thanks to their slightly thicker construction—was to not break as easily when used to scoop up party dip. The product was quietly withdrawn and was never released nationwide.

Meanwhile, back at the lab, we set to work in an effort aimed at overcoming the shelf life obstacle. We abandoned the extrusion system and went, instead, towards a punch-press type mechanism that would cut the chips out of a thin, leather-like sheet of potato dough. The sheets were formed by taking potato dough pellets and forcing them through a pair of huge calendar rolls. This process proved much less risky than the prior extrusion method. In this way, the potato maintained its molecular structure and the breakdown of the end product was delayed resulting in a longer shelf life.

We sought to save time by avoiding the creation of proprietary equipment to stamp out the chips. I located a company in Indiana, owned by Tom Lugar, brother of the future US Senator Richard Lugar, which made cookie-cutting equipment used by the baking industry. We tested their equipment using our potato dough and it just did not do the job in the way we needed it done. So, reluctantly, I set to work designing new chip stamping machinery that would give us the speed and quality control we required. When finished, it worked like a charm. Here's how.

Long sheets of thin potato dough would emerge one sheet at a time from between the calendar rolls onto a short belt. The speed of the belt could be modulated by a servo-motor that maintained the dough sheets at a constant surface tension. Mounted directly above the belt was a synchronized drum covered with cutting dies in the shape of 1 inch by 2 inch ovals. As the "cookie cutter" drum came in contact with the dough, each oval die cut out a single chip that would then adhere to the inside of the die. Getting these proto-chips to disengage from the diehead then became a problem. I devised a camshaft-driven plunger, situated inside each of dieheads, that would gently, and with a slight pop, nudge one piece of dough, and then the next, loose from each die head in clockwork syncopation. Each identically finished oval would then land back onto the belt and be transported further down the production line. The waste, or uncut leftover portion of each sheet, would be directed back into the storage bin where it was folded back into the incoming potato dough.

Once it was in full swing, the device was a true joy to behold. Watching the machine puffing, stamping, and popping out the ovals in perfect rhythm was a sublimely symphonic experience—guaranteed to warm the heart of any mechanical engineer. In addition to increasing the chip's shelf longevity, this cookie cutter method allowed us to produce a significantly thinner chip—something we viewed as a benefit.

Our next challenge was the frying process. In traditional potato chip manufacturing, sliced potatoes are dropped into a vat of boiling vegetable oil. By the end of the day, the oil would break down and need to be replaced with fresh oil for the following day's production cycle. This method would not work for General Mills's round-the-clock manufacturing system. We needed an oil that would evaporate as it broke down and could be replenished via a constant steady keep-fill stream. After much testing, we found the perfect cooking medium for our purposes to be cocoanut oil. Our engineers went to work calculating how much cocoanut oil we would require in order to process 30,000 pounds of potatoes daily. They soon realized that we would need to purchase the entire world's supply of cocoanut oil each week just to keep up with our projections. This problem led to some rather far-fetched proposed remedies, such as one suggestion that General Mills purchase a Hawaiian Island and plant millions of palm trees from which cocoanuts could be harvested and then converted to oil to be used for the production of potato chips. Another school of thought advocated getting rid of cocoanut oil altogether since it has an extremely high cholesterol content. The controversial issue soon became moot as General Mills management began to lose its taste for pre-fab potato chips.

As the chips came off of the assembly line and were dumped into the fryers, I noticed a rather strange phenomenon. Due to the tautness of the original potato dough sheet as it emerged from the rollers, each chip was stretched, like rubber, as it was cut into shape by the assembly of oval cookie-cutter dies. As the tautly stretched chip was fried, the hot oil caused the moisture in the chip to evaporate and, as a result, the elasticity was uniformly relaxed. Because of this unplanned production feature, I observed that each chip came out of the fryer uniformly deformed into the now familiar Pringles parabolic shape—something resembling the brim of a ten-gallon cowboy hat.

I was pondering the implications and value of this interesting and unintended production artifact when we received word that General Mills had sold the entire processed potato chip product line to Procter & Gamble. General Mills evidently felt that with all the controversy concerning the proper cooking oil, we were headed towards another Chippos debacle. In fact, General Mills lost its taste for potato chips altogether and got completely out of the business. P&G, at the same time, was seeking to diversify its product mix away from its traditional consumer laundry detergent products and viewed a long shelf-life potato chip as a golden opportunity to open up a new market category. How right they were.

The first thing P&G did was change the name from Chippos to Pringles. I don't know the derivation of the Pringles name, but it caught on and has today almost become a generic term entering the public domain along with Kleenex, Coke, and Scotch Tape in the pantheon of extremely successful brand name products. The Chippos name lives on in infamy as the favorite potato chip of TV's Homer Simpson.

P&G had used a variety of cooking oils over the years in the production of Pringles including corn, safflower, and vegetable oils. Today, mono-unsaturated sunflower oil is the medium of healthy choice. P&G also understood, perhaps more profoundly than did General Mills, the importance of extended shelf life and suitable packaging. They realized that, thanks to Pringles' uniquely uniform shape, the chips could be easily stacked. This bit of insight permitted Pringles to be packaged in what was called a tennis ball canister. The product's compact and innovative packaging permitted Pringles to perfectly mesh with the needs of modern centralized food distribution. A single canister of Pringles could deliver as many chips as two 8-ounce bags of standard potato chips, taking up one tenth of the shelf space— and without all the air. This efficiency paid off enormously as both grocers and consumers appreciated the space-saving convenience of stackable chips with their freshness preserved inside of an airtight can. The P&G product hit grocer's shelves in 1969 with an unprecedented advertising blitz and a six-month shelf life. The rest, as they say, is history. Pringles today are by far, the top-selling, potato-based retail food product in the world.

I have no regrets about my role in the Chippos/Pringles product development, but I firmly believe that had General Mills held on to the product a bit longer, I would have hit upon the wisdom of stacking and canning the chips. Unfortunately, the product development process got sidetracked and mired down in silly disputes over palm trees in Hawaii and lost sight of the big picture. We had invented a whole new way of making longer-lasting potato chips and we just needed a bit more time to work out the last of the kinks. I was disappointed that, after so much time and energy invested, it was another company that benefited from our innovation. But I guess that that's just the way the potato chip crumbles.

During my nine-year tenure at General Mills I applied for and was awarded numerous patents. Of course, under the terms of my employment contract, any rights protected by such patents became the property of General Mills. Hence, although my name appears on the patent documents for dozens of pieces of production equipment, I can enjoy no financial benefit from my food processing inventions since all rights belong to my former employer. Normally, we would only obtain patents on specific pieces of hardware. We would not attempt to patent any actual production processes. The one exception to this rule involved a sister potato-based product to Bugles known as Daisys. They were named Daisys because their shape, containing six petals, resembled the flower of the same name. Daisys were produced using the extrusion method, similar to Bugles, but the process was complicated by the need to colorize different portions of the snack. There were also consistency issues. Because of its shape, it was difficult for the blade to uniformly slice off individual pieces from the long rope of corn dough coming through the extruder. In order to improve consistency, I developed a moisturizing and drying set-up that permitted the snacks to be created at just the right moisture level to ensure optimal uniformity. This entire process was so complex, and so unique, that I was advised to have it patented, which I did. Several years after my departure from General Mills, my patented production process was put to rest as Daisys were withdrawn from the market due to poor sales.

One of my most unique inventions, thanks to my work under Tak Toshiya, was a vibratory conveyor based on what was dubbed a two-mass system. A two-mass system involved attaching a special flywheel—split along its diameter into two equal semi-circular halves—attached to an electric motor. When the two halves of the split flywheel were in standard balanced alignment, it behaved normally directing its energy outward like the flywheel in a typical automobile engine. But when the two halves were perfectly out of phase, the energy flow from the centrifigal force was reversed and directed inward where it was absorbed by the machines metal frame. By spring-mounting the two opposing flywheels onto the metal frame, I discovered that the resulting vibratory energy could be harnessed and its frequency controlled. The resulting controlled vibration was then used to move product along a metal pan or tube from point A to point B in an assembly line fashion without the need for conveyor belts or wheels of any kind. By controlling the vibratory energy produced by the split flywheel, grain was easily and economically moved along the line. To improve efficiency, I replaced portions of the flywheel with a denser metal such as lead. This additional mass allowed for the production of even more vibratory energy resulting in a more efficient system. In fact, the device was so balanced and so efficient that it could even be suspended from the ceiling without any unwanted vibration.

The original aluminum springs upon which the vibratory conveyor engine was mounted were later replaced by longer-lasting laminated fiber springs manufactured by 3M. Because of their higher elasticity coefficients, these fiber springs would last three times as long as the older aluminum ones. Vibratory conveyors permitted us to move product in new ways—along the ceiling, for example—ways that were impossible to achieve with standard belt-and-wheel conveyors. Today, this two-mass vibratory conveyor technology is widely used in the grain and feed industries as well as many other manufacturing and assembly environments.

Finally, one of the most unusual and most widely used products I ever developed came about, more or less, by accident. As part of General Mills' several ventures into uncharted territory, they decided to take a swing at the beverage industry. Someone came up with the bright idea of placing chocolate syrup into a common soda straw and sealing it at one end. The idea was for the consumer to break off the sealed end, insert the chocolate-filled straw into a glass of milk, swirl it around a bit and wind up with a glass of chocolate milk. I thought the idea was pretty lame, and subsequent consumer testing proved me correct. The novelty of the item soon wore off and consumers were left with a sticky mess and a clogged-up straw.

While the choco-straw idea soon met its well-deserved end, General Mills was not giving up on reinventing the soda straw. Someone came up with the idea of placing a straw inside of a bottle of soda pop as it went through the bottling process. The six-ounce soda bottles would be capped with a soda straw sealed inside of them. Consumers would then enjoy having a handy straw emerge from their soda bottles whenever they would pop one open. They would be spared the inconvenience of searching about for a straw and could get right to business of drinking it without delay. It was felt that this innovation would be welcomed by customers and would serve to stimulate product sales. General Mills was working with third-ranked soft drink bottler, 7-UP, on this project, and they were very interested in offering something new and unique to the public to coincide with their recently launched Uncola campaign and, as always, to further differentiate their product from Pepsi and Coke. But there was a slight problem.

The length of the straw could not exceed the length of the bottle. Hence, with the top of the straw protruding from the bottle in order to permit the consumer to place her lips around the end, the straw would not reach all the way to the bottom of the bottle. Standard drinking straws are normally a bit longer than the container they are intended to empty. In this case it was impossible to place an eight inch straw inside of a seven inch bottle. Faced with this monumental obstacle to their grand design of a world filled with soda-straw stuffed soft drink bottles, General Mills management called in the experts—they called on me and our research engineering team to address this crisis. We were charged with figuring out how to get the last two slurps out of the bottle.

Most drinking straws, we discovered, were made from waxed paper formed into a cylinder. This material was not suitable for what I had in mind. I searched about until I located a manufacturer of a plastic drinking straw. I believed that I could solve the problem by crimping a one-inch segment of the straw into an accordion shape thereby permitting the straw to be compressed and shortened enough to fit into the bottle. Ideally, the straw would decompress when the bottle would open, allowing the user to enjoy the beverage all the way to the very last drop. Even if the user had to give the straw a little tug to get it to extend, this plan seemed to make sense. The trick was how to place a section of accordion folds into the straw itself. I decided to play around with the idea one evening when I found myself alone in the research lab.

First, I took a one-inch thick piece of aluminum and drilled small hole through it roughly the same diameter as a drinking straw. I made sure that the tap I used left clear and distinct thread marks along the length of the hole. I next cut the aluminum block in half making sure the cut divided the freshly drilled hole exactly at its midpoint. Now, I had a mold. I placed both halves around a plastic drinking straw and applied heat slowly for about fifteen minutes and then popped out the straw and let it cool. Presto! There I had the world's first flexible plastic drinking straw. I was able to compress it so it fit perfectly into a six-ounce bottle of 7-UP, and it extended just right so as to allow me to slurp up the very last bit of the beverage from the bottom of the bottle with no problem. I felt like shouting Eureka! But instead I took my accordion straw home and showed it to Anna Ruth.

"That's very nice, Mark," she said. "How many people know about this?"

"Nobody. I made it myself after everyone left tonight," I responded. "I was going to pass it around tomorrow morning."

"I don't know, dear," she said. "This could be something really big. Are you sure you want to hand it over to General Mills and let them get rich from it?"

Mark My Words!

"I know what you're saying, but it's in my contract. Anything I come up with belongs to General Mills. That's the way research works. If I try to sell this to somebody else or to make it myself and they find out, they would fire me and then take me to court. I've got no choice, I'm afraid."

So, the next day I unveiled my latest brainchild—the accordion plastic soda straw—and the place went nuts. People were lined up ten deep to take a sip from a 7-UP bottle with the silly thing stuck in it. It had taken me at the most one hour to make the prototype and you would have thought I had come up with a cure for cancer. The process was so basic and the concept so simple and low-cost that it had eluded the other bright minds in my department. In the midst of all the celebratory enthusiasm, someone noticed something important. Not only did the accordion straw extend and contract, but once extended, it also became bendable. This was an added benefit I had not even considered. With a flexible plastic straw stuck inside a soft drink bottle, the drinker did not have to place his lips directly above the bottle's neck as he did with a standard straight straw. Also, bed-ridden users could easily consume their favorite beverage without having to sit up in bed thanks to my new flexible straw. And what about children seated at a soda fountain? Now they would not have to get upon their knees to reach the soda straw. They could remain seated and simply bend the straw down to meet their lips. The attractiveness of this simple little invention was expanding by the minute. I soon was envisioning a whole new industry popping up and imagined myself on the cover of Fortune Magazine under the banner: "Mark Hasten; Flex-Straw King." Inevitably, the bubble had to burst.

General Mills decided that they were not interested in partnering with 7-UP after all and abandoned their plans to enter the soft drink business. The company attempted to sell the pop-up flex straw concept to 7-UP but failed when it was discovered that keeping a plastic soda straw immersed in a soft drink bottle for an extended time period would affect the flavor of the product. The entire project was abandoned and the rights to my invention were eventually sold to Union Carbide Chemical who began manufacturing a line of consumer Flex-straws. The product was later sold to Procter & Gamble and was marketed under their GLAD trademark. The GLAD product line was recently sold to Clorox who carries on today as the world's leading producer of flexible drinking straws.

Years later, I learned that someone else, a Mr. Joseph Friedman *(no relation to Anna Ruth's step-father, Joe Friedman)*, came up with a paper flexible drinking straw back in 1937. While Friedman was awarded a patent for his invention, the product never caught on. I was completely unaware of Mr. Friedman's Flex-straw and had never before seen a bendable drinking straw at the time I developed my product. It appears that it was necessary to apply the bendable concept to a plastic, rather than a paper, straw before it would become widely adopted.

Not surprisingly, I was becoming increasingly frustrated watching others benefit from the fruits of my hard work and from my bright ideas. You might say that the previously described situation was the "last straw." General Mills, Union Carbide, P&G, and Clorox all made money from my little idea and, because of my status as a company employee, all that I received for my trouble was a citation, my name on a patent application, and the occasional bonus. I started thinking about other opportunities of ownership again. I started thinking about making a change and looking for new directions. The search led, at first, to Cincinnati, Ohio.

Cincinnati was home to Kenner Toys, makers of the Ouija Board and Play-doh, a company that General Mills had acquired as part of General Mills CEO Brewster Atwater's frenetic quest for product diversification. I had been asked in the past to conduct research for some of the toy products that Kenner produced. In particular, I recall working on one of their "educational" children's toys known as the SayIt-PlayIt. It was one of the first talking toys and required that a segment of audiotape be played whenever the child pressed certain buttons. The problem was figuring out how to rewind the tape once it was done playing. After studying the matter, I came up with a machine that produced a never-ending tape loop—a tape that would never require rewinding. By giving the tape a single half-twist and then splicing the end of the tape to the beginning, the machine turned the tape into a Möebius Strip. This arrangement would permit the tape to play on one side, followed by the reverse side and then go back to the first side continually. This technology was later sold by General Mills to RCA who copied it when designing the eight-track audio cassette.

During this period, I was commuting regularly between Minneapolis and Cincinnati. General Mills had loaned my services to Kenner where I was mostly involved in designing and developing equipment for the making of Play-doh. Play-doh is made solely from flour, an anti-spoilage agent, and a coloring solution. The product is so simple to produce it can easily be manufactured at home using a kitchen blender.

Indianapolis, where my brother Hart now lived, was directly along newly opened Interstate 74 that I used as I made my commute back and forth. I would frequently drop in to spend the night with him and his growing family. By this time, I had been transferred from the research lab into the development department. As Chief Design Engineer for Corporate Engineering, I was no longer responsible for personally designing needed manufacturing equipment, but rather for deploying it in order to effectively deliver General Mills products to the marketplace. This move was a step up for me, but even in this new capacity, with its higher pay rate and chance of advancement, I still felt as though I was being cut off from the fruits of my efforts. I recall sitting in Hart's kitchen talking about our futures. Hart had the itch, also. He recognized that there was only so far he could go at Bemis and, because of his strong ambition and powerful work ethic, he felt restricted in his current job. He expressed his feelings to me about striking out on his own.

"You know, Mark," he confided, "we're both making good money, but we're not making it for ourselves—we're making it for strangers. Thanks to your *seychel* (knowledge), General Mills is getting rich and thanks to my hard work, Bemis is making lots of money. I've been thinking about changing that."

"You're absolutely right, Hart," I agreed, "but what do you have in mind?" He proceeded to describe a small business that opened up near his home and how he had become friendly with Bill Wells, the owner—to the point of helping him solve many of his management problems. The business, a nursing home, was not doing too well and Hart felt that it would soon be for sale. He told me confidentially that he was thinking of making Mr. Wells an offer for the business.[4]

In 1965, Hart left Bemis and, with money raised from friends and family *(including $10,000 invested by me)*, he proceeded to purchase the first Colonial Crest Nursing Home from Bill Wells. He and Simona operated it successfully and soon had the facility filled to capacity. Meanwhile, I continued bouncing around the country on trouble-shooting missions for General Mills. Missions that included setting up a "guar" gum processing plant in Kennedy, Texas, for example. I was impressed with Hart's success as an independent businessman, and watching him build up his business helped to boost my confidence that perhaps I could also break off on my own and someday do the same.

By 1967, Hart's success with his single nursing home had overpowered his ability to manage it as a Mama-Papa operation. He was bursting at the seams with a mile-long waiting list and could not handle his growing business on his own any longer. In October, Hart came to Minneapolis for what turned out to be a watershed meeting in both of our lives.

Mark My Words!

"Mark, I want you to come back to Indianapolis with me," he stated right up front. "I want you to say good-bye to General Mills and become a partner in my business. I need you. I'm working seven days a week and I simply can't keep up with it alone." I recalled that Hart and I had spoken before, when he was still at Bemis, about joining forces and going into the printing business. But it all seemed very speculative and we never really pursued it seriously. This time things were different. I just listened as Hart continued to make his case.

"We've got to expand and I've put down an option on the place next door," he went on. "I've only got room for 44 beds right now and I could put in 144 if I had the space for them. You are much more knowledgeable when it comes to real estate and construction than I am, Mark. I really need your help and I need it now." We discussed my leaving my secure job at General Mills and the difficulty involved in relocating our mother to a new city. Hart pulled out his business's financial statements and let me study them. If I was impressed with his accomplishments before then, I was now overwhelmed.

"This is a gold mine, Hart," I whispered in astonishment. I could see that after only two years in business he was earning three times my current salary at General Mills.

"This is nothing, Mark," he said passionately, "compared to what we could do together. If you say 'okay,' I'll turn over half the business to you free of charge. We'll be fifty-fifty partners. By building on the addition to the home, we can add 100 beds in less than six months. Our revenue will triple overnight, but our expenses will only go up incrementally. I guarantee, if you join me, within one year we'll both be making more than I'm making right now by myself." What he said made sense, and suddenly I got it. I understood the enormous opportunity that Hart had just laid out before me. I had to think this over very seriously.

I really was not bothered by the idea of giving up my job at General Mills. I knew that if things did not work out with Hart, as a trained professional engineer with a degree and nine years' experience, I could always find suitable work. If not back at General Mills, then at 3M or some other large corporation.

While some may wonder at my willingness to jump into a business that I knew absolutely nothing about—geriatric care—from an industry that could not have been more different, to me this change was never a big issue. I knew that I was capable of making money for General Mills and I had always believed that I could make even more money for myself if given half a chance. And here was a chance and a half!

I discussed all of this with Anna Ruth and she, naturally, pointed out all the risks, but in the end, she pledged her total support. I told Hart that if we were going to be business partners, it had to be all the way. That meant that we agree, as long as we remained partners, never to go in to any other business ventures on our own. He wholeheartedly agreed with this and we shook hands on it.

That handshake marked the beginning of a business relationship that has endured and flourished for over thirty-five years. A partnership that has taken us to success in the nursing home, real estate, cable TV, and banking businesses . . . plus a few more . . . on an incredible entrepreneurial odyssey. And the first place that odyssey took me was to America's heartland in Indianapolis, Indiana.

CHAPTER SEVENTEEN

My Indiana Home

I could not make the move to Indianapolis immediately. I owned property in Minneapolis that had to be disposed of. My children had to finish out their school years, and housing had to be secured in our new hometown for not only my family, but for my mother as well. We also faced a dilemma regarding Hebrew schooling for the two older boys, Michael and Eddie. Minneapolis had a wonderful Talmud-Torah, as I mentioned, but the Indianapolis Jewish community was much smaller and highly assimilated. It offered considerably fewer Jewish educational options. I began working in Indianapolis in 1967, but we decided not to move the family until 1968 after Edward finished elementary school and was ready to enter high school. With no serious Judaic education opportunities available in Indianapolis for high school age students, we investigated the option of sending Eddie to an out of town Yeshiva for his high school training. The two of us traveled to New York to visit the school and Eddie told me he really liked it. So we signed the enrollment papers on the spot. On the day that the rest of the family packed up and moved to Indianapolis, Eddie headed for New York. Michael attended public school in Indianapolis for the next two years, and when it came time for him to enroll in high school he announced that he was following his brother to New York. Monica also followed in her brothers' footsteps several years later.

It was this conspicuous lack of Jewish educational opportunities that prompted Hart and me to become involved in establishing a day school in Indianapolis.[5] While educational opportunities for our children were, for the time being quite limited in Indianapolis, business opportunities were anything but. The financial risks involved in our rapidly expanding business were one thing, but the more personal risks involved were quite another. To be honest, not only had Hart and I never worked together before, we barely knew each other. Except for short periods in Wloclawek, Ebelsberg, and Minneapolis, Hart and I had not even lived in the same town since I left Alga to join the Polish Army some twenty-five years earlier. I knew that family businesses often failed because the members could not manage to get along with one another and I knew of cases where business disputes would lead to family estrangements and worse. I certainly did not wish for such things to happen in our family. Fortunately, Hart was also mindful of these risks and shared my concerns. Together, we laid down some ground rules that we hoped would help us avoid the common pitfalls faced by many family-based businesses.

First of all, we would work only by consensus. This meant that as fifty-fifty partners, we both had to agree before we could take any sort of major action. Likewise, we both held veto power over any business decision. Of course this policy carries with it a certain risk that if we are unable to agree, we would wind up frozen and unable to act. I am pleased to say that we have never been faced with this sort of gridlock and, while it has not always been smooth sailing, we never permitted our differences to stand in the way of our business's forward progress.

Secondly, and in keeping with the terms I laid down at the outset, both of our financial statements were to be identical. Whatever I had, Hart also had and vice versa. Any debts we incurred would be in both of our names equally. Any property we acquired would be owned by the both of us equally. This policy of full equity made it impossible for any decision we made to either benefit or harm either of us more or less than the other. In other words, we took self-interest out of the equation. If I was in favor of something, Hart never had to wonder if I was advocating it in order to advance my own financial position at the expense of his. If I benefited from a venture, he benefited to the same degree. This policy helped and continues to help keep us focused on the big picture and only ask "Will this move be good for us?" as opposed to: "Will this move be good for me?"

Thirdly, everyone who worked for us had to understand that there was no Mark decision and there was no Hart decision. There was only a Hasten decision. Lines of authority had to be made clear and we did not want an employee who was unhappy with my decision to then run to Hart with an appeal for him to overrule it. If the buck stopped with Hart, I would never overrule him and he likewise would recognize my authority as final whenever I made a decision. We recognized that any other course would soon lead to chaos.

This is not to say that there was no friction between us. We disagreed mightily on all sorts of business matters from bookkeeping methods to computerization. But, we stuck to our guidelines and in so doing we always eventually managed to come to an agreement.

Our first task, once I began working with Hart, was to secure the funding for the adjoining property we had optioned for our expansion. Financing real estate deals was something I had some experience in and so it did not take long before I had met with Arthur Schuster and his son, Stan. The Schusters were in the hospital furniture business in St. Paul and I approached them because I felt they would have a good understanding of the potential profitability of our nursing home operation. In addition to soliciting their advice, I convinced them to sell us furniture on attractive terms through G.E. Financial Credit.

We were successful in negotiating a favorable construction loan from the Speedway Bank working with a Mr. Benjamin Johnson. When the time came for us to build our second 120-bed facility in Greenfield, Indiana, we went back to Mr. Johnson with another loan request—this time for $600,000. After looking at the proposed site *(directly next door to the local hospital),* he approved the loan and gave us a letter of intent. We proceeded to purchase the land and sign the construction contracts. Shortly after we broke ground, I received a call from Bud Hunt who said he wanted to see me right away. Bud Hunt was a loan officer at Speedway Bank and Benjamin Johnson's son-in-law. I invited him right over and we sat down in the nursing home's conference room.

"I'm sorry, Mark," Bud announced, "but we cannot proceed with the loan." I was shocked. I felt like someone had hit me in the stomach with a sledgehammer.

"What do you mean?!" I got out, after catching my breath. "We paid off the last loan on time, didn't we? Why are we a bad risk now?"

"It's got nothing to do with your credit rating. Your rating is perfect. But, our loan committee has reviewed the new note and made a policy decision that we do not wish to finance any more nursing homes. There have been too many business failures in this industry recently and we don't want to get burned."

"But, Bud," I said, "we have your letter of intent. We bought the land. We've signed the construction contracts. We broke ground last week. If we have to cancel this project it's going to cost us plenty. And if the word gets out that we couldn't obtain financing, our reputation will be kaput. We were relying on you to come through with the money."

"I'm sorry, Mark, but if you read the letter of intent you'll see that we reserve the right to cancel for any reason before the note is signed. If you feel differently, you should call your lawyer and take us to court, I guess."

"I guess you're right, Bud." And that's exactly what I did. This development was also a blow to my reputation as a real estate maven. Hart had brought me in primarily as a heavy hitter to secure the financing deals needed for the major business expansion he and I had envisioned. Now here I was, my second time at bat and I was on the verge of striking out with the bases loaded. I immediately contacted our attorney, Herbert Backer, and arranged to meet him at the Columbia Club for lunch the following day.

The Columbia Club is one of Indianapolis's most venerated historic sites. It is located on Monument Circle right in the heart of the downtown area. I explained my plight to Herb and he agreed, very matter-of-factly, to file the lawsuit against Speedway Bank. He expressed his reluctance to take the case before a judge and hoped that the matter could be settled out of court. Herb pointed out that our chances of success were limited based upon the exculpatory language in the bank's letter of intent, but if we could establish that verbal assurances were given to us by the bank in front of witnesses, we could try to make the case that the verbal approval superceded the written terms of the letter. We were discussing all of this as we left the club and began our walk around the Circle heading back to Herb's office. He greeted another one of his clients, Josh Fineberg, walking in the other direction. Herb made the introductions.

"Josh, I'd like you to meet Mark Hasten," he said and then addressed me. "Josh is a major player in the real estate business here, Mark. He's a good man to know." During our sidewalk conversation I recalled that Josh was the trustee for an apartment complex that was in receivership located next door to our first nursing home. We eventually wound up buying that property and it became the first holding of our property management company, Harcourt Management.

I explained to Josh that I had recently come from Minneapolis and he mentioned some people he knew in the Jewish community there. After this brief round of Jewish Geography, Josh mentioned that I looked troubled and asked me what was wrong. I proceeded to tell him that I was about to witness our dream of building a chain of modern nursing homes go down the drain because our bank had pulled the plug. He asked a few questions about the project and then said, "Don't worry about a thing, Mark. I think I know someone that will lend you the dough. Here's what you do." He pulled out a notebook and proceeded to dictate directions as he jotted them down for me.

"Go over to First Federal Savings Bank. Ask for a guy named Jim Life and tell him I sent you." I thanked Josh and did as he directed. Jim Life agreed to see me and asked me to bring in the drawings and the financial projections for the project. After a standard review that took a few weeks, Jim called and informed us that the $600,000 loan had been approved. We got the note signed right away and were able to complete the project on time and on budget.

The relationship that was established with First Federal that day endured for the next decade as they became our principal source for the funding that fueled our company's growth. Once the bank came to understand the profitability, stability, and growth potential of the nursing home business, First Federal and its energetic CEO, Bob McKinney, became our most devoted supporters. They were constantly prodding us into further expansion through acquisition and new construction. First Federal became our partners in growth and profited enormously from our success. At one point, our line of credit with their bank topped $33 million. Over the years, our growth helped to fuel theirs as they morphed from an S&L into First Indiana, a major state-chartered bank. At the time Hart and I sold our nursing home business in 1982, Bob McKinney confided in me that our deal, that included a substantial payoff to First Indiana plus a new note from the buyers at 13 percent interest, was the most profitable deal in the bank's history.

As for Speedway Bank, Benjamin Johnson and his son-in-law, Bud Hunt, eventually sold it to First American National Bank and Ben passed away shortly thereafter. I don't know if they ever came to regret their decision to pull the rug out from under us. All I can say is that they missed the boat on one very amazing and highly profitable ride.

The early days of our business were very hands on. Hart and Simona were in charge of the day-to-day operations of the nursing home and I was focused on designing and executing the new construction. One area where we both would get involved was quality patient care. We believed that the key to our success was the fact that we offered our patients something they would not receive at any competing facility; something called tender, loving care. Hart and I pounded this concept into the heads of our nursing staff as we continually strove to improve the quality of life for our patients. In the prevailing view of that era, nursing homes were basically "warehouses for the elderly." We did everything we could to change that image, from installing on-site beauty parlors to planning nightly social activities for our patients.

At first, supervising operations at a nursing home was a somewhat daunting task for me. After all, how could I, someone with no experience in this field, presume to tell an experienced RN how to do her job. I made up my mind that I would need to once again educate myself and the best resource for this task was right under my nose: my own staff. If I were willing to learn this business from my employees, I would be drawing from a vast experience pool. I even tried to come away from every job interview with a potential employee having learned something new about the industry. This method, along with religiously reading the trade publications, and keeping my eyes and ears open, soon had me up to speed and enabled me to serve as an effective leader.

I was also able to bring my background in industrial engineering into play in the nursing home business. I worked to pinpoint operational inefficiencies and eliminate them. For example, if a scullery worker had to walk all the way across the kitchen with a load of dirty dishes, why not build a pass-through window that would save him fifty steps per hour? I was always interested in devising strategies that would upgrade the quality of care offered at our home. One example: I instituted special containers insuring that every meal was delivered to the patient while it still was hot.

I recall that we had a kitchen chef who could never get along with his staff and would continually wind up firing them one after another. After he burned through a half dozen workers, we finally had enough and wound up letting the chef himself go. The new chef had only been on duty for a few days and had not yet had a chance to meet me face to face. I decided I wanted to see firsthand exactly what was causing the problems in our kitchen area and I also wanted to evaluate the job performance of our new chef. I showed up in the kitchen at 6 A.M. dressed as a normal kitchen worker.

"I'm supposed to help you," I said to the chef. "What would you like for me to do?" He gave me the once over and decided I would do.

"You see all those dishes over there?" he said, gesticulating towards the sink. I indicated that I did. "Those bastards didn't clean up last night. So you need to get busy and get all those dishes washed, dried, and put away. It shouldn't take you more than an hour. Now get to work."

I did just that—finishing the job in about fifteen minutes.

"There you go," I told the chef. "All done. What's next?" The chef was astonished. "Not bad. Next, we need to get all the toast buttered. Here's the toast. Here's the butter. Get going." I finished this job in record time as well. Per his instruction, I next got the egg orders put together and then the cereals. He inspected my work and found no flaws. I could see he was impressed.

"Boy, you're alright," he responded. "You're really fast. I'm going make sure I get to keep you right here with me from now on." He sent someone to summon the facility's administrator who arrived to the kitchen a few moments later. "Where did you find this new guy you sent me?" asked the chef. "The dude is really good and I want to know if I can keep him here with me permanently?"

The administrator could not believe his eyes or his ears. What was I, his boss, doing in the kitchen posing as a scullery worker? Didn't the chef know that I was one of the owners of the entire establishment? And most importantly, how did I wash all those dishes in such a short time?

"Do you know who this is?" asked the administrator, pointing towards me. "Meet Mr. Mark Hasten, one of the owners and our boss." The chef was confounded at first, but then a broad smile came across his face. "You know, " he said through a pained but pleasant grimace, "I thought something was fishy when I saw this guy's shoes. Definitely not government issue." We had a good laugh and both the chef and I came away with a strong sense of mutual respect for one another.

I used this same technique when we purchased a three-story vacant building and converted it into the newest nursing home facility in our chain. Up until this point, we had limited ourselves to one-story facilities. All aspects of our operation were based on having everything on one level. But the economic advantages of a multistory building were enormous. The key question we wanted answered was, "Will the kitchen function properly in a multistory facility?" I devised a floor plan for the kitchen that was based upon an efficient workflow. But to make sure it flowed properly, I had to be right there on site every day observing and tweaking to make sure everything operated smoothly. I'm happy to say the floor plan worked well, and as a result, we overcame our prejudice against multistory buildings and went on to reach new heights in the industry.

Eventually, we were able to employ this hands-on style in a larger context. As our operations grew and we began opening facilities around the state and the region, conducting onsite inspections by car became highly impractical. Hence, we invested in a helicopter that allowed us to make unannounced visits to any of our facilities. Each administrator understood that the owners could drop in suddenly from the heavens at any time for a full inspection tour . . . and they had better be ready if they wished to keep their jobs. We did not adhere to a set schedule and sometimes did not decide where we were heading until we were up in the air.

Operating a round-the-clock facility, such as nursing homes, requires that you come to terms with the fact that you're never off duty. We were never able to just lock the doors for the night and go home. At any given point in time, hundreds of geriatric patients had their welfare, and their very lives, entrusted into our hands. It was a rather intimidating responsibility. In order to better meet this duty, I kept a red telephone "hot line" next to my bed at all times. The phone was connected to a direct line into each of our nursing homes. It was to be used only for emergencies. I knew that if the red phone rang, day or night, it would be a senior staff person with an urgent problem.

One night, the red phone rang around 1 A.M. The manager of our largest Indianapolis home was calling to report that one of the demented patients had wandered off the premises. I immediately contacted our pilot and had him meet me at the chopper. We were in the air within fifteen minutes and began cruising the main drag near the home with our powerful searchlight scouring every shrub and cranny in search of our wayward patient.

When our sky search of the neighborhood turned up nothing, I again questioned the manager on duty.

"Are you sure he's not still in the building," I queried.

"We searched everywhere, sir," he replied. "In the bathrooms, the kitchen, the laundry . . . even up on the roof."

"What about the elevators?" I suggested. Silence.

Sure enough, our errant patient had managed to climb inside an elevator car and had fallen asleep on the floor. He was unharmed and was awakened and escorted back to his bed. I felt like giving the manager "the shaft" because of that elevator incident, but I actually commended him for calling me with the problem. He apologized profusely, but as I told him, "I'd rather have you call me unnecessarily one hundred times than to have you fail to call me one time for something important."

The helicopter turned into a real lifeline during the unprecedented blizzard that hit central Indiana during the winter of 1977-78. Most of the state was entirely shut down. Hart was in Israel at the time, and I was in Washington, D.C. and needed to return home to deal with the crisis. I was able to take commercial flights as far as Louisville where I had arranged for our chopper pilot to pick me up. As I approached Indianapolis, the only other vehicle I could observe moving was a military helicopter carrying the mayor of Indianapolis as he surveyed the snowbound city. I immediately established a crisis command post and worked around the clock distributing needed medication and food by helicopter to our patients. I feel certain that had we not had the use of the chopper during that crisis period, we would surely have lost some of our critical patients as the food and medication ran out.

I soon learned that the key to being effective in this business, or any other business, for that matter was "responsibility." The reason we succeeded was because neither Hart nor I were afraid to accept the required responsibility. Responsibility for the very lives of the patients entrusted to our care. Responsibility for the welfare of our workforce. Responsibility to our community and to ourselves to make sure that we exercised both ethical and, at the same time, profitable business practices. Accepting this sort of responsibility requires a willingness to do whatever is required, at any time, to make sure that you never let down those who are counting on you. It is also helpful if you have a little arrogance, a little chutzpah, and a lot of self-confidence in order to convince yourself that you're capable of handling such a critical and demanding responsibility.

Another key to our success was our insistence on hiring the most capable and knowledgeable people in our field to fill key positions. Neither Hart nor I had any sort of training in geriatric care. But we both were willing to spend what it took to attract the top people in this field into our employ. And we were never afraid to learn from them. I would observe how some business owners refused to hire anyone more knowledgeable than themselves for fear of being upstaged by one of their employees. They wrongly believed that in order for them to be in a leadership position they had to have all the answers and therefore surrounded themselves with only "yes-men" and ego-stroking sycophants. Business owners with this type of mindset would either remain in the minor leagues indefinitely or eventually suffer failure.

If I do enjoy any special skill, it is my ability to quickly assess a potential employee and place him or her into the proper spot. Give me fifteen minutes with a new hire, or a loan applicant, or a buyer or seller of real estate parcel and I am usually able to quickly determine the person's strengths and weaknesses.

When it came to employees, neither Hart nor I were ever intimidated by a candidate who knew more about the business than we did. We felt that as leaders, it was our job to structure proper incentives so as to motivate the person towards doing his or her best. And again, the key word is responsibility. While our operations were always highly centralized, we soon recognized that we could not be available for every day-to-day decision that had to be made at each of our facilities. This meant that we had to delegate many of them to others. Hart and I took responsibility for all operational matters personally in the beginning. But eventually, in order to achieve growth, we had to begin delegating these responsibilities to capable key people in our organization. Finally, we had to remain vigilant to insure that those who were charged with these responsibilities were carrying them out properly. That's why we would continually conduct performance reviews of all of our key staff members.

So with those three watchwords, Motivate, Delegate, and Evaluate, Hart and I succeeded in building up a smoothly structured and highly profitable organization over the ensuing ten years.

Another key to our success was our observance of an important rule: Don't Panic. We never fell apart or became hysterical in the face of any sort of business crisis. Calm, steady-as-she-goes management became our style, and this style has served us very well up through today. Whether it's a lender who decides to suddenly renege on a funding commitment or a key employee who turns in his resignation at the worst possible moment—both Hart and I strove to keep tempers in check and calmly talked over the problem and arrived at the best solution.

CHAPTER EIGHTEEN

Leading and Learning

As explained in the early chapters of this book, my own schooling was interrupted because of the war. I was in the fifth grade when the Russians rolled into our town and I was unable to resume my formal education until I was married with two children and enrolled at SMU. The values of our family, and of our people, place the highest priority on learning and education. My grandfather, my Zayde, was known as a highly respected Talmudist—more knowledgeable in the many areas of Jewish law than even the rabbis of our shtetl. Unlike some other religions, it is possible for a Jew to be both a Talmudic scholar and a businessman, and that exactly described my Zayde as well as his own father, Hertz Halpern, who was revered as a Chassid in addition to being a very successful lumber mill operator. My uncle Psachye, who owned the bicycle shop where I worked as a child and who was known as an accomplished photographer, was also highly educated, not only in Jewish law, but in civil law as well. Had it not been for the anti-Semitic sanctions of the day barring Jews from practicing law in Polish courtrooms, Psachye would have been a top-flight attorney. As it was, he served as a *metzenas*, or a para-legal, drafting documents for his clients, but always forced to find a gentile lawyer to provide the legally binding signatures and seals. The emphasis on education in the shtetl paid off for many Jews at a time when the illiteracy rate among the general population was over 80 percent. Jews, because of their ability to read and write—even if only in

Yiddish—enabled them to enter the United States as refugees under the provisions of US immigration laws.

Within our family, education was also a priority for women. I remember my mother telling stories of her childhood and how she would cross a river twice a day—hopping from stone to stone since there was no footbridge—in order to reach her rebbe's house for her daily Torah lesson. I recall how as pre-school children, my brother and I would be carried on the back of a behelfer who would pick us up at our door and carry us to the home of the rebbe for our aleph-bet sessions. In this way, we were already able to read and write by the time we were enrolled in school. Education was a fundamental cornerstone of our culture. The love of learning was in our blood.

Learning the Hebrew of the Torah and the prayer books was part of every Jewish child's upbringing in our corner of the world. In addition, in our family, the children learned Ivrit b'Ivrit, Hebrew in Hebrew. This was conversational, rather than liturgical Hebrew. Similar to the difference between Shakespearean and modern-day English. Studying modern Hebrew was considered a progressive political act in our shtetl. If you taught your kids Ivrit b'Ivrit, it meant that you were a confirmed Zionist and that you were preparing your children for life in the future Jewish homeland in Palestine.

Of course, the war and its aftermath disrupted both my secular and Jewish schooling. Obviously, when you're concerned about your very survival, Jewish observance and study have to take a back seat. Once life began to get more stable and normalized and as I settled down and started a family, I once again felt the need to re-connect with my Jewish heritage. Initially, I was rather indifferent when it came to Jewish observance in our home. I told Anna Ruth after we first were married, "If you want to keep kosher, that's fine, and if you don't, that's also fine." My focus during those early years was earning a living for my family. Jewish observance was regarded as a nice luxury, if one could afford it, but at that point, we had more pressing business to attend to.

Anna Ruth, on the other hand, was much more involved with Judaism after having spent her teenage years under the tutelage of her adoptive grandparents, the Rabutniks. The Rabutniks, as well as the entire Roberts family, were pious Jews—keeping kosher, observing the Sabbath and all Jewish holidays. Anna Ruth had grown very close to her adoptive grandparents, and from this grew a deep appreciation for the Jewish way of life.

During the first year of our marriage, living in the dusty outskirts of Dallas without so much as a Jewish calendar, we were both dismayed to discover that we had overlooked the observation of the holiest day of the Jewish year, Yom Kippur, the Day of Atonement. This lapse turned into a real wake-up call for both of us. It upset Anna Ruth so much that she put her foot down.

"From now, on we're going to be Jewish," she declared. "This is a *shanda* (disgrace) and it will never, ever happen in our family again." From that point on, our home was a kosher one, and we always kept a current Jewish *luach* (calendar) within easy reach. We immediately stopped buying non-kosher meats, and little by little, we moved towards having a completely kosher home.

Like many Jews before and since, we were pushed more closely towards our Judaism as the result of trouble in the land of Israel. In 1956, Israel was again attacked by her Arab neighbors, and this hostility caused Jews around the world to rally to the Zionist cause, Anna Ruth among them. Although she was kept very busy with our two toddler sons and remained somewhat isolated from the Jewish community—since I had not encouraged her to learn to drive—Anna Ruth prayed fervently for Israel's safety and welfare. I admired her for this and gave her my unequivocal support.

By the time we made the move back to Minneapolis in 1959, we had already made a strong turn back towards our Jewish heritage. I wanted to create the same major emphasis on Jewish learning that I had experienced during my upbringing back in Europe. As mentioned, both of our boys, Edward and Michael, were enrolled in an excellent Talmud-Torah afternoon school. In addition, Anna Ruth saw to it that Eddie studied with a private teacher who taught him how to properly chant from the Torah using the ancient notation system called *trop*.

Paying for this private Jewish education for our kids was, of course, a major burden. When we first moved back to Minneapolis we elected to live in an old, but quite clean, one-room apartment rather than purchase a home. This move made it possible for me to afford paying for the kids' tuition and tutoring fees.

I began attending Rabbi Ginzberg's synagogue regularly along with my parents. As we became more observant, Anna Ruth insisted that the kids keep the TV turned off on Saturdays in observance of the Sabbath. Although the children missed watching Howdy Doody, they soon understood the value of setting aside one day each week for quiet, rest, prayer, and study. After we moved to Golden Valley, the outlying suburban neighborhood, we would travel to my mother's house on Friday before sunset and spend the night. Doing so permitted us to walk to the nearby synagogue on Saturday morning and kept us from violating the Sabbath by riding in a car.

As our children became more educated about Judaism, our family discovered something that many others have learned: Judaism is hereditary—you pick it up from your kids! I made it a point to learn as much as I could about Jewish law and history so as not to appear ignorant when my children asked me questions about these subjects. I delighted in reconnecting with my Jewish upbringing. Thanks mainly to the influence of Anna Ruth, I actually believe that I became something of a "born-again" Jew.

My connection to Judaism continued to grow after our family relocated to Indiana in the late 1960s. It was during one of my many visits to Indianapolis during the year prior to our move that Hart referred me to the rabbi of the local Orthodox synagogue. I phoned Rabbi Nandor Fruchter, of Congregation B'nai Torah, and told him plainly, "Rabbi Fruchter. I'm a Jew who is moving his family to town, and I need a synagogue." He paused for a long time and then responded.

"Mr. Hasten, no one has ever told me before that they *need* a synagogue. Usually it's the other way around with me telling them that they need one. You have impressed me as a serious Jew and I'd like to meet with you at once."

Rabbi Fruchter proudly showed me around the newly constructed, modern *shul* situated in a pleasant suburban section of the city. It was nearly time for the Jewish High Holidays, so the rabbi suggested that I return during a special Yom Kippur appeal that was planned. I would be able to meet all of the synagogue's leadership and get to know many of the congregants. I did as he suggested and observed as a major gift of $70,000 was announced by local industrialist, Miklos Sperling, which would be used to pay off a note used in the construction of a new chapel that today is still known as the Sperling Memorial Chapel. I got a flavor of the place and decided that I would consider joining B'nai Torah. I decided to stop in for Sabbath services the following Saturday morning. I was dismayed to discover that the services were mostly attended by old-timers and being held in the chapel and not in the large sanctuary. The synagogue's leadership apparently did not wish to absorb the cost of heating and cooling a large hall and so decided to keep the main sanctuary shut off. In looking around the place further, I detected the musky odor of mildew. Despite the fact that the synagogue was housed in a relatively new building, the sanctuary smelled of decay. I approached Rabbi Fruchter after the service.

"Rabbi, I'd like to join your congregation, but things need to change and I'm the guy that can help you make those changes." I had his attention, and he nodded for me to go on.

"The first thing is you must open the main sanctuary," I insisted. "We pray on Shabbos in the big hall, even if we only have ten members present. Secondly, we put on a kiddush after the service. We bless the wine and the bread and offer some herring and fruit to the members after prayers." At this, the rabbi raised an eyebrow as if to ask who would pay for this extravagance.

"I'll pay for the next ten weeks myself," I told him. "Don't worry, by the tenth week, our membership will have gone up so that you can pay for the herring from the extra dues we're bringing in." Rabbi Fruchter liked my idea about the kiddush, but then pointed out another problem.

"You know, Mark, if we begin attracting families for Shabbat services, we'll have a problem with the children. They make noise and make it hard for the members to conduct their prayers."

"Rabbi," I responded, "that noise is music to my ears. It tells me that Judaism is alive and has a future. Our services must attract young families who will teach their children the value of coming to the synagogue regularly. A bunch of old men sitting in a small room, closed off to the world . . . I'm sorry, but that's not my idea of Judaism."

Over the coming year, these and other innovations were implemented by the synagogue and the dividends began to pay off in increased membership. The shul was growing into its role as a community service facility as well as a house of learning and prayer. This growth, of course, placed new demands on the shul's clergy. B'nai Torah enjoyed the services of a skilled cantor, Yitzhak Jade, who held a full-time job as a manufacturer's representative. Although the Board considered offering him a full-time position, it could not match his salary requirements. Nevertheless, as Rabbi Fruchter explained to me, he needed help to manage the affairs of the congregation. Although he had been a one-man-show for many years, he now believed that he needed the services of an assistant rabbi.

Nandor Fruchter was a German-Jewish immigrant who had escaped Europe shortly after Kristallnacht in 1938. Working at first as a *shochet* (ritual slaughterer), he and his wife, Ruth, eventually wound up serving as the spiritual leaders of B'nai Torah and its antecedent congregation, for some twenty years. His proudest achievement was the construction of the new building on land donated by a non-Jewish real estate developer. The developer had donated the land to the synagogue in order to placate the membership and keep them from remonstrating against a neighboring apartment community that was being erected. In fact, the small street alongside the new building is still named Bauer Lane, in honor of the generous builder.

Fruchter was totally dedicated to *yiddishkeit* or Jewish culture. He was known to personally drive to the homes of his congregants and transport them to services if necessary. Fruchter was beloved by the synagogue's older generation. He eschewed spontaneity and believed that order and structure must prevail throughout his domain. This Germanic penchant for fastidious organization made him appear as severe and over-bearing—particularly to the younger members of community. I felt that if an assistant rabbi was to be hired, we should try to attract a fresh young face who would counter-balance Rabbi Fruchter's more established, old-world sensibilities.

By 1970, I had been offered and accepted the vice-presidency of the synagogue's board of directors, and I made it my business to conduct a nationwide search, in coordination with Rabbi Fruchter and the Board, for a new assistant rabbi. I eventually contacted the rabbinic seminary at Yeshiva University in New York and spoke with Rabbi Norman Lamm, its president. Over lunch, I explained our needs to Rabbi Lamm and asked if he knew of any graduating rabbis who might be well suited for the rigors of promoting Orthodox Judaism in the remote wilderness of Indiana. Rabbi Lamm said that he felt he had the perfect candidate—a brilliant young man from Atlanta named Ronald Gray. He was described as Modern Orthodox—meaning that while he strictly abided by Jewish law and tradition, he remained sensitive to the needs of the modern world. He was recently married, and the father of a six-month old child. After reviewing his résumé, I phoned him up.

"Rabbi Gray," I said after introducing myself, "how would you like to be a pioneer?" He seemed intrigued. I went on.

"You know, there's a whole country out there west of the Hudson River, and it's filled with Jews. Indianapolis is not New York, not Philadelphia, not New Jersey. It's the hinterlands . . . but we still have Jews and we need an Orthodox rabbi." He agreed to come have a look and I arranged a flight and drove to the airport to pick him up. Rabbi Gray impressed me tremendously right off the bat. He was friendly, gregarious, and very devout. In fact, although I wished for him to lead Shabbat services so our congregants could get a look at him, this proved impossible because of a microphone. Rabbi Fruchter had permitted the installation of a sound system in the main sanctuary that was typically used during services. In the opinion of Rabbi Gray, and others, this represented a violation of the Sabbath sanction against performing any sort of labor during the Sabbath. The action of the microphone, triggered by the human voice, which in turn led to the electrical signals leading to the amplifier and connected speakers, were viewed as breaking the prohibition against the use of any sort of electrical equipment. Thus, Rabbi Gray was introduced to the congregation after the Sabbath ended on Saturday night. The reaction was overwhelming and positive. Here was a tall, good-looking young man with a powerful speaking ability and a warm personality. The congregation fell in love with him at once. I was directed by the board to negotiate salary terms with Rabbi Gray and issue him a letter of engagement. I did so and we were easily able to come to terms on all matters except one. He would only take the job if the sound system were removed. This question came up during his final interview with the board who also asked him about his requirement that the *mechitza*, or barrier wall separating the male and female sections of the sanctuary be maintained and strengthened. When questioned about his unwillingness to compromise on these two points, Gray told the board:

"I have a very loud speaking voice, so we really don't need a microphone to make me any louder. And, more importantly, I plan to teach Torah during the service, and I will make the Torah so interesting and so fascinating that no one will strain to hear me and no one will even notice that they are not sitting next to their husband or wife."

Another board member wanted to know if Gray was in the habit of wearing a long gown during services as was sometimes customary. "Tell me, Rabbi Gray," she asked, "do you wear a robe?"

"Yes. Right after I take a shower," he shot back.

These answers charmed the board who viewed him as a refreshing counter-balance to the stern and serious Rabbi Fruchter. They agreed to Gray's terms and quickly offered him a contract.

During the early years of Rabbi Gray's tenure, the shul lost both of its spiritual leaders as both Cantor Jade and Rabbi Fruchter passed away. Within a very short period, Rabbi Gray, somewhat unexpectedly, became the congregation's main rabbi. Working together, we accomplished a great deal over the ensuing years as we strove to reconstitute what had once been a thriving congregation but had devolved into a private club for old-timers. Had Rabbi Gray not brought his enthusiastic brand of Jewish exuberance to our community, I am 100 percent certain that by now there would be no Orthodox synagogue in our community.

Gray understood the need to integrate our shul into the fabric of community life. He made quick friends with the other Conservative and Reform rabbis at the much larger congregations—even serving as their tennis and racquetball partner. In short order, Rabbi Gray's stature as a community leader was established, and his leadership succeeded in bringing a new vigor and vitality to B'nai Torah. I convinced the board to construct a new house on a lot adjoining the synagogue to serve as a parsonage for the rabbi and his growing family. During most of Rabbi Gray's fifteen and a half years of service to our synagogue, I served on the board and we developed a very close working relationship—and a strong personal friendship—that I cherish to this day.

Thanks to Gray's efforts, we were able to conduct a daily prayer gathering every morning and evening as proscribed by Jewish law. Perhaps his greatest accomplishment was helping to found our community's only Jewish day school, the Hasten Hebrew Academy.[5] During the twelfth year of his rabbinate, he was awarded a one-year Israeli sabbatical, which was our way of expressing the gratitude felt by the congregation for Rabbi Gray's dozen years of dedicated service. By the time Rabbi Gray departed Indianapolis to accept a position in New York with Boy's Town Jerusalem, the membership of B'nai Torah had quadrupled to over 200 families. This astounding growth was directly attributable to the efforts of this dynamic and dedicated clergyman.

As mentioned, my introduction to Rabbi Gray came about, thanks to my contact with Rabbi Lamm of Yeshiva University. Another noted Yeshiva University educator at the time was a Dr. Bernard Lander who would eventually leave Yeshiva and found an institution with which I have proudly been associated for many years: Touro College.

My involvement with Touro College came about, thanks to my daughter, Monica. She had learned about Touro in New York during her high school years as a member of NCSY. Once out of high school, she enrolled at Touro and became a standout student. One day in 1977, I received a phone call from Dr. Lander, the school's president and founder.

"Mr. Hasten, this is Bernard Lander. I'm in Indianapolis, and I'd like very much to meet you since Monica has told me so much about you."

"Fine," I said. "Come on over for dinner tonight." He accepted, and after dinner I explained to him how I was involved with Jewish day school education in Indianapolis.

"That's what I wanted to talk to you about, Mark," he said. "I want you to do me a favor. Please don't say yes or no, just agree to think about it. I want you to become a member of our board at Touro." He explained that the current chairman of the board was a man named Max Karl from Milwaukee. Evidently, Karl had heard some things about me and recommended to Lander that I be invited to sit on the board.

I promised Dr. Lander that I would think it over. He proceeded to educate me a bit about how Touro College got started. At one time, Dr. Lander, a former rabbi and professor of sociology at Notre Dame University, served as the vice president of Yeshiva University in New York. When an opening arose for the president's post, Lander was disappointed that a Dr. Lamm was selected to serve instead of him. Expressing his dissatisfaction with this choice in the most dramatic way, Lander resigned from the university, and in 1971, launched his own competing school. Touro began with only thirty-five liberal arts students and has grown steadily to its current enrollment of over 14,000. Dr. Lander, since founding the school, has served as New York City's first commissioner of human rights and is today a nationally acclaimed lecturer on Jewish studies.

While some might suspect that the motives behind Dr. Lander's invitation for me to serve on Touro's board may have had something to do with fund-raising, I knew this was not the case. He did not ask me for one dollar then or ever since. Any philanthropic support I have directed towards the school was done at my own initiative and never because Lander or anyone else solicited my support. Actually, Touro University, while qualifying as a charitable organization, generates enough money from its secular academic activities to underwrite the Jewish education components that operate at a loss. For example, the Touro medical school at Vallejo, California generates roughly three million dollars in profit a year, while the Touro College for Men, a religious seminary loses about the same amount. Lander has guided the school to success after success, until today, it conducts accredited higher study programs in law, medicine, business, and other disciplines at cam-puses throughout the United States and around the world Touro's real estate holding's are substantial and serve as th school's financial foundation.

Lander told me how he selected the name for the college. He decided to name the school after Judah and Isaac Touro in order to underscore the fact that this school was to embody the ideal of the Judeo-American experience. The Touro brothers were eighteenth century leaders of colonial America. Since they were inspired by the democratic ethos enunciated by George Washington at Newport, Rhode Island, when they visited Touro Synagogue in 1790, the Touro family provided major endowments for universities, the first free library on this continent, community health facilities in the United States, and pioneering settlements in Israel.

Lander explained that as a Touro College board member, I would be serving in some rather prestigious company. Besides Max Karl, the board included two United States Congressmen and New York Supreme Court Justice Fuchsberg, among others. After conferring with Anna Ruth, I decided to accept the invitation and I have served on the board ever since. We meet regularly in Manhattan, and over the years, I have seen the college undergo unbelievable growth. For example, I watched at the Flatbush College grew to enormous size in a very short time period. Touro operates, among others, a School of Health and Science, a School for Young Women in downtown Manhattan, a Law School with an enrollment of 2,000 students, and Touro University International, an online Internet School based out of California that offers a Master's Degree in Business Administration.

In 1995, I was honored to succeed Max Karl as Chairman of the board, and during the intervening years I am pleased to say that Touro College has continued to flourish and enjoy steady growth. As the result of a donation from our family to the school of a Manhattan real estate parcel located at Sixtieth and Tenth Avenue, Touro will be able to relocate their School for Young Women to this upscale area. The land was sold to a developer who will build 40,000 square feet of street–level, rent-free space for the new school, and then develop the upper floors for himself.

Despite his advanced age and despite the fact that he suffers from Macular Degeneration, a disease that has robbed him of much of his eyesight, Dr. Lander still oversees the day-to-day operations of Touro College today. I am extremely proud to be affiliated with such an exemplary organization as Touro, headed by a truly extraordinary Jewish leader like Dr. Bernard Lander.

Another outstanding Jewish leader it has been my honor to know is the Toshover rebbe. Our association goes back over fifty years to the days when I was a youngster growing up in the Ebelsberg DP Camp *(see chapter 5)*.

Next door to our unit in Ebelsberg lived a pious young man named Levi, a Hungarian survivor of the death camps. Levi and his sister were the only surviving members of his large orthodox family from the Hungarian shtetl known as Tosh. Levi himself was a pious Jew who clung to his deep religious convictions throughout the long night of the Shoah. He was descended from a Chassidic dynasty going back ten generations, and before long, he sought to pick up the mantle of rabbinic leadership that was his birthright. The Toshover Rebbe, as he became known, developed a cadre of *Chassidim* (students) who studied under him and were known, not surprisingly, as the Toshover Chassidim. I recall attending a Yom Kippur service held at Ebelsberg where the Toshover Rebbe was leading the prayer service. It was an unforgettable display of religious fervor. I watched as he shrieked, sweated and beat his breast with his fist and his head against the wall. What passion! What drama!

I recall vividly how my little brother and I helped the Toshover Rebbe build the first *sukkah (*booth) at Ebelsberg. Since we lived on the first floor of the high-rise, we were able to lay the branches across the roof of the Sukkah from our apartment window. The Toshover Rebbe spent all day and all night in the Sukkah in compliance with the biblical commandment.

The Toshover Rebbe developed a strong friendship with my father, who soon attained a leadership role in the camp hierarchy. It was Tatu that organized a memorial to the victims of the nearby Matthausen death camp, arranging to send a symbolic box of ashes to Palestine where it still rests today at Yad Vashem, the Jerusalem Holocaust memorial.

Years later, I heard that the Toshover Rebbe had immigrated to Montreal, where he had established a large thriving seminary. As recounted in chapter 10, I too found myself in Montreal in the early 1950s and in something of a predicament. I had just gotten married to Anna Ruth, and we were trying to determine if we should live in the United States. or remain in Canada. At this point, my entry visa application was pending before the US Immigration Service. Unfortunately, during my days as a bachelor in Montreal, I had garnered a few enemies. One such enemy, a former landlady, claimed that I had defaulted on a lease agreement after I got married and that I now owed her money for unpaid rent. She threatened to expose my crime to the US immigration authorities and thereby thwart my efforts at entering America. Anna Ruth and I discussed the problem, and since I did not have enough money at the time to satisfy the landlady, I really did not know where to turn. "Why don't you call up your old friend, the Toshover Rebbe?" suggested Anna Ruth. "He knows every Jew in Montreal. Maybe he can suggest something."

Both the rebbe and his wife remembered our family well from Ebelsberg and were anxious to help us with our problem.

Mark My Words!

Although the rebbe was only a few years older than me, I treated him with deference and respect as I handed his wife the little scrap of paper *(kvitel),* that described my reason for consulting with the rebbe. The rebbe, who now sported a long beard, sat surrounded by his children and sliced off pieces of black bread for each one as we spoke. I explained the details of the situation and made my case why I felt I had to move out when I did. The rebbe looked towards Anna Ruth and spoke, "You moved out so you could marry this beautiful Jewish girl. Am I right?"

"That's correct, Rebbe," I replied.

"And you plan to have children and raise a fine Jewish family in America?"

"With G-d's help," Anna Ruth replied.

"Then the landlady must understand that you left her house for a holy purpose and that such a purpose has a price above rubies," he stated. "*Gey. Gey avek* (off with you) to America. I will speak to the landlady and you'll not have any more problems, I promise you." We thanked the rebbe and his wife and bid them farewell. As we were walking away, Anna Ruth said, "You know, we really should get them something to show our appreciation, Mark." I agreed, but what could we get them? Since it was right before Passover, Anna Ruth suggested that we buy them a crate containing twelve dozen eggs and a fifty-pound bag of potatoes and have it delivered to their door. I thought it was a great idea and made the arrangements with the kosher grocer. Needless to say, I entered American soil without incident and I never heard from the disgruntled landlady again. But I did hear from the Toshover Rebbe again—many, many years later.

It was a summer evening in 1993 when Anna Ruth and I were sitting at home in Indianapolis and a knock came at the door. I looked out and saw a not altogether unfamiliar sight: two bearded gentlemen in black hats and long black coats standing on my doorstep. Since I was known to occasionally offer financial support for various Chassidic movements, such traveling *schnorrers* (fund-raisers) often beat a path to my door. I invited them in and offered them a cup of tea. I looked out towards the driveway and I saw no car or taxi.

"How did you get here?" I inquired.

"Don't worry about it," replied the senior fellow. "We're not here for money. I just wanted to meet you and bring you regards from the Toshover Rebbe in Montreal. He told me the whole story about the eggs and the potatoes and it brings a smile to his face even today." I was pleased to hear this, but I was still curious about their mode of transportation. Finally, I sneaked outside and went out to the street where I spotted their waiting stretch limousine parked behind some shrubbery. "Impoverished beggars," I thought to myself. "Riding with their hands out in private limousines. I can't believe it." The schnorrers got nothing more than a cup of tea from me that day, but I did ask them to relay my warm greetings to the rebbe when they called him from the backseat of their limo.

I learned that my visitors were father and son by the name of Neuman. The Neumans own a very successful clothing manufacturing concern in Montreal and were considered the chief financial supporters of the Toshover Rebbe. In fact, the Neumans were responsible for managing the growing religious seminary that the rebbe had founded.

A few years later, I finally accepted an invitation to visit the rebbe in Montreal. To date, I had not been solicited for any financial support and had given them nothing. The rebbe and the Neumans urged me to come visit the grounds of the massive theological seminary they had built outside of Montreal and that they had named Tosh. When my commercial flight was cancelled, the rebbe sent his private plane to pick me up at Indianapolis airport.

As the venerated rebbe, now in his eighties, showed me around the vast complex, which served as home and school for some 5,000 theological students, I could not help but be impressed with the scope of his operation. I was greeted with school children singing songs of greeting in Yiddish. I'll never forget their faces as I distributed the candy I brought for these angelic *kinder* (children).

The reaction I received from the assembled children and followers of this respected rebbe was exuberant beyond belief. Dancing, clapping, singing. The province of Quebec had given the Toshover Rebbe a vast parcel of land outside of Montreal upon which he was now expanding his operations. To think back and remember that this was the same man we had observed sleeping in the Sukkah at our doorstep made me marvel again at G-d's power. I became a supporter of the Toshover Rebbe and his work at that point and continued to extend what help I can to this extraordinary *tzadek* (righteous person).

A completely different affiliation came about through my long-standing association with the Masonic movement. In 1963, shortly after moving to Minneapolis, Anna Ruth's uncle, Nate Roberts, recommended me for membership in a local Masonic Lodge. I was accepted and "went through the chairs," a process by which I was familiarized with the rites and rituals of Freemasonry. I was impressed by the humanitarian and philanthropic purpose of the Masons and my admiration has grown steadily over the years.

After becoming a third degree Mason, I was invited, in May of 1966, to join the "Ancient and Accepted Scottish Rite of Freemasonry." The rituals of the Scottish Rite were established in France during the seventeenth and eighteenth centuries as Freemasons from Scotland sought refuge there. The name became associated with American Freemasonry in the early nineteenth century. While there is much Christian symbolism and mysticism woven through the Masonic order, it is not so surprising to find many observant Jews, such as me, among the ranks. In fact, the Masons trace their roots all the way back to the builders of King Solomon's Temple in ancient Jerusalem.

After attaining my standing as a thirty-second degree member of the Scottish Rite, I was now eligible to become a member of the Shriners. This worthwhile organization is devoted to putting on grand performances to benefit sick children throughout the world. The Shrine of North America, and its 500,000 members, currently operates a network of twenty-two children's hospitals that provide orthopedic and burn care for children under eighteen.

Today, although I enjoy an emeritus, or non-active, status with the Masons, I still endorse them and give them all the support I can. I strongly urge others, Jews or non-Jews, to do the same.

After I moved to Indianapolis in 1968, Hart and I both became members of Rotary International. We were recommended for membership by a business associate and well-known architect, George Barr. The Rotarians extend membership based upon a person's profession. I'm proud to say that Hart and I were the first representatives from the nursing home industry to join the local Rotary Club. We are both considered non-active these days, but we both strongly support the fine humanitarian social welfare activities of the Rotary.

Affiliations such as these, along with a growing interest in Jewish education, helped to shape the next unforeseen chapter of my career.

CHAPTER NINETEEN

The Other Side of the Desk

Running parallel to my involvement with Jewish education was the continuous acceleration of our business interests. Over the years, as Hart and I erected our nursing home enterprise, we had frequent occasion to sit down with bankers and other lenders in order to put together all types of financing deals. As the years wore on, I began to wonder more and more often what it must be like on the other side of the desk. Obviously, whenever you negotiate with someone, it's important to put yourself into their shoes to gain an understanding of their motives and objectives. But this was more than just a "know your enemy" sort of desire. I was a trained research scientist and it was due to my nature, as well as my training, that I enjoyed a very healthy natural curiosity . . . about everything. "What were these guys thinking about as they pored over our financial projections? What questions are running through their minds as they sit in judgment of us?" I wanted to know, as they say in Yiddish, *Fun Vannen Die Fees Vaxen* (from where their legs do grow).

I had some background as a research engineer in running cost analysis studies for a given piece of equipment. At General Mills, I often had to determine if the cost of designing, constructing, operating, and maintaining a particular piece of manufacturing equipment was justified by the anticipated revenue the machine was likely to generate. It seemed to me that this sort of cost analysis was not all that different from what bankers went through in analyzing business loans. I also had a real love and a respectable talent for real estate development. I was able to eval-

315

uate a given piece of real estate, be it commercial or residential, and accurately determine its profit potential and anticipated return on investment. I felt that these skills would serve me well if I ever decided to enter the banking business.

Hart and I put our heads together, and I pointed out that we would be in a much better situation if we had more control over our own financing. By this stage of the game, we knew exactly how much money we needed to raise per bed for any new nursing homes we wished to build. We also knew exactly how much money that bed could be expected to produce, assuming that it was kept full most of the time. Based upon cost and anticipated return, we were able to secure all the funding we needed as long as we could demonstrate that we had the know-how to maintain our occupancy levels and keep the beds filled with paying patients. And since we had long waiting lists at each one of our "Convalescent Care Centers," this never was a problem. There came a point where we could no longer continue to plow our nursing home profits back into the business. This forced us to seek out other places in which to invest our money. Not surprisingly, we turned to real estate.

We became involved in some rather exotic leveraged real estate deals in those days that permitted us to keep on steadily building our business without having to pump in any new money. While appealing on the surface, this practice was not without its downside. As I explained to Hart, the only way to reduce that downside is to sit on the other side of the desk. I felt that we should use our investment capital to break into the banking business. Hart agreed, and I started spreading the word among business brokers that we were interested in looking at any banks in the area that might be for sale.

Now it might seem that we were being presumptuous in assuming that since we were successful in operating a nursing home business, we could also be successful in running a bank. The fact is that Hart and I did enjoy a banking background. Our beloved Zayde was, among his many other roles, the investment banker for the Jewish community of our shtetl. Jews in those days could not open or manage a bank account and did not feel comfortable turning over their savings to a bunch of gentile strangers who might easily make off with them. There were no Jewish banks available, so individuals in our hometown who wished to safeguard their savings often turned them over to our Zayde. A common situation was a father saving up for his daughter's dowry. A father would come in to Zayde's store with one hundred Zlotys and say "Avraham Yechiel Mechel, I've got a little extra money here that I won't need till my daughter gets married. Could you hold it for me till then?" Zayde would accept the money and give the father a formal IOU, or *wexel*, on a little slip of parchment. He would make a record of the transaction on another piece of parchment for his own files that he folded up in a particular manner and then filed in an elaborate system of wooden drawers in his desk.

Zayde kept detailed records about each account he managed in his desk, and whenever anyone wanted his money withdrawn, Zayde made sure he got it back right away. He would aggregate the money he held and place it into banks and other secure investments in order to make it grow. Zayde would pass the earnings back to his "depositors" after deducting a small fee for his services. He also issued small loans to members of the community who he felt were deserving and likely to pay it back—never once charging the borrower any interest. He recognized that it was a violation of Jewish law for one Jew to charge interest to another. As he saw the gathering Nazi threat on the horizon, Zayde managed to put much of his people's holdings into what he hoped would be secure safekeeping. He transferred all the money he was holding into a Swiss bank account so as not to permit it to fall into the hands of the Nazis. After the war, he intended to retrieve the money and return it to the citizens of Brotchin who had entrusted him with it. Of course, Zayde did not survive the war and neither did most of the Jews whose money he stashed away in Switzerland. I have made numerous efforts to retrieve these funds over the years, but to date, I have been unsuccessful primarily because I do not know which specific bank was used, because I do not know the account numbers and because of the general reluctance of the Swiss banking industry to return money collected from Jews during the Holocaust. I also don't know how much money Zayde put away. I don't believe that if I were handed over the proceeds today, that I would be able to locate all the rightful heirs and return their portions to them. But I also don't believe that the money should sit in a Swiss bank account indefinitely. I would much prefer to see the money directed to a worthwhile cause benefiting Holocaust survivors and promoting awareness. I feel that Zayde would consider this a proper use of the money.

Zayde was able to operate his one-man banking operation for one reason only—he was considered to be a worldly and trustworthy individual by everyone in the community. He and his father, both, had been entrusted with the interests of the entire Jewish community in its dealings first with Emperor Franz Josef in Vienna and later with the Polish government in Warsaw. It was this quality of total trustworthiness that Hart and I understood we would need to develop in order to be successful in the banking business.

Over the years, we had developed strong relationships with several of our community's leading lenders. As discussed, our construction financing was most often arranged through First Federal, but our permanent financing was shopped around and the one bank that always expressed an interest in garnering our business was American Fletcher National Bank. Thanks to an unusual opportunity, they finally succeeded in getting us as customers, and at the same time, we succeeded in getting ourselves into the banking business.

Mark My Words!

In those days, Indiana banking regulations required that all banks operate under the "one bank, one holding company" rule. It was illegal to hold multiple banks under a single holding company. Despite this restriction, most banks had established holding companies in anticipation of the day when this rule would be done away with, and they would be free to begin acquiring other banks.

In order to get around the restriction, AFNB's president, Frank McKinney Sr., established a holding company made up of AFNB employees. While AFNB was not permitted to acquire any other banks, because of their supposed "arm's length" relationship, the new entity was free to do so. The holding company purchased a small bank in Kokomo, Indiana, about sixty miles due north of Indianapolis. The purchase, not too surprisingly, was financed through AFNB. This strategy worked for a while until the Federal Reserve looked into the practice and deemed it "phantom-like." The "phantom" holding company was ordered to divest itself of the bank, and this placed the First National Bank of Kokomo up for grabs. AFNB listed the bank with a business broker who made a connection with us.

Once Frank McKinney learned that we might be interested in the Kokomo bank, he jumped on the opportunity to bring us in to the AFNB family. While they never came out and said so, it was assumed that if we purchased the Kokomo bank, we would finance the deal through AFNB. And that's exactly what we wound up doing.

Now, it may seem strange that AFNB was willing to loan millions of dollars to two fellows who wanted to buy a bank, when the two knew absolutely nothing about operating one. Perhaps they were counting on us to fail. Since the note was secured by the assets of the bank, our failure would benefit AFNB very nicely. They would be forced to foreclose and wind up holding the assets of a bank they originally wished to own, but couldn't because of regulatory restrictions. It was a clever way of side-stepping the restrictions and all we had to do to oblige was go broke.

There's an old Yiddish expression: "The only animal that walks backwards is a goat." Well, we were not interested in walking backwards. We did not acquire First National of Kokomo just so we could give it up in six months. We had a very clear picture of what we wanted to do. We wanted to own an investment that had a limited downside and an unlimited upside. Although we were unfamiliar with the intricacies of the banking business, we had the necessary confidence to take on a challenge of this sort.

I recall telling Hart, "Operating a bank is like dealing in a commodity business. You buy and you sell. It so happens that what you're buying and selling is money. The only differences between the nursing home and the banking businesses are that, in the case of banking, the assets do not have to be fed and cared for, they don't die on you and on Friday afternoon at five o'clock you can close the door and go home for the weekend. Best of all, when you open the doors again on Monday morning, there will be somebody there who needs your product."

Of course, if all the people lined up at the front door of our bank on Monday morning were there to withdraw their money, we would have a real problem. I'll never forget the evening we closed the deal. We were having dinner with the bank's board of directors. One of the board members took me aside and whispered something that shook me up. He said that he feared once the word got out in Kokomo that two Jewish brothers from Indianapolis had bought the First National, there would be a run on the bank. He may have been overly alarmed, but his point was a good one.

I recognized that in order for us to succeed at operating our new acquisition and avoiding disaster, we had to impress and instill confidence into our employees, in our board of directors, in the business community of Kokomo as well as our individual bank customers. As I told Hart:

"You're good at communicating to the public, Hart. You built up our nursing home business by talking doctors into referring their elderly patients to our care. You can do the same thing when it comes to banking. You should get out there in the spotlight and do some serious public relations for our bank." Hart saw the importance of enhancing our image and agreed to take on this important assignment.

Our first stop was at the local newspaper, the Kokomo Tribune. We sat down and introduced ourselves to the editor and came right to the point.

"We want you to put an article in the paper announcing that the Hastens have bought First National bank," Hart told him.

"You guys are kidding, right?" said the editor. "I happen to be on the board of Union Bank, your major competitor. There's no way I'm going to publicize your bank."

As we were leaving I told Hart, "It's better he doesn't write anything about us because no publicity is better than bad publicity. This *mamser* (bastard) might have written something derogatory about us." It was clear that this fellow was typical in his belief that Hart and I were Jewish carpetbaggers and had no business running a business we knew nothing about in a community we were not a part of. We were going to have to work very hard in order to prove ourselves. What really got us through this difficult period was our unshakable confidence in our own management skills. We believed that if we were capable of constructing a successful management organization in the nursing home business, we could translate those skills to any business we chose. It was simply a matter of applying common sense techniques to a new set of challenges.

For example, shortly after taking control of First National, I was visiting our branches and introducing myself to each of our employees. I sat down at one fellow's desk and asked him what he did here at the bank.

"I'm the Ag Loan officer," he told me. "I review all the loan applications placed by farmers from around here."

"I see. You must know a good deal about the farm situation in this area," I commented.

"Yes, I sure do," he said. "In fact, I'm glad you stopped by, because I was wondering if you were interested in purchasing some farmland not far from here." This question threw me.

"What do you mean?" I inquired. "Is our bank in the business of selling farmland?"

"Oh no, of course not," came his reply. "In addition to working here at the bank, I'm also a real estate agent for farmland." This did not seem right to me and I went to take up the matter with the bank president.

"What's this fellow doing here?" I asked him. "He's not lending money, he's buying and selling farmland on our time and to our customers. I don't think he belongs here, and you need to get rid of him." The fellow was let go and replaced with someone who promoted the bank's agenda, and not his own, while on duty.

Despite a minor crisis when our bank president turned in his notice on the day after we closed the deal on the bank,[7] we soon started earning the respect and trust of our board, our employees, and our customers. There was no run on the bank, and in very short order, our public relations efforts and our community involvement started to bear fruit. With one exception, we kept the existing board of directors intact. Hart and I each had one vote, just like every other director, despite the fact that we were the majority stockholders. We insisted that Jack Fell, the prominent Kokomo attorney who sold us his controlling interest in the bank, stay on as chairman. Jack has served on the board continuously to this day. We selected a new president, Conrad Uitts, a bank employee who had worked his way up through the ranks and who served faithfully for over twenty-five years before retiring. He serves today as the Executive Chairman of the bank's board of directors.

Over time, Hart became very involved in the day-to-day operations of the bank, overseeing such areas as marketing, employee training, and customer relations. I was more attracted to the back office and enjoyed learning about the inner mechanics of loan approval, risk assessment, regulatory compliance, auditing procedures, computerization, and portfolio management. We both strove to institute efficiencies that would improve both our level of customer satisfaction and our bottom line. Before long, our efforts began to pay off and we started experiencing substantial growth. This growth had to be managed and required more space than we currently occupied. We began an expansion program that enlarged our main branch through acquisition of adjoining properties until we wound up occupying the entire city block in downtown Kokomo. Because of the rapid pace of this growth, the expansion was not managed as well as it should have been. After several years, I looked around and observed a slapped together hodge-podge—a Rube Goldberg contraption—and anything but an efficiently operating business environment. I spoke with Hart.

"Hart, enough is enough," I proclaimed. "We can't keep on patching here and pasting there whenever a need for more space arises. We've got to build ourselves a new building from scratch." It took some time, but we opened our new facility in 2000 and then donated the old bank building to the city for use as a community center. By this time, our main competitor, the Union Bank, whose owner, the local newspaper editor, had led the resistance to our acquisition of First National on the basis that we were out-of-town "carpetbaggers," had now changed hands three times—being sold each time to ever larger out-of-town concerns. We are now considered the community's "hometown" bank in the eyes of the Kokomo business community.

Our entry into the banking business has to be regarded as highly successful. So successful, in fact, that within one year, we were looking at a second bank to purchase. In November of 1976, we bought our second bank in Martinsville, Indiana from the same parties we had dealt with for Kokomo—Jack Fell and his partners. For the first seven years of our involvement in the banking business, we continued to operate Colonial Crest Convalescent Centers. While initially we got into banking as an investment vehicle, both Hart and I loved it so much that we kept getting more and more involved in operations, to the point that we went from being nursing home operators with an investment in banks to bankers with an investment in nursing homes. We experienced a true shift in fields between our background and foreground businesses. While the banking business eventually evolved into an exit strategy from the nursing home business, we did not get into it with this intention in mind. It was simply an attractive place for us to park the money we were generating in the nursing home business. But once we began to get involved, Hart and I both found it to be much more attractive and lucrative than nursing homes.

This situation led to our conscious decision in 1980 to put our nursing home business on the block. We wanted to cash out because we feared that anticipated government regulation and bureaucracy would place too great a burden on our operations. We were anxious to get away from the highly labor-intensive, round-the-clock management requirements of the nursing home business before we both became totally burned out. But our major motivation in selling was to allow us more time to devote to our real interest, the banking business.

Some questioned our decision to bail out of a highly successful nursing home business. Colonial Crest enjoyed a huge market share and was facing enormous growth opportunities throughout the Midwest and beyond. Our operational innovations had earned us the respect of the entire industry as well as the government agencies that regulated it. We had investigated taking the company public and had been advised that we could raise tens of millions in exchange for a small portion of our equity. And yet we chose to exit and take another, less stressful path. Why did we choose this course?

At some point in life, a man has to give himself what is called, in Hebrew, a *din v'cheshbon* (a full accounting). I sat down and engaged in some serious introspection in order to clarify to myself what is and what is not truly important in my life. I put together a personal balance sheet in order to identify my assets, my liabilities, and ultimately my bottom line. Not in financial terms, but in personal terms. I listed my family as my most valuable asset. I also viewed my Jewish identity as a cherished keepsake of enormous value. In terms of liabilities, the largest was the toll that the nursing home grind was taking on my time and my health. Putting it all on the scale, I could see that my bottom line, while still in the black, needed some serious improvement. I regarded our decision to get out of the nursing home business and devote our energies full-time to our banking and real estate interests as the most positive step I could take to enhance the value of my life. Today, I regard that decision to be one of the best ones I ever made. Do I feel any regret because we did not continue to build our business up to the next level? Do I ever wish that the Hastens had become the dominant force in the US nursing home industry and not others such as the Beverly Company? Yes, these thoughts do cross my mind from time to time, but I can honestly say that not one iota of remorse or regret exists in my heart over this road not taken. A heart, by the way, that has remained much healthier, thanks to the reduced stress brought about by our departure from the pressure-cooker world of geriatric care.

Ultimately, our bank holdings grew to include seven Indiana banks, each with its own governing board of directors. In 1995, as banking regulations in our area began to relax, we were permitted to consolidate all the banks under a single holding company, Hasten Bancshares. While the economies and efficiencies of this move have been great, I, nevertheless have some second thoughts about this move. Merging the state banks and the national banks under the rubric of First National has brought with it a new level of complexity as we attempt to fully integrate our operations. Secondly, our banks situated in the northern half of the state do not blend too smoothly with our southern banks.

It's mostly a clash of cultures and banking styles between rural and urban environments. Eventually, I see us moving away from a centralized management model and developing a strategy that allows for independent local control, while at the same time allowing each bank to benefit from the centralized back office resources. In this way, the economies brought on by consolidation will still be enjoyed *(i.e. computers, marketing, training, etc.),* while each bank's management team will enjoy local autonomy and the flexibility they need in order to be effective in the markets they serve.

In 1989, I was appointed by Governor Evan Bayh to serve as the chairman of the board for the Indiana Department of Financial Institutions—a post I held for the next nine years. My position was the state equivalent of the federal government's controller of the currency. I was responsible for setting and maintaining Indiana's monetary policy. The IDFI also serves as the main regulatory agency for all Indiana state-chartered banks. While it might seem odd that someone such as me, an owner of state-chartered banks, be appointed to head the watchdog agency that oversees compliance with state banking regulations, in actuality, state law requires that this post be held by an experienced banker. While the other six members of the IDFI board of directors could come from all walks of life, according to state regulations, the chairman was required to be drawn from the banking industry.

It was true that among the 250 state banks that we regularly reviewed, several of them were owned by Hart and me. How could I seriously be called upon to objectively examine the accounting practices, reserve levels, management practices, etc. of my own bank? Didn't this pose an obvious conflict of interest? Actually, no. I sat and listened to examination reports about my own banks just like I listened to reports from dozens of other banks throughout the state, and if they had been found in violation of any state regulations *(which they were not),* they would have received an MOU *(Memorandum of Understanding)* and been required to remedy the problem or face serious sanctions. And the fact that the bank happened to be owned by the chairman of the department would have made absolutely no difference. Whenever a routine examination report about one of our banks appeared on the agenda, I made it a point to erect a mental wall between my interests as a banker and my responsibilities as chairman. Because of my position, I had to be almost "holier than the Pope." I made sure all of our state banks dotted every *i* and crossed every *t* when it came to regulatory compliance. The last thing I wanted was to pick up a newspaper to read a headline that screamed, "IDFI Investigates Banking Irregularities at Bank Owned by Its Own Chairman!" After nine years of monthly meetings and after having reviewed the practices of hundreds of banks, mortgage companies, savings & loans, and the like, I felt that I had had enough and informed Governor O'Bannon that I would not be available for a renewal of my appointment due in 2000.

In 2002, Hasten Bancshares consummated the fourth largest Indiana business merger of the year when we acquired the Harrington Bank chain based out of Richmond, Indiana. Thanks to this acquisition, we are now among the top ten largest banking institutions operating in the state and the largest which enjoys full local ownership. At the risk of sounding like my message in the annual stockholder's report, I must say that despite the muddy economic environment we now find ourselves in and the persistence of all-time record low interest rates, our banks are all operating profitably and we are looking ahead to a period of continued strong performance and growth.

CHAPTER TWENTY

Politics and Priorities

As mentioned in the previous chapter, I was appointed to the chairmanship of the IDFI by Governor Evan Bayh and reappointed by his successor, Governor Frank O'Bannon. These appointments came about as a result of my years of support for the Democratic Party both in Indiana and nationally. My introduction to Democratic politics came about, thanks to Evan Bayh's father, Birch, during his run for re-election to the US Senate in 1968. I had agreed to host a fund-raiser in his behalf at my home and met both the senator and his late wife, Marvella, for the first time. They were both such disarming and engaging people, we soon became close friends. What most impressed me about Birch was his profound support for the State of Israel. He was deeply involved with the Israeli-American Friendship Society—a relationship that has endured to this day.

I have observed that typically American politicians have three basic reasons for supporting Israel. One is because they have a substantial and well-heeled Jewish constituency and they know that an outspoken defense for the State of Israel will earn the politician the respect and the financial support of this segment. Secondly, many Christian American politicians support Israel for religious reasons. They regard Jewish sovereignty in Jerusalem as the fulfillment of Biblical prophesy and a harbinger of the Second Coming. Finally, most American politicians support Israel for political, strategic, and ethical reasons. They correctly regard Israel as the only country in the region with true democratic institutions, a free economy, and a strong military.

Birch Bayh fell in to the first and third categories. He supported Israel because it was the morally right thing to do . . . but also because it earned him the support of people such as me and, more significantly, of a man who became Bayh's mentor and financial sponsor, a successful Hungarian immigrant industrialist, Miklos Sperling.

One evening in the spring of 1978, Birch and Marvella were dining at our home along with Hart and Simona. This was strictly a social visit. I wasn't asking for any favors and he wasn't doing any fund-raising. Just relaxing and making conversation. Birch asked if we were still in the nursing home business. I replied that we were and that we were pleased with his strong positions in support of Israel. Hart mentioned that we were friends of Menachem Begin's, the newly elected prime minister of Israel and that he was sure that Begin would be pleased to meet with such a strong Israeli advocate from the US Senate. Birch pointed out that he had never traveled to Israel but that he had always wanted to go. We said we would try to arrange for a meeting in December if Birch was willing. They pointed out that their son, Evan, was going to celebrate his twenty-first birthday in December and that a family trip to Israel would be a terrific way to mark the occasion.

Anna Ruth and I accompanied Birch, Marvella, and Evan on a whirlwind tour of Israel. We celebrated Evan's birthday at the King David Hotel in Jerusalem with a huge party attended by a host of Israeli VIPs. Marvella had recently finished her biography *(MARVELLA, A PERSONAL JOURNEY, 1977)* and was distributing copies to the dignitaries and Israeli politicians we met including Yigael Yadin and Misha Arens, the minister of defense. We visited the newly erected Holocaust memorial in Jerusalem, Yad Vashem, and I could see how moved the Bayhs were by this heart-wrenching presentation. When we visited the Knesset, Birch entered Menachem Begin's office and the two men exchanged shoulder hugs. Birch shook Begin's hand

and announced, "Mark Hasten has brought us over here mainly to meet you and to ask you one question—how can I help you?"

"Senator, I know you are great friend of Israel," said Begin in his typical gracious manner. "Come in, sit down, let's talk." I exited myself as the two men spoke behind closed doors. I'm not sure what was said, but on the very next day, Birch unexpectedly flew to Tangiers to meet with the king of Morocco on his own—not accompanied by his family. It was known that the king was one of the few moderate Arab leaders in the region who was not continually calling for the death of the State of Israel. I can't be sure, but I suspect that Senator Bayh may have been carrying a peace feeler that Begin was extending at that time in an effort to bring Egyptian president Sadat to the bargaining table.

Of course I had considered myself a disciple of Menachem Begin's since long before our paths crossed at Kfar Vitkin onboard the doomed Altalena in 1948. I first became aware of Menachem Begin years before when he served as the leader of the Betar Revisionist youth movement in Poland during 1930s. After the war, Begin migrated to Palestine with the Polish military after being interned by the Russians in a Siberian prison. He took over the reins of the Irgun from Yaakov Meridor in 1943. I again learned of his activities through David Speigel, the man who had recruited me into the Irgun back in Salzburg, Austria in 1946. Begin's words of Jewish liberation were distributed via leaflets and flyers throughout the DP camps of Europe during those last days before Israeli statehood. His message served to kindle the spirit of many young men and women like me who were anxious to create a new breed of Jew. A Jew who had endured generations of victimhood but would do so never again. A Jew who had not only emerged from the flames and ashes of the Holocaust, but had also evolved from a lamb of sacrifice into a lion of Judah. Begin's words gave that new Jew a voice—a passionate and a very powerful voice.

After the Altalena debacle and my loss of innocence on the homeless streets of Tel Aviv, I slowly surrendered my youthful idealism that had been stoked by Begin's rhetoric and Jabotinsky's heroic writings. By the time I made the decision to leave Israel in disgust, I had pretty much written off Menachem Begin and the whole Herut right-wing movement *(see chapter 9)*. Ben-Gurion was firmly entrenched, and although Begin had formed a small opposition party to the ruling Labor, or Mapai, Party, I felt their chances of ever coming to power were nil. With only six seats in the Israeli parliament, I concluded that Begin and his Herut followers would soon be forgotten forever and be regarded as nothing more than another lost cause and a footnote in Israeli history. Like many others, I had greatly underestimated the determination and tenacity of this man.

I did not meet Menachem Begin again until June 1973 during the summer months before the Yom Kippur war in Israel. I had come to Israel to attend a twenty-fifth anniversary reunion of the *Oleh* Altalena (*Altalena* immigrants). We were scheduled to meet for a reunion ceremony, but I had arrived a few days earlier in order to escort my mother on her first visit to Israel. She indicated that she wished to look up Dr. Josef Burg, who at that time was serving as the Israeli Minister of the Interior. Burg, who for many seemed to embody the religious Zionist ideal of serving as a bridge between the religious and secular worlds, claimed to have been born in Berlin, Germany. But my mother believed him to actually have been born next door to us in our hometown of Brotchin. She explained that Burg left Brotchin when he was one year old when his father, a leader of the Mizrahi Movement, moved to Germany before the first World War. Burg served for nearly forty years in the Knesset, a tenure during which he distinguished himself as a pragmatic, centrist politician known for his oratorical skills and sharp wit. In the 1930s, Burg was a leader of Youth Aliya and a member of the executive committee of the Palestine Office in Berlin. In November 1938, on

Mark My Words!

Kristallnacht, Burg's landlady saved him from arrest by the Gestapo, and he came to Palestine the following spring on a student visa. At the end of World War II, Burg returned to France and became director of the Paris-based Central European section of Mizrahi. Burg returned to Israel in 1949 as a leader of the National Religious Party, and was elected to the first Knesset. He served continuously until 1987 when, at almost eighty, he stepped down. Among the ministerial positions he held were Health, Posts, Social Affairs, Religion, Police and Interior. At the time of his death at age ninety in 1999, Burg was a revered elder statesman of Israeli politics and of Religious Zionism. He was the longest serving member of Knesset—from the first Knesset until the eleventh, a span of almost forty years.

I contacted Burg and he agreed to meet with me and with my mother. During our get–together, I told Burg about my background and my experiences aboard the Altalena. He suggested that I go see Menachem, who was at that time a member of the Knesset and the leader of the "loyal opposition" Herut party. Burg recommended that I contact Yechiel Kadishai, who I knew from the Altalena and who was now serving as Menachem's chief aide. Although I expected to see both Kadishai and Begin at the Altalena reunion, I anticipated that they would be featured speakers and I would not have an opportunity to speak with them privately. So I phoned Yechiel and explained who I was and that I very much wished to meet with Menachem. Yechiel did not remember me specifically after twenty-five long years, but he nevertheless said he would be happy to arrange for a meeting for the following day at the Metzudat Ze'ev or Herut Party Headquarters.

As soon as Mother and I arrived the next morning, Begin greeted us and asked us to join him for a cup of coffee. He inquired about my brother, Hart, who Menachem had gotten to know initially through his work in behalf of the Israel Bond organization. Hart and Menachem had hit it off and formed a very strong friendship that continued for the balance of Begin's life.[8] Begin was extremely courteous and exuded old-world charm as he spoke to my mother about life in Poland before the war. He and I chatted a bit about the Altalena and about the upcoming reunion. How could twenty-five years have flown by so quickly? We spoke about his current political situation and about the need to compensate the widows and orphans of the Irgun fighters who were killed during the war of independence and who received no pensions from the Labor government. He did not solicit me for any financial support at that meeting. That would come a few years later when Begin again ran for the prime ministership.

In 1976, I attended the bi-annual convention of the Orthodox Union in Washington, D.C. I was accompanied by Anna Ruth and our rabbi, Ronald Gray. The featured speaker on the program was Menachem Begin, and I was asked to introduce him to this audience made up entirely of Orthodox Jews. Once Begin arrived to the convention site, the famous Watergate Hotel, he phoned me and asked that I come to his room on my way to the dinner. When we arrived, he was shaving and cleaning up after his long plane trip from Israel. He offered us some orange juice and indicated that he was pleased that I would be introducing him that evening.

We chatted a bit as he finished getting dressed and then we walked out, along with his security officer, heading towards the main banquet hall. Just as we turned a corner into the main corridor, a smallish man jumped into our path holding a large portrait on canvas. I could see that it was a rather mediocre watercolor rendering of Begin.

"Excuse me, Minister Begin," said the man in perfect Hebrew, "I wanted you to have a look at this painting I created especially for you." I had seen this fellow before in the exhibit hall hawking his unexceptional Judaica water colors. Begin stared at the painting and finally said, "Very nice."

"I'm glad you like it. It is for sale, you know," proclaimed the artist.

"How much does it cost?" asked Begin.

"Ten dollars," came the reply. Begin searched his pockets and found only Israeli lirot. "I'm sorry," he said apologetically, "but I just got off the plane and I don't have any American money." He looked over to the security officer. "What about you? Do you have ten dollars?"

"I just got off the same plane you did, *Mar* Begin," he pointed out. I decided to step into the fray. I took out ten bucks and smashed it into the artist's hand, saying to the fellow, "Don't bother Mr. Begin right now. He has to go. Now here's ten dollars. Please get out of our way." I grabbed the masterpiece and later had it delivered to Begin's room. I suspected that Begin probably left it behind in the hotel room when he checked out.

At the dinner, I gave Begin a truly enthusiastic build-up and a stirring introduction ending with the words: " . . . and now ladies and gentlemen, it is my great pleasure to introduce to you the next prime minister of the State of Israel, Minister Menachem Begin." The crowd literally went wild. Cheering, whistling, screaming. I recall observing Rabbi Gray jumping up on top of the table to express his excitement and approval. After the crowd settled down, Begin gave a speech in English that illustrated why he enjoyed a reputation as a skilled orator. He spoke from the heart about the roots of Zionism and the yearning of the generations for redemption and renewal. His words touched the audience like no speaker before or since. I was seated next to Baron Edmond de Rothschild, who I could tell was very moved by Begin's words. Begin spoke for over two hours until well past midnight, but the crowd would not let him go. After concluding his remarks and attempting to sit down, the audience kept banging the tables and silverware until he relented to an encore, returning to the microphone for another hour to discuss the current state of Israeli politics.

After the dinner, close to 2 A.M., Begin and I were walkin
back to his hotel room and he stopped, looked at me, and sai
"Mark, you introduced me tonight as the next prime minister."

"Yes, sir. I believe that to be a true statement," I responded.

"Well then, you've got to help me make it happen. I want yo
to serve on my campaign cabinet." I was shocked because
knew his cabinet met in Israel. "Don't worry about th
distances," he advised. "Your job will be to raise money in th
United States and then we'll tell you where to send it." I agree
on the spot, and Begin said Yechiel would get back to me wit
the details.

About six months later, I flew to Israel to attend the first meet
ing of the campaign cabinet. The meeting was held in Tel Avi
on Rehov Rozenberg No.1, Menachem Begin's private apar
ment. I was greeted at the door by Begin's wife, Alla, wh
brought me in to meet the others. Of course, Yechiel Kadisha
was there as well as Yitzchak Shamir, Ezer Weitzman, Eli Ber
Elisar, and Chaim Ladau. Before I could sit down with the Heru
High Command to map out Menachem's upcoming campaig
strategy, I was first stopped by Alla who pulled a slip pf pape
from her purse.

"Mark, I've been carrying this note around until I had a chanc
to meet with you," she said.

"What is it?" I asked.

"It says here that we owe you ten dollars because you bought
painting for Mr. Begin the last time he was in Washington.
figure that's eighty Lirot, so here you are." She held out the cas
and I balked.

"I don't want to take it," I said.

"You must," she stated. "Menachem says it's yours and I mus
give it to you." I could see that she was serious about this, an
that I risked offending her if I did not agree to accept the money
I thanked her and placed the eighty Lirot in my pocket.

Once the strategy meeting got underway, it became quit
intense-lasting for over two days. We developed a whole cam-

paign structure and a series of specific fund-raising targets. I was assigned the task of identifying and soliciting wealthy Begin sympathizers in the United States. Unlike today, back then an American citizen could make unlimited donations to an Israeli politician. I approached many of my contacts from the OU who had cheered him so wildly at the conference. I called on my nursing home contacts. I called on everyone I could think of explaining why Israel needed Begin and why Begin needed their support. The campaign was a success, financially exceeding our targets in almost every sector.

The money we raised not only helped to reduce the party's outstanding debt accrued by providing financial support to the families of fallen Irgun fighters—families who received not an "agurah" from the Labor-led ruling party. The funds also served to finance Begin's successful bid for the prime ministership and his election ushered in a new chapter in Israeli politics. History has well recorded Begin's accomplishments in the macro-arena of world events. His monumental achievement of forging a peace agreement with the largest Arab state in the region earned him the Nobel Peace Prize and his well-deserved place in history. But, Begin's accomplishments in the micro-arena were not as well heralded, yet in many ways, even more significant. For example, he altered the Israeli policy concerning foreign bank accounts that had bedeviled Yitzhak and Leah Rabin. Israelis at that time were not permitted to leave the country without first obtaining permission from the government. Furthermore, they were unable to carry more than $100 with them when they left making it impossible to purchase anything when abroad without first establishing a secret foreign bank account. Hence, most Israelis of means who were able to travel extensively all had illegal foreign bank accounts in several countries. Begin eliminated this whole absurd system. Israeli citizens were free to travel out of the country unrestricted by visas and currency limits. Now anyone could own a bank account anywhere as long as they revealed it openly. As one Israeli pundit put it, "Overnight, we stopped being little *ganovim* (thieves)."

Begin instituted a series of economic reforms that succeeded in inching Israel away from its collective socialist roots towards a free market economy. It was a formidable task at which Begin met only limited success. Anyone familiar with the inner workings of the Israeli political/economic system understands that there exists a decades-old, highly entrenched, bureaucratic infrastructure that is by and large impenetrable regardless of the political orientation of the top leadership. Like an iceberg, the visible portion of the true Israeli power structure represents only a small portion of the total. The vast submerged and immovable block, existing as it does just below the surface, is too well insulated via its own vested interests and too dedicated to its own self-perpetuation to ever risk being melted down. I recall meeting with Begin's finance minister, Professor Yoram Aridor, a brilliant theorist and free market economist. He wept on my shoulder that he could not accomplish anything in terms of fiscal or monetary policy to curb the skyrocketing inflation rate because of the entrenched network of apparatchiks who didn't give a damn about anything other than when the next coffee break was scheduled. If he tried to remove non-productive workers from any sector, the country was immediately crippled by a vast strike. He opened my eyes to the fact that the most powerful man in Israel is not the president, not the prime minister, not the chief rabbi . . . but the head of the Histadrut (national labor union) who can wiggle his finger and shut down the entire country in a heartbeat. My own heart went out to this poor frustrated and tragic figure and I was beginning to understand the vice-grip in which the country was held by the left—a condition that was the result of forty years of Ben-Gurion-style socialism.

Any American attempting to conduct business in Israel quickly comes to understand who really holds the keys to the kingdom. I recall our futile efforts at acquiring and operating a ank in Israel. The *Histadrut* representative confided in me, "I ʌant to be your partner in this venture, Mr. Hasten."

"How can you be my partner when you're charged with looking out for the interests of my workforce?" I asked him. "You've ɔt to make up your mind. You either need to be a socialist or a apitalist. You can't be both. They don't go together."

What he really wanted was to collect regular weekly dues from ιy labor force while at the same time collect a share of the rofits from the management. I soon learned that the Histadrut tands firmly between labor and management with one hand in ach of their pockets.

I hope someday this would all change and Israel will join the ιodern world and abandon its vestigial socialist underpinnings. I ɛel it will happen eventually, but it will not be easy to shake the ountry loose from this long-term legacy.

My involvement with the Begin campaign in 1977 led to my ιngoing role with the Herut Zionist Organization of America, an dvocacy and fund-raising group devoted to promoting Israel's ιghtist agenda. I was fortunate to serve as the organization's ational president, succeeding my brother Hart's long and roductive tenure in that office.

My interests during recent years have not been restricted to usiness and politics. My penchant for innovation that was put to uch productive use during my years at General Mills has always ɛmained alive and well within me. As a result, I was awarded et another patent in 1999, but not for a piece of factory ιachinery this time. No, this patent was for a device that puts a ew twist on an ancient religious artifact.

As I became more involved with Judaism, primarily through ιy wife and children, I continued my learning about the customs nd rituals that constitute Jewish religious observance. One of ιe oldest and most widely observed customs is that of the ιezuzah which literally translates to "doorpost of a house." ⅞ore broadly, mezuzah refers to a scroll of parchment affixed to the doorpost of a Jewish home. This custom derives from a direct commandment in Deuteronomy *(Devarim)* 6:9 that states: "And these words that I command you this day . . . you shall write them on the doorposts of your house and on your gates." As retold in the Torah, Jews were commanded to identify their homes in ancient Egypt so that the angel carrying the tenth plague *(killing of the firstborn)* would "pass over" the homes whose doorposts were so marked.

Ever since, Jews have marked their doors by affixing a scrap of parchment to the entryway. Most mezuzot bear two biblical inscriptions from the Book of Deuteronomy *(6:4-9 and 11:13-21)*. For centuries, doorposts were made of stone, and the mezuzah scroll was inserted into a small indentation carved into the right side of the masonry. With the advent of wooden frame architecture, the custom evolved so that the mezuzah scroll was placed into a decorative vertical case, about four to six inches long. This case was then affixed to the upper third of the doorframe using glue, nails, or screws. Tradition dictates that the mezuzah lean inwards with the top of the case pointing the way in, towards the home. Most mezuzah cases also bear the Hebrew letter *Shin*, which stands for Shaddai, one of the Almighty's biblical names meaning "Creator of the Natural Law." Observant Jews typically affix Mezuzot to all the doorways in their homes *(with the exception of doorways to the bathroom)* and this was the custom we practiced at our home in Indianapolis. In 1997, we re-modeled our house and refinished many of the wall surfaces and doorways with a fine maple paneling. After re-attaching the first of nearly one dozen Mezuzot throughout the house, I discovered a problem. To be certain that the parchment had not deteriorated, I was advised to check the contents of each mezuzah case every year. This process involved unscrewing and then re-attaching all of the Mezuzot thereby causing serious damage to our beautiful wood paneling. There had to be a better way to both comply with the religious commandment and keep from destroying our newly installed woodwork. After pondering the matter for a few days, I sat down and made a rough sketch of new-style mezuzah that I thought might solve the problem.

The mezuzah I came up with consisted of two wooden components—although metal or plastic could also be used. The base piece was a flat rectangle that permanently affixed to the doorframe with two screws. This piece was designed to remain in place indefinitely. This base piece contained two groove tracks and a protruding stopper at the bottom. The second component was the actual housing for the scroll. The scroll could be rolled up and inserted into an opening located at the bottom of the housing. The housing contained a tongue-in-groove track along its back that dovetailed with the groove tracks on the first piece. Once the scroll had been placed inside the housing, the housing itself could be slid into place along the groove track until it was halted by the stopper. The stopper also served to seal the housing and protect the scroll from the elements. With one of these Hasten Mezuzot, I could easily remove the housing from its bracket, check the parchment, and put it back into place without having to disturb the woodwork.

I set to work to prepare the finished drawings and arranged for a prototype to be built. After building a few and testing them out, I wanted to make sure that they did not violate any Jewish laws. I solicited official opinions from rabbis and learned scholars from around the world and received a uniformly positive response. Anything that assists people in the performance of *mitzvoth* (biblical commandments), is by definition, a good and holy thing. I next showed the prototype to a patent attorney who conducted a search and discovered that nothing like this had been previously registered with the patent office. I felt that if this item became popular, I wanted to have control over its distribution. I did not wish to see it being merchandised for profit as a tourist souvenir item, for example. Hence, I instructed the attorney to proceed and apply for a patent that was granted by the US Government on May 16, 1999. I was later also granted a patent by the Israeli government. As far as I know, this is the only patented device in the world whose primary purpose is to facilitate compliance with instructions issued by the G-d of Israel to the Jews in Egypt some 3,200 years ago!

Since obtaining the patent, I have produced quantities of the Hasten Mezuzah and donated them to Jewish charitable organizations for use as fund-raising incentives. The local Jewish Federation, for example, awards a Hasten Mezuzah to every donor to its endowment fund. Recently, I was contacted by the Menachem Begin Heritage Foundation. They wish to obtain nearly two hundred Mezuzot for use at their soon-to-be-completed Begin Heritage Museum in Jerusalem. They also plan to sell the item at their gift shop. I'm hopeful that readers of this book will make the museum a stop on their next trip to Jerusalem and pick up a few Mezuzot when they do. The Hasten Mezuzah is styled in a beautiful contemporary motif and is sure to invite comments and compliments.

Hasten Mezuzot are now affixed to Jewish doorposts in the minuscule Jewish community in a place that once was called Stanislawow. This is due to an amazing journey that my brother and I recently undertook back to our hometown of Brotchin as recounted in the following chapter.

CHAPTER TWENTY-ONE

Return to Brotchin

In the summer of 2002, I was finally able to fulfill a dream that I had carried with me for over sixty years. My brother and I returned to our old hometown, Bohorodczany. Hart had visited there nine years before, but for me, this would be my first look at the town of my childhood since the night our family stole out of town just ahead of the Nazi onslaught. Our purpose in visiting the Ukraine was to dedicate a stone monument at the spot where most of the Jews of Brotchin were buried. The marker, or *matzeiva* would be unveiled on the sixtieth anniversary of the date we believe the killing occurred in a place then known as Stanislawow and now named Ivano-Frankovsk. Hart arrived from Israel and I came from London to our meeting spot in Warsaw where we made ready for our journey back to Brotchin.

After reaching the Ukraine, we traveled directly to Brotchin by van, not stopping in Ivano-Frankovsk. Once there, Hart and I got out and began walking from one end of the main street to the other. We passed the church and the town well, both landmarks from our youth that enabled us to precisely pinpoint the location of our former family home. The site today houses the community post office. I attempted to locate the old walnut tree in our backyard that I was always climbing as a child, but it was gone. We observed that our old public schoolhouse now served as a sports club. Next door stood a building that once housed the Jewish-owned apothecary. The people who then owned the shop were one of the few non-observant Jewish families in our town. None of them survived, including my friend whose father owned the establishment. I went searching, in vain, for the old sports and community center, or *sokol*, where I used to study the trumpet as a child. The skills I developed there enabled me to serve to this day as our synagogue's *Bal Tokaya* or "Blower of the Ram's Horn" during the high holy day services.

Looking at the large Ukrainian Orthodox *(formerly Catholic)* church, I remembered how it used to house a monastery between the wars, populated primarily by an order of gay monks. My grandfather would curse them as these "faigele friars" as they incessantly beat a path across our property in order to enjoy a shortcut into the churchyard. Driving huge hay wagons, they would roll across the back of our property in order to enter the churchyard from the back through a large arched gateway. This traffic resulted in a constant destruction of the brick retaining wall we used to separate their property from ours. Every time they knocked off a piece from the wall, we would be forced to repair it while Zayde filed a complaint with the monastary's leadership. He would beg them to drive a little further and use the front gate around the corner to avoid traveling across our property. But to no avail. After closing the back gate for a short while in response to my Zayde's complaints, in very short order, it would be reopened. The monks seemed to enjoy taking the back route across our yard simply to torment the old Jew. The problem went on for years on end. It got so bad that Zayde attempted to employ court action in order to restrain this constant stream of marauding monks. But a Jew trying to find justice in a civil court in those days was more or less a lost cause. Zayde decided to take this annoying problem up to a higher authority.

From the nearby community of Chortkow, near Bucacz, there came an illustrious rebbe known, not surprisingly, as the Chortkow Rebbe. The rebbe had moved to Vienna to carry out his studies, but he still had a large family and a contingent of *bochers* (students) back in Chortkow. Once a year, the Chorkow

Rebbe would return to his hometown for a visit and while there he would grant an audience to whoever wished to confer with him. Throughout the early 1930s, Zayde would make a pilgrimage to Chortkow to visit the rebbe whenever word came that he would be there. As was customary, Zayde would provide a small financial token to the rebbe along with a kvitel. This kvitel was a scrap of paper upon which the person coming before the rebbe would write down a request or a message for the rebbe to pass on high. It was believed that since the rebbe had a direct pipeline to the Almighty, passing a request on in this way was more expeditious than mere prayer. For several years, each time Zayde went before the rebbe, he handed him a kvitel with the same request: "Stop those monks from trespassing across my property and knocking down my wall." Typically, the rebbe read the note and then, after asking a question or two, would agree to work on the problem. Finally, after several years of this, the rebbe had become annoyed. His face turned into a frown as he again read my Zayde's message and looking up, he summoned him:

"Avraham Yechiel Mechel *(my Zayde's name)*," he announced in Yiddish. "Come up here." Once Zayde arrived at the front of the room, the rebbe looked directly at him and castigated him:

"Year after year you come in here and give me this same kvitel about the monks and your wall. Enough, already. It will be done when it's done. Meanwhile, I don't want to see this kvitel anymore—not ever again. Understand?" As he uttered the final word, he took the scrap of paper and tore it up and cast the pieces to the floor. Zayde returned home sadly and recounted the story to us. It appeared that he would never be able to remove this stone from his shoe. But then fate . . . or something like it . . . intervened.

A few weeks after my Zayde's disappointing visit to the rebbe, the monks once again were bringing a wagonload of hay into the churchyard and they again drove across our property, knocking into our brick fence on their way through the massive stone archway that led into the churchyard. The wagon was filled to overflowing, with hay piled as high as it would go and drooping off both sides of the straining wagon. One monk sat in the driver's seat and controlled the team of horses pulling the wagon. Another sat high atop of the haystack in order to keep it compressed with his body weight as the wagon moved along. Just as the wagon was making its way under the stone arch, the horses became spooked and started to buck and gallop. As they did, the topmost monk's body was forcefully smashed against the stone arch and the man was horribly decapitated. His body was torn to pieces just like my Zayde's kvitel that was destroyed by the rebbe. From that day on, the back gate was permanently closed off and all wagons entered the churchyard via the front gate—totally bypassing our property. Of course, among the superstitious Jews of our shtetl, this incident proved the mystical power of the Chortkow Rebbe.

Evidently, word of this matter traveled throughout the world. Many, many years later, I was contacted by the Chortkow Rebbe's followers in Israel who asked me to recount this story on tape. They felt that it was evidence of the miraculous power of their leader's *moffsim*, or miracles.

Perhaps it was more of the rebbe's otherworldly moffsim that I felt as we strolled the dreary streets of Brotchin in the late afternoon drizzle. We strolled by the building that once had held our community's *Mikveh*, or ritual bath. Today a large sign identified it as the *Banya* or public bathhouse. The block near the marketplace that once was home to all of the town's five synagogues, long since burned down, today houses the municipal police headquarters. The memory of the ornate and imposing *Groisse Shul* (big synagogue) standing next to the smaller *Stretner Shul*, where the town's Chassids would convene, began coming to life in my mind's eye. How this street was filled with life every Sabbath. Today—no sign, no marker, no mezuzah. Nothing to show that Jews danced, cried, laughed, and prayed on this street for over one thousand years. What crime did we commit to deserve such a punishment? To be wiped away without a trace as if we never even existed? Sometimes the cruelty of history is too much to bear.

Although I had been told that the old pre-war Jewish cemetery no longer existed, I still wanted to see the place for myself. I kept walking in the rain until I arrived at a signpost noting the distance to many of the nearby towns. "You've walked out of the town, you know," our guide informed me.

"I know," I replied, "but this should be where the Jewish cemetery used to be. Where my *Bubbe* (grandmother) is buried." I scanned the countryside, and finally, my eyes fell on the remains of an old iron fence.

"That's it!" I exclaimed. "I know that fence. That's the spot. That's where the cemetery was. I'm sure." Not a gravestone or marker of any sort identified what appeared to be nothing more than an empty pasture with a few houses nearby. I recognized one of the houses as the residence of the non-Jewish caretaker who used to maintain the cemetery grounds. Towards the front of the field, the government had erected some sort of gas conversion utility plant. Is it possible that the city fathers, when selecting the site for this gas factory, in a morbid twist of black humor thought it appropriate to locate it atop the abandoned Jewish cemetery as if to say: "Gas and dead Jews . . . they go together?"

Hart did not have an umbrella and by this point had returned to our van. Our guide huddled under my umbrella and asked if I wanted to see something. "Of course," I said, and he guided me towards the edge of the field towards a hollowed out tree stump.

"See this tree? Two hundred Jews are buried beside this tree, right here." He explained that during the German occupation of Brotchin in 1941 and before the one thousand surviving Jews were deported to Stanislawow in July 1942, this spot held a large communal grave. Bodies of Jews, killed through torture, starvation, shootings, and other privations were dumped here, often a dozen at a time. I feel certain that this must be the spot where my beloved Zayde's body was dumped after being publicly executed for bravely refusing to serve on the *Judenrat* (the German-mandated Jewish community council that was forced to administer the ghetto and organize the deportations to the camps in every community that fell under Nazi control.)[9] I said Kaddish for my grandfather and the others and slowly walked back to our van for the ride to Ivano-Frankovsk.

Once in Ivano-Frankovsk, we made our way to the site where the remainder of Brotchin's Jews were buried. They had been marched to a spot called Rudolf's Mill that the local Ukrainians had converted into a slaughterhouse for Jews. During the summer of 1942, hundreds of defenseless, innocent Jewish men, women, and children were marched into the building and attacked with whatever tools were available: knives, axes, pistols, hammers in a non-stop bacchanalia of blood. Their still-warm corpses were transported by wagon to one of the burial pits previously dug by other Jews where they were stripped of valuables and dumped to rot. Our monument, or matzeiva, marked the final resting place of these unfortunate Jews . . . many of them members of my extended family.

We conducted a simple dedication ceremony of the marker, noting that for exactly sixty years this spot has remained unmarked, and that from this day on passers-by and visitors will know of the martyrs who perished here. We had prepared lists of names of the victims and Hart and I took turns reading the lists until each one was read aloud. As Hart recited the names of the victims one by one, he paused, and looked up at me as he read the name of Berta Hammer. As he did so, a stab of memory shot swiftly through me. Berta Hammer was the town midwife. She was a strapping handsome woman who had delivered hundreds of babies, both Jewish and non-Jewish, safely into the hands of their mothers. It's quite likely that, in the end, she was sadistically murdered by one or more Ukrainians who she had personally brought into this world. Those vipers repaid her gift of life with a blow of death.

My earliest childhood memory involved Berta Hammer. I was a five-year-old boy, playing with my friends on a bright April day when Berta Hammer found me and told me I should go home because the stork had just left a package at our house. I ran home and saw my baby brother for the first time. Now, more than seventy years later, here he was reciting her name and honoring her memory.

Aside from this flash of feeling concerning Berta Hammer, I experienced no apparent emotional reaction whatsoever during the ceremony. I did not weep or become otherwise overcome in any way. I felt blasé, hollow—devoid of feeling—almost estranged from the situation. Had I run out of tears? Had I become so callous and indifferent? I was almost in a dreamlike state. Floating. Disconnected. Alienated from both the current reality, but moreover, alienated from the reality of 1942.

In looking back and trying to conduct some self-analysis about my feelings—or more correctly, lack of feelings—at that moment, I believe I now have a better understanding of what was going on. I see the hardening of my heart as a defense mechanism against the forces of hatred that had wiped out our people back then. I feel it also provided a defense against the current crop of Ukrainians who have seen fit to wipe their slate clean of Jews. "If you have no place in your heart or in your memories for my people, then I must not allow myself to weaken with sentimentality. If you can push the Jews into the dirt so deeply that no one will remember that we were here, then I will also scrape clean any vestige of affection I may have held for this place." Just as the boy was taken out of Brotchin so many years ago, so Brotchin was taken out of the boy somewhere along the line. I had made up my mind when I crossed the Atlantic to make a new home in North America, that I would torch all of my Old World memories until all that was left was a smoldering black hole. I felt as though I must be born again as an

American and become completely Americanized. I accomplished this metamorphosis and in the process said good-bye to any vestigial emotional ties I may have had to my past. While I made a conscious effort to burn away my old European persona, I never gave up my identity as a Jew.

During our visit to Ivano-Frankovsk, I discovered that ours was not the only monument marking the spot of destruction. Before the war, the family Rothenberg operated a lumber business in Bohorodczany. Their home was directly opposite the market square from us. We could look directly ahead from our front door and easily spot it. Unlike my grandfather, who was involved in the harvesting of trees for lumber, the large Rothenberg family dealt with the actual milling of the wood. I recall how one of the Rothenberg brothers had been killed in the 1930s by an anti-Semitic Petlurist bandit. Another brother, Avraham, survived the Holocaust by posing as a Christian monk. For over three years Avraham, or Brother Abe as he was called, roamed the countryside in a horse and wagon, disguised behind a scraggly hair-do and a long beard, and wearing a large, heavy crucifix around his neck. He sold needles, thread, buttons, and other sewing notions door-to-door.

I discovered that another sister from the Rothenberg family had survived the war. I learned this many years later as I was walking down the street in Montreal with my new bride, Anna Ruth. It was in the fall of 1952 when I thought a passerby looked very familiar. I stopped short in my tracks, deliberated for a moment, and then said to Anna Ruth, "My G-d. That's Ida. That's Ida Rothenberg from Brotchin!" I called after her and she turned to face me. A look of bewilderment melted into shock as my identity dawned upon her.

After a quick reunion, I learned that Ida had immigrated to Canada and had never married. Ida put me in touch with Avraham who was now living in the US. At this point, I was unable to enter the US, so Avraham and I communicated by mail and by phone. It was during a phone conversation that Avraham told me the following story about the fate of another of his siblings. This sister, whose married name was Friedlander, along with her two children, paid a Polish citizen to hide all three of them in his underground bunker during the German occupation. One of her children was a polio victim and partially disabled. The child was the same age as my brother, Hart, and I reminded Avraham how Hart had carried his young nephew to school every morning back in Brotchin using a little makeshift wagon. The threesome sat in hiding during the long, dark war years waiting for liberation. Amazingly, they were not discovered and they managed to emerge from hiding alive at war's end.

When liberation finally arrived, at the hands of the Red Army, the Pole—the erstwhile rescuer of the little family—fearing that the sister may inform the Soviets that she had given him a good deal of cash, brutally and tragically murdered her and the two children in order to ensure their silence. Avraham told me the tale of how he found their poor bodies and, with some difficulty and in secret, brought them to Stanislawow in order to bury them close to the common grave housing the rest of his family's remains. Burying them in Brotchin was out of the question since there was no proper burial spot any longer. All of the pre-war Jewish graves had been desecrated and the Jewish cemetery turned into a cow pasture.

When we visited the burial site in Ivano-Frankovsk *(the former Stanislawow),* I made a point of looking for Avraham's hand-made grave marker. With the help of Rabbi Kolesnik, who corroborated Avraham's account of the atrocity, I found the blacktopped matzeiva, which looked like it had probably been hurriedly created and put into place. It consisted of a large marble slab topped by a black softer stone into which I could make out the traces of three hand-chiseled names—although they were too worn to be legible. Together with my brother, Hart, I recited Kaddish for these three and thought "At least we know where your bodies are located. With the other victims, who were dumped here, we'll never know who is buried where."

Ida Rothenberg was not the only person I discovered alive in Montreal during those days. I recall visiting the local synagogue at Succoth and there, seated in one of the pews, was another survivor from Brotchin, Benjamin Reuben. Benjamin was an old family friend and neither of us knew if the other was dead or alive or that we both were living in Montreal as well. I informed Benjamin that Ida Rothenberg was alive and living in Montreal. He insisted we all get together for a Brotchin reunion. Like Jews all over the world during those bittersweet post-war years, we clung to each other and tried to weave together any life-threads we were able to pick up. We were delighted to find ourselves among the living, of course. But when we stopped to realize that most of us from that world were gone—our hearts grew leaden and filled with tears.

As we sat around Reuben's dinner table, we attempted to account for those who survived and those who did not.

"I always thought that if anybody would survive it would be Nathan Wasser, the baker's son, he was such a big guy. But he didn't make it."

"What about the other baker, Buzsi Koenigsberg? He made it, didn't he?"

"Yeah, he was always close to the shiksas in town. One of his shiksas probably saved him."

"What about the shuster's son, Naftali Gold? What happened to him? I heard he died in a Jeep accident in Italy after the war after having hidden in the woods and fighting with the partisans for years."

"Have you heard about that Israeli politician, Yosef Burg? Did you know that he was from Brotchin? Sure. Sam Hipschman told me the whole story. He was born there and his parents took him to Berlin when he was one year old. One of Burg's cousins, I think it was, was a big Communist and he was sent to Kartos Bereza prison in Poland before the war. Once the Russians took over, the fellow came back and started making a lot of noise, so the Russians sent him off to Siberia. Why did the Russians send fellow Communists to prison? Who knows? Maybe he was the wrong flavor. Maybe they only liked Stalinists and this guy was a Trotskyite. Go figure. Anyway, by putting him in a Russian prison camp, they saved his life since he avoided being killed by the Nazis."

"Did you know the Luster family? I think they made it. You remember them. They lived next to Lapis and his family. They were also in the lumber business. I met Luster when I was in Israel. He's alive. He's making ladies' dresses in Tel Aviv. He made it the same way as me, in the Russian army."

"Speaking of Lapis, did you know his two brothers were also in the Russian military. Yeah, poor boys were killed in combat in Eastern Prussia during the last days of the war."

"That's what happened to Schechter, too. And do you remember Professor Koppelman *(who changed his name to Stern)* and Chaim Bru? They're both alive and well in Israel."

"Do you remember the Reuben woman. She had one leg shorter than the other. Yeah, she survived. She left with us at the same time. We were in a wagon, but she and her husband were on foot. I remember the husband. He used to buy leather sheets from my father and fashion the tops of shoes with them. He would sell the tops to the town cobblers who stitched them onto the soles. They sat out the war in Russia, just like we did, and afterwards they made it to Israel."

"I remember you parents, Benjamin," I said to Reuben. "Your father, Naftali, was a Chassid and your mother wore the tichel and they sold apples by the bushel in the marketplace. Right?"

"That's right," he said. "Do you remember my brother?"

"Of course. Your brother, Chaim," I responded. "One of his sons, your nephew, was my best friend growing up."

"Does anyone remember David Schmertzler? He lives in Dayton, Ohio now. He says he's a relative of mine, but I don't claim him," I said. This brought out a laugh as we concluded our sail across this sea of memories.

By the end of the evening, we had pretty much listed every person from Brotchin who had survived the war. Maybe altogether, fifty people out of two and a half thousand were left alive. What was the common characteristic? Why did these fifty live and the others all die? In some cases, of course, it was luck. It may not have seemed lucky to Yosef Burg's cousin when he was shipped off to the Russian Gulag, but yet he managed to stay alive as a result. For others, like my father, it was a rational decision based on credible information coupled with his level-headed unwillingness to delude himself into thinking he could somehow manage under Nazi rule. Some, like Koenigsburg, went into hiding and survived. Others, like Friedlander and her two sons went into hiding and did not. I tend to believe that only G-d really knows the answer to the question of why some were destined to live while most were slated to die. I don't think I will ever fully understand it, but somehow being there, on the soil that had been drenched with the blood of so many of my people, I felt powerless and prideful at the same time. I was powerless to change the cruel fate of my family and friends and yet I was proud of the fact that we had not forgotten about them.

These memories from Reuben's kitchen flooded over me as I walked back to the grave marker we had erected. As I walked through the rain, I spotted a row of fruit trees—apple and pear— lush large trees that would soon produce ripe fruit. I stopped and stared as a memory washed over me along with the steady drizzle. In my mind's eye, I saw a group of boys and girls, no more than five or six years old. Sweet, angelic Jewish children following their teacher to the woods behind their school—a school that once stood where I now was standing so many decades later. The teacher is handing out seeds to the children. Some have apple seeds and some have pear seeds. Some, like me, have both. The little boy that is me, the little boy they call Munjee, wants to plant both seeds just to see what will happen. How many of those little children who planted the trees I saw that day lived long enough to see them bear fruit? None but me. The other little boys and little girls were turned to ashes years ago. Should I cry for them? Should I let my tears water the trees they planted so long ago? I cannot. I feel nothing. No sadness. No regret. Nothing. Nothing but a numbness that will surround my heart till I die.

I walked back to town as the rain subsided, got into the van, and drove away without looking back. I will not be returning to this place again. Not in this lifetime.

CONCLUSION

The stories I have catalogued in this volume may be viewed as just that and nothing more—a series of simple episodes, snapshots pasted into my album of experience. Or they may be viewed in a larger context, as one thread in the fabric of the Jewish experience of the twentieth century. It is this second view that I prefer—not out of arrogance or grandiosity. After all, there are many whose stories are more fascinating, heroic, and colorful than my own. Each of us cares to believe that our own life has meaning and it is this search for meaning that prompts some of us to record our life's key moments in a memoir such as this one. So we may fairly ask not "What is the meaning of life?" but rather, "What is the meaning of *this* life?" Or, more precisely, "How did this thread enrich the fabric into which it was woven?" I will leave it to others to answer these questions. However, I do feel the need to share some of my personal reflections about my family, my community, and the road ahead. These are the aspects of my life that provide it with the truest meaning.

First, like many Jews who emerged from the flames with their bodies intact but their spirits shattered, I feel a strong desire to do all I can to reconstitute what was lost in some way. Some may call it a Holocaust Mentality, but I have an overwhelming urge to resurrect the Hasten/Halpern families in some fashion. Ours was such a dynamic and diversely exceptional family before the war. I yearn to see that same lust for life and strong family cohesiveness preserved among Hart's and my children, grandchildren, and great-grandchildren. It was for this reason that Hart and I drafted a family mission statement in 1999 that sought to lay down some of the family values that we wished to pass on to our progeny.[10]

Linked to this urge is a profound appreciation for the democratic institutions and political liberties we are able to enjoy as citizens of the United States. Unfortunately, in order for most people to gain an appreciation of the freedoms they enjoy in America, they must first have them denied. Anyone who has lived under oppression, be it Soviet communism, German Nazism, or Hussein-ism understands and cherishes the opportunities afforded to us as Americans. As I write this, the television screen is filled with non-stop images of jubilant Iraqis throwing off the yoke of tyranny in the wake of their country's liberation at the hands of American and British forces. Only someone who has lived under such a yoke can fully empathize with those rejoicing Iraqis. Unfortunately, no American troops came to liberate us from Nazi tyranny until most of us had been thrown to the flames. The fact is that the opportunities available to us in the United States—and to a lesser degree in Israel—were never available to us in the shtetl. To ignore such opportunities and not exploit them to the fullest is a tragedy.

What I mean by "reconstituted" is the act of being brought back from impoverishment to full bloom—in every aspect of life. When we emerged from the Shoah, there were only the four of us, penniless and constituting but two generations. Today, I am able to say that I have been involved with seven generations of my family spanning over 150 years across three different centuries. I remember my great-grandfather, and, of course, my grandfather, and my father. I also have lived long enough to know my children, grandchildren, and great-grandchildren and if I can manage to live a bit longer, it's possible that I will know an eighth generation as well. Given that all of Jewish history covers only 120 generations, knowing eight of those is a rather signifi-

ant fraction. We must not squander the opportunities we have
een handed. Instead we need to leverage those opportunities to
ontinue reconstituting our family in every way possible.

I'm not only speaking of spiritual redemption, but also
conomic and physical renewal as well. If we, as parents, are
ble to give our kids "a leg up" when they're starting out, we
hould definitely do so. Raising the "reference line" permits a
randchild to begin their career from a point beyond the entry
evel. It is hoped by permitting our children to begin their career
oads at a more advanced point than we were able to, they will
kewise be able to go further than we did.

But more important than monetary assistance, it is imperative
or adult members of our family to lead by example. We must
xemplify the values we seek to impart to our children.

As discussed in an earlier chapter, our first son, Eddie, was
orn in 1953 when my wife, Anna Ruth, was only nineteen.
ddie received his MBA degree in accounting from the Kellogg
chool of Business at Northwestern University and worked for
any years as our company's Chief Financial Officer. In 1973,
ddie made up proud when he volunteered for civil service in
srael during the Yom Kippur War. He is the father of three
onderful children: Sam, who is currently serving in the Israeli
ilitary; Amanda, who is a student at Washington University in
t. Louis; and Bianca, a student at North Central High-School.
ll three children graduated from the Hasten Hebrew Academy
efore attending high school. Today, Eddie is an avid deep-sea
cuba diver and marine photographer, traversing the globe in
earch of exotic underwater venues.

Our second son, Michael, was born in Texas a year and a half
fter Eddie. Given his passion for Judaic studies, I was not
ntirely surprised when Michael informed me that he wished to
ttend Itri Yeshiva in Israel after graduating from high school.

Once there, Michael began following a more Orthodox reli-
ous way of life. Early marriage is typical among the observant,

community and so it did not come as a shock when Michael, still in his early twenties, phoned from Israel to tell me, "Papa, I found the girl I want to marry." He began to describe Shulamit, his beloved, and then dropped the bombshell, "And by the way, her father is Laibele Weissfish."

Weissfish was well-known, to the point of being notorious, for his connection with an anti-Zionist sect of Judaism known as the *Naturei Karta* (Watchmen of the City). Followers of this group believe that Jewish sovereignty in Jerusalem may only be attained through messianic—and not secular—means. Their marginalized adherents were regarded as Israel's lunatic fringe. While Shulamit's father had been associated with the group during his youth, years before Michael met his daughter, Weissfish had long since disassociated himself from them. Nevertheless, the stigma lingered primarily because Weissfish had become well-known for traveling to the United Nations in 1951, calling himself the foreign minister of the Naturei Karta, in order to vocally protest against Israel's conscription of women into its military.

"Papa, he's no radical," Michael assured me. Michael explained that his prospective father-in-law descended from a family who had lived in Jerusalem for at least six generations. The man was an articulate scholar and a respected Talmudist besides being one of the world's leading authorities on the life and work of philosopher Frederick Nietzche. Michael described him as a modest, humble Jew—a father of eleven children—who made his livelihood producing and selling handmade *t'fillin* (religious phylacteries) and lecturing about Nietzche.

Naturally, when the news media in Israel learned about the betrothal, they jumped on the story with zeal. "Son of American Zionist Leader to Wed Daughter of Former Naturei Karta Foreign Minister," shouted the headlines. The senior Weissfish and I were painted as mortal enemies and the romance was given a complete "Montague versus Capulet" spin. Actually, the truth was far less colorful. Flying to Jerusalem to meet my future in-laws, I found Weissfish, living in the Shomrei Emunim sector, to be anything but the rabid radical as characterized by the press. He was a simple, old-world pious Jew and when the conversation turned to the past, he was candid and clear:

"I have nothing to do with them anymore," he explained, referring to his former affiliation. "Today, I live simply, as you can see, and consider myself to be a member of the State of Israel. Like every other Israeli, sometimes I agree with the government, sometimes not. Some of my family members are right-wing and some are left-wing-they're all my family. I have not stood in the way when some of my children decided to serve in the army."

More important than my impressions of her father, Anne Ruth and I were completely taken aback by Shulamit, our future daughter-in-law. She was, and remains today, a striking beauty whose poise, charm, and genuine warmth won our hearts just as they had captured Michael's. The marriage has lasted over twenty-six years and produced six wonderful grandchildren. First came the twins, Dina and Dovi, followed by Esther, Tzvi, Yisroel, and Yonatan.

Dina and her husband, Itamar Cohen, live in Indianapolis with their two children, Ari and Yael. Dovi and his wife, Tali, live in Israel with their daughter Yehudit. Esther and her husband, Shlomo Chill, live in Munsee, New York, with their son, Yedidyah. Tzvi also resides in Israel with his wife Rachelle.

Michael has developed into a noted Talmudist in his own right. He dutifully maintains the largest library of Judaic legal and philosophic texts in the state of Indiana.

With the emphasis our family has always placed on Jewish education, I was not too surprised when our older daughter, Monica, expressed her desire to follow her brothers on a course of advanced Judaic study. "Papa," she told me, "You've got to do for me what you did for the boys." We agreed and Monica came home with more than an excellent Jewish education. She met her future husband, Dr. Stephen Rosenfeld, while she was a student at Touro College in New York and he was enrolled at th Einstein School of Medicine. Steve had been a high school stu dent at the Ner Israel Yeshiva in Baltimore and, because highe secular education was frowned upon by his religious community he secretly enrolled into Johns Hopkins University's pre-me program. After Steve completed his anesthesiology residency a Queens College Hospital in New York, he and Monica settled i Indianapolis. Today, Steve is regarded as a brilliant anesthesiol ogist and serves on the faculty of Indiana University School o Medicine. Monica earned her Masters in Library Science an today works as a librarian for the Bureau of Jewish Education i Indianapolis. She has developed a reputation as a beacon o hospitality and a true community resource in the area of Kashru and Jewish ritual observance. Monica and Steve are the prou parents of six of our wonderful grandchildren:

Shalom, Esther, Aaron, twins Ephraim and Cyril, and Rachelle. Currebtly, Shalom and his wife, Leah, live in Baltimore witl their son, Joseph Pinchas.

Our youngest, Judy, recently celebrated her fortieth birthday She and her husband, Neil Kaye, a successful South Africai hotelier, live in Ranana, Israel, and have four wonderfu children: Moshe*, Gabriel, Benjamin, and Zaki.. Judy is deepl involved and devoted to numerous worthwhile philanthropi activities both in this country and in Israel.

Of course, each child and grandchild must be afforded th freedom to express his own individuality within a certain define context. Part of that context is a discipline and respect for on another that serves to strengthen the family bonds. Trust betwee the generations is another means of building those bonds Sometimes it is easier for a child to trust a grandparent than parent. A grandparent must always be ready to listen to whateve problem is on the grandchild's mind.

Our Judaism binds and protects us from life's paths o destruction. I believe in G-d who takes an active role in our

*Moshe now serves in the Israeli Defense Forces.

lives. But each person's relationship with the Almighty is up to that person. It is more the common Judaic heritage than the common philosophy that holds us together. As Jews, we share a very rich and proud legacy, and while our own family history may be marked by enormous tragedy, it is taking pride in our Judaism in spite of that history that strengthens and revitalizes us. I believe our greatest strength and our greatest obligation is to teach each succeeding generation about the language, history, customs, and ethics of our people. Without this aspect, we are simply a group of relatives. It is only as serious and committed Jews that we achieve true strength as a family. As we are instructed in the daily Shachrit prayer before we recite the Sh'ma, our children must be taught to learn the Torah and the Talmud *B'ahavah* . . . with love. This is perhaps our greatest obligation.

As explained in the early chapters of this book, Hart and I grew up in a kosher home that would today be called observant although back then we just viewed ourselves as normal . . . just like everyone else. As explained in the middle chapters, after I came to America my level of observance diminished as I sought to shed the mantle of Old World refugee and become a full-fledged, red-blooded, assimilated American. In later years, thanks mostly to Anna Ruth who was greatly responsible for my re-discovery of my faith, I have become more closely attached to Judaism's original fundamental teachings and, in this way, I find enormous comfort and strength in dealing with the many unknowable and unanswerable questions of my existence. For example, in coming to terms with the loss of millions of Jews, including my own family members during the Shoah, how can I resolve this crime and still believe in an all-powerful and just G-d. To answer this, I look to the concept of *gilgul* (the reincarnation of souls) or rolling under the ground. The midrash teaches that while only Joseph's bones were carried to Eretz Yisroel during the Exodus from Egypt, in fact all the bones of all the Jews buried there during their enslavement were "rolled underground" by G-d, all the way to the holy land where they remain. I believe the same holds true for the millions of Jewish martyrs. Their *neshumot*, or spirits, are with us and enjoy an exalted place in Israel today. Unlike some Holocaust survivors, I was never angry at G-d. I did not seek to place G-d on trial or to accuse Him of revoking the covenant. While there were particular bitter periods of my life, particularly in Israel during the late 1940's, my anger and my anguish were always directed towards other men and never towards heaven.

Concerning the road ahead, I happen to be tremendously optimistic. I see a golden era of world peace and progress as country after oppressed country shakes loose *(sometimes with a little military help)* from the grip of its tyrants and dictators. The days are numbered for these vestigial artifacts from the twentieth century. We have no place for the likes of Castro of Kim-Jung II or Arafat in the twenty-first century. And as the world becomes more democratic, it will become more politically stable and hence more economically advanced. One only needs to look to China to witness the impact of personal liberty on the standard of living. I am hopeful that Israeli political leadership will emulate the actions of President Bush in eliminating dangerous regimes such as the Afghani Taliban and Hussein's Baathists and replacing them with democratic ones more favorable to the West. I believe that this is exactly what needs to be done in the territories. Arafat must be deposed and recognized as the terrorist dictator that he has always been before any resolution of the Palestinian issue can hope to be achieved.*

I also foresee our family's continued growth from strength to strength as we rebuild and reconstitute ourselves into the future. And that, I suppose, is the main reason I wanted to write down my story. So that when I am no longer here, future family members will read my words and understand why things are as they are and why we must do what we must do.

* Now that this book has been reprinted, Arafat is no longer alive.

Mark My Words!

Like most Americans, I consider myself to be a patriot. But unlike some, I don't take the blessings that we enjoy in this country for granted. Because of my immigrant background—because I became an American by choice—my love of country is more tangible and possibly more passionate than most. I view myself, along with my parents and my brother, as being among Emma Lazarus' "huddled masses, yearning to be free." I honestly believe that G-d has blessed our country and that those blessings have been extended to me and to my descendants. Looking back, it's fair to say that there has never, in the history of the world, been another nation that has so been regarded by mankind as a beacon of liberty and a provider of opportunity than the United States. Looking ahead, I feel that despite the current rising tide of anti-American sentiment sweeping the Arab world and elsewhere, our country will, with the help of G-d, continue to endure in this role.

If my vision of tomorrow's world turns out to be accurate, remember that you heard it here first. Whether you are a member of our family or not, I urge you to take my words to heart because they all came straight from my own.

Finally, I am indeed grateful to you for taking the time to read and consider my words. It is hoped that you will find them acceptable and of some value. By so doing—by agreeing to Mark My Words—you honor me and the memories of those who have gone before. For this, I am very grateful, and extend my most sincere thanks.

Shalom alechem,
—Mark Hasten
April 2003

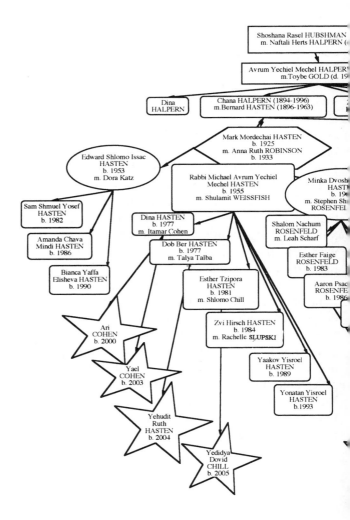

Shoshana Rasel HUBSHMAN
m. Naftali Herts HALPERN

Avrum Yechiel Mechel HALPERN
m.Toybe GOLD (d. 19

Dina
HALPERN

Chana HALPERN (1894-1996)
m.Bernard HASTEN (1896-1963)

Mark Mordechai HASTEN
b. 1925
m. Anna Ruth ROBINSON
b. 1933

Edward Shlomo Issac
HASTEN
b. 1953
m. Dora Katz

Rabbi Michael Avrum Yechiel
Mechel HASTEN
b. 1955
m. Shulamit WEISSFISH

Minka Dvoshi
HASTE
b. 19
m. Stephen Sh
ROSENFEL

Sam Shmuel Yosef
HASTEN
b. 1982

Dina HASTEN
b. 1977
m. Itamar Cohen

Shalom Nachum
ROSENFELD
m. Leah Scharf

Amanda Chava
Mindi HASTEN
b. 1986

Dob Ber HASTEN
b. 1977
m. Talya Talba

Esther Faige
ROSENFELD
b. 1983

Bianca Yaffa
Elisheva HASTEN
b. 1990

Esther Tzipora
HASTEN
b. 1981
m. Shlomo Chill

Aaron Psac
ROSENFE
b. 1986

Zvi Hirsch HASTEN
b. 1984
m. Rachelle SLUPSKI

Ari
COHEN
b. 2000

Yaakov Yisroel
HASTEN
b. 1989

Yael
COHEN
b. 2003

Yonatan Yisroel
HASTEN
b.1993

Yehudit
Ruth
HASTEN
b. 2004

Yedidya
Dovid
CHILL
b. 2005

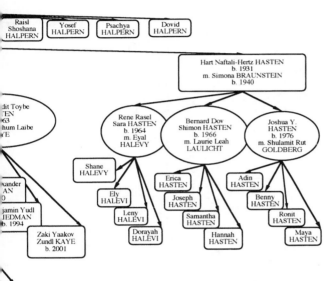

Raisl
Shoshana
HALPERN

Yosef
HALPERN

Psachya
HALPERN

Dovid
HALPERN

Hart Naftali-Hertz HASTEN
b. 1931
m. Simona BRAUNSTEIN
b. 1940

dit Toybe
TEN
63
hum Laibe
'E

Rene Rasel
Sara HASTEN
b. 1964
m. Eyal
HALEVY

Bernard Dov
Shimon HASTEN
b. 1966
m. Laurie Leah
LAULICHT

Joshua Y.
HASTEN
b. 1976
m. Shulamit Rut
GOLDBERG

Shane
HALEVY

xander
AN
0

Erica
HASTEN

Adin
HASTEN

jamin Yudl
IEDMAN
b. 1994

Ely
HALEVI

Joseph
HASTEN

Benny
HASTEN

Leny
HALEVI

Samantha
HASTEN

Ronit
HASTEN

Zaki Yaakov
Zundl KAYE
b. 2001

Dorayah
HALEVI

Hannah
HASTEN

Maya
HASTEN

a
)

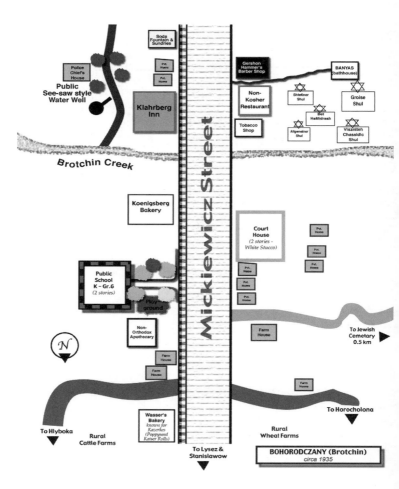

Soda Fountain & Sundries

Pvt. Home

Pvt. Home

Police Chief's House

Public See-saw style Water Well

Klahrberg Inn

Gershon Hammer's Barber Shop

BANYAS (bathhouse)

Non-Kosher Restaurant

Shtetiner Shul

Groise Shul

Bet HaMidrash

Tobacco Shop

Allgemeiner Shul

Visznitleh Chassidic Shul

Brotchin Creek

Mickiewcz Street

Koenigsberg Bakery

Court House
(2 stories - White Stucco)

Pvt. Home

Pvt. Home

Pvt. Home

Pvt. Home

Public School K – Gr.6
(2 stories)

Pvt. Home

Pvt. Home

Pvt. Home

Play-ground

Non-Orthodox Apothecary

Farm House

To Jewish Cemetary 0.5 km ▶

N

Farm House

Farm House

To Horocholona

To Hlyboka ▼

Rural Cattle Farms

Wasser's Bakery
known for Kzerkes
(Poppyseed Kaiser Rolls)

Farm Home

Rural Wheat Farms

To Lysez & Stanislawow ▼

BOHORODCZANY (Brotchin)
circa 1935

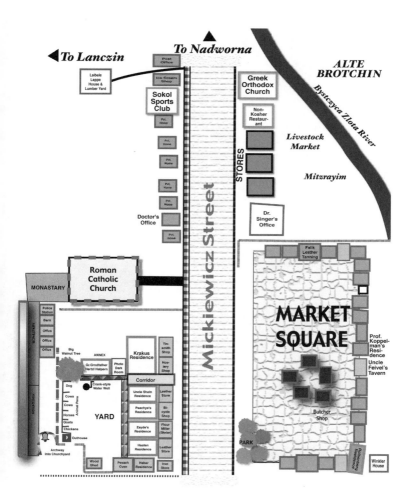

Glossary

A

Aleph-bet (Hebrew) (lit., A–B)—
The first two letters of the
Hebrew alphabet. A child's
primary studies.

Aliyah (Hebrew) (lit., ascent)—
1. Immigration to Israel. 2.
being called up for a Torah
reading.

Aliyah Bet (Hebrew)—Illegal
immigration to Palestine.

Amcha (Hebrew)—"I am from
your people."

Ashkenazi—A Jew of European
heritage; non-Sephardi.

Ayne Breyrah (Hebrew)—"We
have no choice."

B

Bal Tokaya (Hebrew)—Person
assigned to blow the ritual
ram's horn during the Jewish
New Year.

Balagan (Hebrew slang)—Great
disorder.

Banya (Russian)—Public bathhouse.

Bar Mitzvah (Hebrew)—A
Jewish boy's coming of age
at age thirteen.

Behelfer (Yiddish) (lit., helper) -
An aide or assistant.

Betar (Hebrew)—Acronym for
"Brith Trumpeldor,"
Revisionist youth move-
ment.

Bez borznik (Russian) (lit.,
There is no G-d)—Popular
Soviet slogan.

Bricha (Hebrew) (lit., to run
away)—1940s underground
organization to promote illegal immigration to Palestine.

Bubbie, Bubbe (Yiddish)—
Grandmother.

C

Challah (Hebrew)—Traditional
Sabbath plaited bread.

Chassid (pl.: Chassidim)
(Hebrew derivative)—an
observant Jew who is a
follower of a particular
rebbe or religious leader.

A member of the Chassidic movement.

Chassidism (adj. chassidic) (Hebrew derivative)—A stream or movement in religious Judaism that arose in Eastern Europe (primarily in Poland) during the seventeenth century. (*see* Chassid)

Chaulent (Yiddish, from the French)—1. A hot baked bean casserole prepared before the Sabbath and kept warm until it is consumed as the Sabbath mid-day meal. 2. (from German) "Shulamt" or end of the synagogue service.

Cheder (Hebrew) (lit., room)—Religious school.

Chumash (Hebrew)—Book containing the text of the Torah (five books of Moses).

Chuppah (Hebrew)—Wedding canopy.

D

DPs—*See* Displaced persons.

Deutsch—German.

Displaced person—A stateless individual.

E

Eretz Yisroel (Hebrew)—Land of Israel.

Etzel (Hebrew acronym)—Abbreviation for Irgun Tzvai Leumi (*see* Irgun).

Etzelnik—Member of Etzel.

G

Ganvenin (Yiddish)—Thievery.

Gehaims Polizei (German)—Secret police.

Gemarah (Hebrew)—The main body of the Talmud, consisting of a record of ancient rabbinical debates and constituting the primary source of Jewish religious law.

Gilgul (Hebrew)—The reincarnation of souls (also: gilgul neshamot).

Goldeneh Medina (Yiddish) (lit., the golden country)—A euphemism for America among Jewish immigrants.

Goy (Yiddish)—Slang for non-Jew.

Greener (Yiddish)—Greenhorn, pejorative term for new immigrant.

Groisse shul (Yiddish)—Large synagogue.

Groshen—Polish coinage. One hundreth of a Zloty.

Gulag (Russian)—Prisoner camp.

H

Hafugah (Hebrew)—Cease-fire.

Haganah (lit., defense)—Jewish para-military defense organization in British Mandate Palestine.

Halacha (Hebrew)—Jewish law.

Hatikva (Hebrew) (lit., the hope)—Israeli national anthem; name of Tel Aviv neighborhood.

Havlagah (Hebrew)—Self-restraint.

Herut (Hebrew) (lit., freedom)—Right-wing political party in Israel.

Histadrut (Hebrew)—Israel's trade union umbrella organization.

Hoch-Deutsch (German)—German language in its proper spoken form.

Handling (Yiddish)—Bargaining, negotiating a price.

I

IDF—Israel Defense Forces.

Irgun Tzvai Leumi (Hebrew) (lit., national military organization)—Jewish underground organization in British Mandate Palestine.

Israel Bonds Organization—Association issuing commercial bonds for the benefit of the State of Israel.

Ivrit b'ivrit (Hebrew)—Conversational modern Hebrew as opposed to liturgical Hebrew.

J

JDC—*See* Joint Distribution Committee.

Jihad (Arabic)—Holy war.

Joint Distribution Committee—US Jewish organization providing assistance to needy Jews world-wide; arm of the Jewish Agency (*see* Sochnut).

Judenrat (German)—Jewish council appointed by the Nazis to administer ghettoes internally.

K

Kashrut (Hebrew)—The law of ritually permitted foods.

Key-pee-tauwk (Russian)—Hot running water.

Klezmer (Yiddish)—Style of Jewish folk music.

Knesset (Hebrew)—Israeli parliament.

Komsomol (Russian)—Young Pioneers. Soviet youth organization.

Kopeck (Russian)—Russian coin; 100th of a Ruble

Kosher (Hebrew-Yiddish)—Ritually permitted [food].

Kova Tembul (Hebrew) (lit., dunce cap)—popular Israeli headwear.

Kristallnacht (German) (lit., Night of Broken Glass)—Massive, Nazi-incited anti-Jewish pogroms that ripped through Germany in November 1938, marking the onset of the Holocaust.

Kvitel (Yiddish)—A private note written on a scrap of paper and submitted to a rabbi for transmission to the Almighty.

L

Landsmen (Yiddish)—People from one's country of origin.

LaShon (Hebrew) (lit., tongue)—Slang for an enemy informer.

Latrune—Site of battle near Jerusalem during Israeli War of Independence.

LEHI (Hebrew acronym)—Militant Jewish underground organization in British-mandate Palestine.

Likud - Right-wing Israeli political party.

Lokshen (Yiddish) (lit., wide pasta noodles)—Slang for US dollars.

Luach (Hebrew)—Calendar.

M

MACHAL (Mitnadwey Chootz L'aretz), Machalniks (Hebrew)—Non-Israeli nationals enlisted as volunteers into the IDF.

Mapai (Hebrew)—One time Israeli labor party.

Mapainik—Member of Mapai.

Mar (Hebrew)—Mister.

Marshalek (Yiddish)—Interlocutor or emcee at a Jewish festive event.

Masada—Site of Herod's fortress near Dead Sea; in 73 A.D., after a two-year siege by the Romans, its defenders committed mass suicide.

Matzeiva (Hebrew)—A stone marker or monument.

Mechitza (Hebrew)—Barrier separating men from women in a synagogue.

Metzenas (Polish)—Paralegal aide.

Metzudat Ze'ev (Hebrew) (lit., Ze'ev's citadel)—Likud party headquarters.

Moffsim (Hebrew)—Miracles.

Moshav (Hebrew)—An Israeli cooperative farm where, unlike a Kibbutz, members enjoy private ownership and a less communal lifestyle.

N

Naftali—One of the twelve tribes of Israel.

NKVD—Soviet secret police (abbreviation).

O

Olim (Hebrew)—Immigrants.

Orthodox Union of Jewish Congregations of America—Body representing Orthodox congregations in the United

States and Canada; known also for its provision of kashruth certification.

Ostjuden (German)—Jews from Eastern Europe, the Balkans, and Russia.

OU—*See* Orthodox Union.

P

PLO—Palestine Liberation Organization

Palmach—Elite striking force of the Haganah established in 1941.

Parsha (Hebrew)—Weekly Torah portion.

Petlurist (Polish)—Follower of Ukrainian strongman, Simon Petlura.

Pirkei Avot (Hebrew)—Ethics of our Fathers; studied on Sabbath afternoons from Passover through Rosh Hashana.

Policia Granichna (Polish)— Border police.

Pumphosen (German)—Trousers with gathered hems favored by golfers and young boys in early 20th century; knickerbockers, knickers.

S

Schnorrer (Yiddish) (lit., beggar)—Fund-raiser.

Schwab (German) (lit., frog)—

Slang for ethnically German person.

Seder (Hebrew) (lit., order)— Festive meal on first night of Passover at which the story of the Exodus from Egypt is re-told.

Shabbos, Shabbat (Hebrew-Yiddish)— Sabbath.

Shanda (Yiddish)—Shame, scandal.

Shenel (Russian)—Overcoat or great coat as worn by the Red Army.

Shiddach (Yiddish/Hebrew)—A match between a man and a woman typically arranged by a matchmaker.

Shiker (Yiddish/Hebrew)— Drunkard

Shmate (Yiddish) (lit., rag.)— Garment.

Shoah (Hebrew) (lit., burnt offering)—The Nazi Holocaust.

Shoichet, shochet (Yiddish/Hebrew)—Kosher slaughterer of animals

Shomrei Emunim—Residential district of Jerusalem favored by Chassidic (observant) families.

Shtetl (Yiddish)—Little town.

Shtubak (Yiddish)—A slow student held back in school.

Siddur (Hebrew) (lit., arrangement)—Hebrew prayer book.

Simcha (Hebrew)—Joy, joyous occasion.

Sochnut (Hebrew)—The Jewish Agency. International Jewish welfare organization engaged in rescue, resettlement, training, relief and humanitarian aid.

Spekulatzia (Russian)—Speculation, commerce for profit.

Stern Group—See LEHI.

Svennaya TuShonka (Russian)—Spicy canned sausages, sometimes known as Vienna Sausage.

T

Talmud (Hebrew)—Compendium of Jewish Oral Law.

Tanakh (Hebrew)—Hebrew Bible; the 24 books of the Torah, Prophets and Scriptures.

Tatu (Yiddish)—Father.

Te'udah (Hebrew)—Membership card.

Tichel (Yiddish)—Woman's headscarf.

Torah (Hebrew)—Five Books of Moses; Pentateuch.

Torah Umesorah (Hebrew) (lit., Torah and Tradition)—National Society of Jewish Day Schools.

Totach Hakadosh (Hebrew)—Holy cannon.

Tzedakah (Hebrew) (lit., righteousness)—Charity, contribution.

Y

Yahrtzeit (Yiddish)—Memorial day for deceased relative.

Yeshuv (Hebrew)—Term referring to Jewish settlement in British Mandate Palestine.

Yom Kippur (Hebrew)—Day of Atonement, holiest day on Jewish calendar.

Z

Zayde (Yiddish) —Grandfather.

Zionism—Political movement seeking to return Jews to their Biblical homeland.

Zloties (Polish)—Polish currency.

Zsid (Russian/Polish)—Jew [derogatory].

INDEX

ENDNOTES

1   For a detailed account of my family's escape from Alga, see pages 29–31 in "I SHALL NOT DIE!"

2   For a detailed account of this incident, see pages 38–39 in "I SHALL NOT DIE!"

3   For a detailed account of the death of my father, see pages 96–97 in "I SHALL NOT DIE!"

4   An account of this episode may be found on pages 113–115 in "I SHALL NOT DIE!"

5   A detailed account of the founding of the Hasten Hebrew Academy of Indianapolis may be found in Chapter 11 of "I SHALL NOT DIE!"

6   A detailed account of the founding of the Academy, and Rabbi Gray's instrumental role may be found in Chapter 11 of "I SHALL NOT DIE!"

7   A detailed account of this episode may be found on pages 186–187 of "I SHALL NOT DIE!

8   For a detailed account of Hart's relationship with Menachem Begin, see Chapter 13 of "I SHALL NOT DIE!"

9   See the Preface of "I SHALL NOT DIE!" for a detailed account of my grandfather's murder at the hands of the Nazis.

10   The Hasten Family Mission Statement may be found in the Appendix (pp. 339–344) of "I SHALL NOT DIE!"